KT-169-053

Heinemann Studies in Sociology
General Editor Donald Gunn MacRae

A Sociology of Religion

Jubuum.
Jan 1973
from Jill and
Paul.

Heinemann Studies in Sociology

A Sociology of Religion

Michael Hill

Lecturer in Sociology
London School of Economics

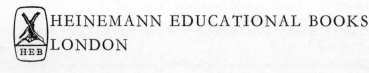

HEINEMANN EDUCATIONAL BOOKS
LONDON

Heinemann Educational Books Ltd

LONDON EDINBURGH MELBOURNE TORONTO
AUCKLAND SINGAPORE JOHANNESBURG
HONG KONG NAIROBI IBADAN NEW DELHI

ISBN 0 435 82410 4
ISBN 0 435 82411 2 (paperback)

© Michael Hill 1973

First published 1973

Published by Heinemann Educational Books Ltd
48 Charles Street, London W1X 8AH
Printed in Great Britain by Butler & Tanner Ltd
Frome and London

Contents

To Andrew and Stephen

Foreword

THERE IS a sense in which there is, at least potentially, a sociology of anything and of everything. Mostly what is meant by saying that there is a sociology of something is that the something, let us call it *x*, is influenced by the institutional arrangements and presuppositions about values, uses, virtues and vices of a particular society at a given time. In this sense one could have a sociology of, say, bananas: how they are perceived, used and obtained. (Probably today, however, one would not call it the sociology of bananas but rather the ethnobotany of the banana in Jamaica or Coventry, or wherever. This, however, is a mere convenience of labelling.) Now such 'sociologies of *x*' are not merely trivial and they are often of great importance in providing data for administrators, opinion-makers and politicians. This interest is, though, usually limited, and any sociology of sociologists—an example of what I am talking about—would be forced to admit that many 'sociologies of *x*' are largely protective specializations and territory-claiming by nervous and ambitious academics.

Not such the sociology of religion. The academics who are concerned with this topic in Britain—and they are many and distinguished, and Dr Hill gives full reference to their works—are not nervous, but confident, active and numerous, even if not the favourites of the bodies that give grants for research. Indeed it is in the sociology of religion that I would see one of the three major, unique strengths of British sociology in recent times. What is more, this is appropriate. There is no society, however formally secular, in which religion is not a major component of both the structural and the cultural life. If, as I think, surrogate religions are genuinely religions from a sociological if not a theological viewpoint, we live not in an age of secularization but rather are accompanied by the perils and delights of an age of faith—or faiths.

What is more, as all the greatest sociologists and anthropologists have realized, religion is at the core of the understanding of all social cohesion and much social change. The major names here are Durkheim and Weber. I incline more to the position of the former than does Dr Hill, but that is not of much importance given our agreement on the salience of religion in society. Even those who accept that religion is illusion—no necessary conclusion of the sociology of religion—must remember that man is the one animal which lies, which is capable of deception and being deceived. *Mundus vult decipi:* the sociological consequences are enormous whether or not one thinks that the Devil is the Father of Lies or holds with Charles Kingsley, from whom Marx got the phrase, that religion is the opium of the people. Sociologically, religion is precisely central.

It is also amusing. As William James knew, the varieties of religious experience are not only intrinsically important, poignant and terrible, they are also to the observer funny and sources of delight in the human and social capacities of our kind. Dr Hill has written a textbook which should be immediately accessible to anyone knowing either a little about sociology or a little about religion—it cannot be quite a beginner's book. Unlike other textbooks on the subject this one, to repeat a phrase I have gladly used in other contexts, is genuinely a contribution to its own subject matter; that is to say it is both a text—and a rich one—and an addition both to knowledge and understanding which seems to me to gain by its being unafraid of humanity. Much sociology endistances us by learning or by technique from reality. This is a good, learned and systematic text which brings us closer to the varieties of ways in which society is possible, is changed, and relates itself to itself and also to the gods.

Highgate, 1972   DONALD G. MACRAE

Preface

A BRIEF EXPLANATION of the format of this textbook is required, because it uses a slightly different method of footnoting from the more familiar kind. Two related aims in writing this book have been to evaluate the literature on a number of central issues in the sociology of religion and to provide as comprehensive a bibliography as possible. It seemed sensible to link these two aspects by listing at the end of each chapter not only those sources that have been cited or quoted in the text but a broader spread of books and articles that bear directly on the issues in question. Thus the lists of references contain much relevant literature which has formed the background to this book but which has not always been explicitly dealt with. There will obviously be gaps and omissions in these lists, though I have tried to make them as accurate and as detailed as possible. Each list is numbered, and where necessary page references are given: thus the note [16:3] would signify a quotation from page 3 of the source numbered 16 in the list at the end of the chapter in question. Where reference is made to a number of sources without detailed page references they will be separated by a semi-colon, thus [16; 40; 51].

I am immensely grateful for the generous advice and guidance of two people in particular. Professor D. G. MacRae has been a constant source of encouragement and criticism, and without his support I could hardly have completed this book. Professor D. A. Martin, who first introduced me to the sociology of religion, has given the manuscript a detailed and perceptive reading and made countless valuable suggestions. Their influence on the way this book took shape has been decisive: for the imperfections that remain I alone am responsible.

The suggestions and criticism of colleagues and students have also sharpened my understanding of some of the issues raised in this study, and to them I owe a large debt of gratitude. To my colleagues Leslie Sklair and John Peel I am especially indebted, since they very patiently allowed me to pick their brains and try out different interpretations. The same is true of my students, both at the London School of Economics and in the Southwark Ordination Course, where I soon learned the dangers of uninformed trespassing on theological territory. Again, I take responsibility for the final product.

The typing of the manuscript was begun by Pat Martin and completed by Rosemary Wiltshire, both of whom saved me endless hours of correction by their accuracy. Miss Wiltshire was also largely responsible for compiling the bibliography.

Finally, I owe a considerable debt of gratitude to my wife, who knows more than anyone what this book involved in terms of domestic disruption. As well as tolerating me *and* a manuscript which demanded much of our leisure time, she helped in reading and correcting the text. Our children were completely indifferent to the whole project, and in return for their sobering influence the book is dedicated to them.

London School of Economics, March 1972

I

Sociology and Religion

THE SIGNIFICANCE of religion for understanding the theoretical contributions of 'classical' sociologists like Durkheim, Weber and Pareto is now a generally accepted part of the sociological tradition. In the early growth of sociology religion was a central issue; indeed, it can be argued that it was *the* central issue. This basic principle has important implications for a textbook on the sociology of religion, since it suggests that any approach that divorces the empirical study of religious beliefs and activities from the theoretical context within which these phenomena can be given a sociological interpretation is a misconceived enterprise. The same principle is true of any specialist area in sociology, but in recent years it has been clearly highlighted in the sociological study of religion. While 'classical' sociology gave religion a central place, its position in much sociological writing until the early 1960s was fairly marginal. At the same time, the 'boundaries' of religion, rather than being defined in terms of theoretical criteria, became increasingly identified with the boundaries of institutional Christianity. The result was the growth of denominational 'religious sociologies'.

One reason for the reversal of this tendency in the last few years has been the persistent decline in institutional Christianity in Western industrial societies. Even when this did not involve a substantial decline in institutional participation—as in the United States—it was clear that the content of traditional religious beliefs had been substantially transformed. Therefore, if the institutional boundaries could no longer be regarded as the area in which sociologists of religion were broadly interested, some other source of boundary-definition was needed. Since an important function of any theory is to specify the limits within which its propositions are applicable, it was to sociological theory that studies of religion increasingly turned within the main tradition of sociology.

However, the reinstatement of these central theoretical concerns involved certain problems, and one of the most important of these was the process which might be termed 'conceptual drift'. To take an obvious example: Weber's study of the relationship between Calvinistic Protestantism and the spirit of capitalism, written in 1904–5, contained a number of insights that were inseparable from the rest of his theoretical contributions. With the exception of his colleague Ernst Troeltsch, and with the major exception of the American sociologist Talcott Parsons, who translated Weber's work in 1930, theologians and economic historians treated 'the Weber thesis' very much as a point of controversy. Some of them, as will be shown in chapter 5, failed to see the significance of Weber's argument because they detached it from its wider theoretical context. As a result, it is still quite difficult to get beyond the basic assumption that the Weber thesis has been 'disproved'. Perhaps even more difficult to shake off is the cumulative effect of second-hand versions and partial reinterpretations of 'classical' theories, which often arrive at a very different position from that of the original theory. Again using the Weber thesis as an example, one quite recent account regards the supposed demonstration of a link between Protestantism and capitalism as having acquired the status of a 'received doctrine', [12] meaning by this that it has been uncritically accepted as part of the mythical baggage of sociology. As it happens, the writer himself criticizes Weber's thesis on the basis of evidence which on important theoretical grounds is explicitly *deemphasized* in the original work (namely, the evidence of Calvin's *own* theological position). Thus through a process of 'conceptual drift' and the acceptance of substitute versions of basic arguments the links with a central core of sociological theory become increasingly tenuous.

In order to trace some of the most productive continuities between 'classical' theory and contemporary studies in the sociology of religion I have adopted a closely defined perspective. This is especially necessary since the discussion will point to important links between the study of 'religion' as narrowly defined and other areas of sociology, principally the study of political movements, social change and the role of ideas in different historical perspectives. To attempt this and simultaneously to adopt an unlimited scope in the specific area of the sociology of religion would make the task unmanageable. Thus I will not be concerned with all of the sociology of religion (whatever that might mean in substantive terms) but with an interlocking group of issues which broadly stem from *Weberian* theory. Very recently, a number of translations and studies of Max Weber's work have appeared, and it is important to develop the connexions between his general theory and his studies of the major significance of religion, especially as a source of social change.

This textbook will only be marginally concerned with religions other than Christianity and there will thus be a fairly brief discussion of primitive religion, although the problem of the rationality of magic and ritual, which is raised in chapter 2 and again in chapter 10, involves a discussion of the criteria on which primitive and modern systems of rationality may be analysed. Nor is the main focus of the book on the functions of religion for social categorization, or on theories of myth, although the relationship between the sociology of religion and the sociology of knowledge is discussed in chapter 12, where the element of continuity between 'classical' theory and contemporary explanations is traced in the work of Berger and Luckmann. If any justification is needed for concentrating on Christianity it might perhaps be given by contrasting the present approach with the even closer demarcation of the field made by the American sociologist Everett Hughes, when he pointed out that 'Nearly everything sociologically speaking has happened in and to the Roman Catholic Church'. [6:124]

The scheme of this book is organized around a number of centrally located and connected issues. In this chapter the relationship between sociology and the study of religion will be outlined in terms of three possible approaches. In chapter 2 the early development of the sociology of religion is similarly shown to have depended on the extent to which a particular theoretical approach was adopted. Chapters 3 and 4 trace the development of typologies of Christian organization in the work of different sociologists and draw attention to the importance of contextual criteria in elaborating typologies. In chapter 5 a detailed account is given of the theoretical background to the 'Protestant Ethic' thesis and the importance of this for interpreting the historical links between Protestantism and capitalism, which are explained in chapter 6. Chapter 7 takes another aspect of Weberian theory, that ideas may exert an autonomous role on the process of social change, by outlining the theory of charisma, and the applicability of this in the case of religious movements is argued in chapter 8. Closely related to Weber's study of Protestantism and capitalism is Halévy's thesis that the influence of Methodism prevented a revolution in England, and this, together with its subsequent elaborations and criticisms, is the subject of chapter 9. Broadening this discussion to the study of millennial movements, in chapter 10 we consider the variety of relationships between political and religious radicalism and the extent to which religious action can be regarded as 'rational'. Chapter 11 goes into the range of meanings—and their implications—which sociologists have attached to the term 'secularization'. Finally, the synthesis of 'classical' sociology in the work of Berger and Luckmann on secularization is discussed.

This book is not intended to provide an overview or a summary of the whole field, but it will attempt to start at a basic level and explore one set of important theoretical possibilities in a systematic way. Taking the most basic issue first, the rest of this chapter will be largely devoted to establishing that the sociology of religion exists as a legitimate area of study.

It might seem strange to a textbook reader that the first chapter should be concerned with the problem of whether or not a subject exists. There are good reasons for beginning this way in the sociology of religion, as I hope to show, and the type of radical questioning to which sociologists of religion are prone is neatly exemplified by the article in a recent issue of the *Journal for the Scientific Study of Religion* which puts the disturbing question, 'Is the sociology of religion possible?' [13] In the rest of this chapter I will suggest that the sociology of religion is indeed possible, but that it involves a particular attitude to the relationship between religious explanations and sociological explanations; it will also be suggested that some of the approaches taken by classical and contemporary writers are more valuable for the sociological study of religion than others. As in most areas of sociology, the problem of definition is a central issue, involving not only the concepts within the field of study but also the nature of the field itself. Thus we will need to look at different approaches to the study of 'religion' and their implications as far as a sociological treatment is concerned. We will forgo in the present context any discussion of the possible reasons for the current general upsurge of interest in religion, with which the growing popularity of the sociology of religion is closely associated, and for the moment will concentrate on the *sociological* aspect of the enterprise.

This is a necessary starting point. Although there is less recognition of the fact than there should be, it is nevertheless true that many of the basic methodological issues with which sociologists of religion are found grappling are common to sociology as a whole. This will form a persistent *leitmotiv* in the present chapter, because what often appear to be fundamental criticisms of the sociology of religion can in most cases be redirected so that they highlight problems which face all sociologists. At its crudest level, the issue can be depicted in terms of an adjective before or a noun after: religious sociology or the sociology of religion? There is an important difference between the two, which will be treated at greater length later. What is worth noting at this point is that 'religious sociology' as a discipline is a significantly different enterprise from 'the sociology of religion'. 'Religious sociology' (as far as it is a recognizable tradition) is best seen as a form of research which takes its basic orientation and attitudes from a theological rather than a theoretical sociological source. Thus the ultimate assumptions of this discipline do not come within the scope of an internal sociological debate. While sociologists as a group are continually engaged in arguments about the extent to which the different sociological traditions imply certain *a priori* assumptions about the nature of man and his place in society, this must of necessity exclude the 'religious sociologist' because the debate about the basic assumptions used by the latter takes place in an entirely different milieu. Since in the last analysis the orientation of 'religious sociology' is acknowledged to be external to sociology and is strictly beyond the scrutiny of other sociologists, the understanding of the word

'sociology' in this context is that of a *method* rather than an autonomous intellectual activity.

The implications which are suggested by this distinction might
equally be applied to other fields of sociology. The labels 'political
sociology' and 'industrial sociology' usually go unquestioned:
do they, however, reveal the extent to which the assumptions of
different political philosophies or economic creeds have percolated
into the theoretically autonomous discipline of sociology? Certainly, much of the more interesting theoretical debate in the
study of politics is concerned with the extent to which the different
perspectives adopted by sociological writers are closely related to
particular political orientations. Similarly, some of the early
work of the human relations school of industrial sociology in the
United States was criticized for its apparent acceptance of what
might be called the 'management-based' criteria of efficiency and
maximization of production. Much the same kind of problem
seems to have arisen in the sociology of education, for a recent
account suggests that 'separate use of two terms, "educational
sociology" and "the sociology of education", might be maintained
in order to preserve the distinction between an emphasis upon
educational or social problems and an emphasis upon sociological
problems'. [19:4] The writer goes on to claim that, although the
more rigorous examples of 'educational sociology' have brought
considerable sociological insight to bear on educational problems,
the subject in the main 'has tended to be hortatory rather than
empirical, inspirational rather than objective, and synoptic rather
than analytic'. [19:4]

None of these observations need be in any way surprising.
Most academic disciplines which pursue the goal of a rigorous
and systematic investigation of the empirical world sooner or
later come up against the 'pure' and 'applied' dichotomy, and the
fact that the sociologist is in an important sense part of the phenomena he studies makes it all the more likely that he will encounter
this problem in a clearly defined form. The question at issue is one
of personal values: how far can these be identified in the work of
any sociologist? The answer seems to be that the more crystallized
are the value-systems in the social phenomena being studied—
and this would be particularly true of differentiated religious
groups, in which the value content tends to be distinct and co-

herent—the more self-conscious becomes the problem of value in the observer, and in the study of religion there is the rather unusual situation that the elaboration of a 'pure' and 'applied' division has become formalized. Of course, this does not mean that the work which goes on in the sociology of religion is thereby 'value-free'. What is interesting is that there should be such an explicit declaration of value orientation by the exponents of 'religious sociology', a feature to which we will shortly return.

Some of the central issues in the sociology of religion can be understood in terms of three basic perspectives which the observer of religious phenomena may adopt. There is at one extreme of this continuum of attitudes the quite unequivocal position in which religious phenomena are regarded as beyond human scrutiny, above any influences which the social environment might exert, and therefore outside the scope of an empirically oriented discipline such as sociology. This position may be called a theologically conservative, fundamentalist or ultra-orthodox perspective, since religion comes to be regarded as an autonomous, self-regulating segment of human experience and activity which is set apart from the more mundane segments of economic, social and political activity and, therefore, cannot be 'touched' (in this context meaning contaminated) by these other spheres of human activity. This position effectively eliminates the socio-logical observer since his task can be seen as at best misguided or more likely as presumptuous: 'the proper study of mankind is man' seems to epitomize the position described here. It follows logically from this point of view that the sociology of religion, at least as understood by sociologists, becomes impossible. While this attitude, if generalized, would put the whole of religion beyond sociological investigation, it is more often found in a selective variant applying to some religious groups but not others. In this case, the argument usually takes the form of a defence of one's own religious commitment by placing it firmly beyond sociological scrutiny and an application of the techniques of sociological enquiry to other religious traditions. Special pleading of this sort becomes highly polemical when the 'sociological' criterion applied to other religious groups takes the form of a thoroughgoing and misguided materialistic critique which attempts to 'explain away' their activities and beliefs.

One of the more obvious recent examples of this technique is to be found in the writings of the Catholic sociologist Werner Stark, which contain a very clear Roman Catholic apologetic. [18] The basic structure of his argument is not difficult to summarize. Stark views the history of Christian development in terms of a dialectical opposition between the polar types of established church and sect. The established Church, which forms the *thesis* of a dialectical triad, is depicted by Stark as a compromised institution based on the fundamental contradiction that although Christianity explicitly rejects the notion of 'living by the sword', this is precisely what is attempted by Caesaropapism. In order to fill the vacuum created by the contradictions within Caesaropapism, it is necessary to inject pagan ideas, and this process is illustrated in Stark's two main examples of established churches (and reactions against them)—Anglicanism and Russian Orthodoxy. The *antithesis* of established Christianity is sectarianism, and this form of religious expression is claimed to arise only in protest against established churches: hence, the observation that sects apparently arise in Catholic cultures is ingeniously disposed of by the contention either that these were not *really* Christian sects or that the dominant form of religious organization was not *really* Catholicism.

The imposing *synthesis* of the dialectical triad thus becomes only too predictable: it is the universal Church, and Roman Catholicism is its foremost example. In fact, Roman Catholicism and Calvinism are given as examples of the universal Church, but since Calvinism is seen as 'an attempt' [18c:410] which largely failed to materialize, there is a full discussion of Catholicism only. What is highly significant for the present argument, however, is the way that Stark steps outside his sociological role when he is discussing the universal Church and becomes the committed apologist. Thus the universal Church is depicted in the following way: 'It refuses to be turned by the influences which impinge on it from the secular environment: it keeps its eyes on the beyond, in relation to which the here-and-now appears relatively so valueless, so uninteresting, as hardly to merit any attention, let alone to justify intensive preoccupation.' [18c:5]

The implications of this statement are quite staggering: Stark is in effect demanding that whatever judgements may be made about other Christian groups on sociological criteria—and it will be shown that Stark's notion of a 'sociological' judgement in the case of sectarian groups goes to the extreme of materialism—the same kinds of judgement are illicit in a treatment of Roman Catholicism. If the latter, embodied in the universal Church, is in Stark's view explicitly out of range of and disconnected from social influences, then one might logically conclude that it is also beyond the scope of sociological enquiry. This attitude to Catholicism seems a particularly clear example of the first position described above—that which postulates the complete separation of religious phenomena from any other form of organization or belief. The observer with this orientation will usually deny to the uncommitted sociologist any right to meddle in things which do not concern him. Thus I think it is quite significant that at one point in his text Stark refers to 'Troeltsch and Weber, and with them the whole throng of the semi-educated . . .' [18c:96], because this sums up the attitude of the passionately committed participant towards the dispassionately inquiring observer. It shows also that there is a very poor basis for the sociology of religion in this approach because it is inextricably involved in making extra-sociological judgements.

A somewhat similar problem, though on a much less polemical level, is raised by the tradition of religious sociology—which often goes under its French name of *sociologie religieuse*, since it is so closely associated with the work of the French sociologist Gabriel le Bras. Although le Bras himself has set out the programme of *sociologie religieuse* as 'to embrace every religion, whether living or dead, ancient and modern'; adding: 'In our view it is essential to get the co-operation of every science. We find demarcation disputes objectionable' [3:133], the characteristic interests of the discipline as it now exists are for the most part institutional, Roman Catholic and in many respects service-oriented (since the 'problem-defining agency' for many socio-religious research institutes is quite often the religious hierarchy itself). This 'inner-religious' orientation is distinct from that which sees sociology as an irrelevant incursion on forbidden territory because it regards the posture of social science as a legitimate and necessary one; but to the extent that the content of theological dogma is taken *as given* rather than as part of the problem to be defined, it would appear—as was argued earlier—to set its basic assumptions beyond sociological discourse.

An account of le Bras's work highlights this extra-sociological aspect:

> It is apparent from a perusal of his writings that le Bras accepts the theological dogma of the religious society *as a starting point*. As a practising member of the particular faith under scrutiny, he wittingly makes his studies 'inside' the faith. Enormous advantages are evident: intimate knowledge of meanings, of structure, of administrative process, of goals, along with the relatively facile access to both quantitative and qualitative data. As a result, the studies are carried forward with sympathy, precision, penetration and responsibility. On the other hand, the risks of an 'inside' study need to be weighed also. How can the researcher transcend a debilitating naïveté toward the phenomena? How can he be truly 'objective', eschewing temptations to utilize only data which promote the faith? Indeed how can he achieve a balanced, critical and sophisticated evaluation of the religious society which he studies? [15:81]

As the writer of this article goes on to point out, this is not a new problem in history or sociology. At the same time, the procedure articulated by le Bras of adopting both theological assumptions and the discipline of the social sciences is not in itself a solution to the problem. To demonstrate the type of criticism which le Bras circumvents rather than answers, two examples from the work of Ernst Troeltsch and Max Weber—which will be outlined in greater detail subsequently—can be given. In his elaboration of the church–sect dichotomy, Troeltsch took doctrinal statements as a 'starting point' to the extent that he traced the legitimate pedigree of both types of Christian organiz-ation to complementary elements in the New Testament. It is also clear that Troeltsch tried to rescue these terms from theo-logical controversy. [20:333–4] However, this does not in itself guarantee that his interpretation is thereby value-free, and recent criticisms of his early work have directed attention at Troeltsch's tendency to regard sectarian religion as in some sense more 'real' because of its spontaneous, other-worldly characteristics: as a corollary, church-type religion is given the evaluative label 'compromised'. Similarly, Weber's image of the Israelite prophet has been challenged as a Protestant view in that Weber relied largely on the historical evidence of Protestant scholars (which, admittedly, was almost all he had at his disposal), whereas a less theologically-weighted body of evidence might suggest quite different interpretations of the role of prophecy. [2] What these examples reveal is the extent to which sociological concepts can be criticized and developed by *detaching* them as far as possible from underlying theological assumptions, rather than *locating* them so firmly in such assumptions. The criticism which can be made of *sociologie religieuse* is much the same as the criticism which can be made of the philosophical critique of sociology of Peter Winch. [24] While it is true that the 'understanding' which a *member* has of either his religion or his society is an important component of any explanation which attempts to incorporate aspects of the social actor's meaningful reality, it does not follow from this that the only way a sociologist can 'understand' the particular religion or society is by himself *becoming* a member.

Rather, it would only follow if it were maintained that nothing more than a single integrated 'understanding' was possible within any one social context (and the actual definition of what constitutes 'one social context' would seem to involve some external criteria). Thus, the only 'understanding' of a religious group must necessarily involve being part of it and sharing its definitions. Even this position gets us very little closer to a solution of the problem, because the question then arises: what *kind* of member is it necessary to be?—clergy or lay?—centrally involved or marginally involved? There is a solid body of evidence—from those 'inside' as well as those 'outside' the different religious institutions—which shows that radically different 'understandings' of the institution may persist *within* it. One need only point to the distinct schools of churchmanship within the Church of England [7:181–7], to the different meaning which may be attached to membership within the same religious group [1;4;17], or to the differential commitment to ecumenism among clergy and laity [22] to indicate that this is so.

An analogy by J. M. Yinger is a useful way of anticipating the line which will be followed in a later section of this chapter. He asks the question, 'How is it possible . . . to see a stained-glass window from the outside?' [25:1] The negative answer to Winch might be paraphrased by noting that even from the *inside* a stained-glass window can be seen from many different angles or may be totally obscured by pieces of architecture, and that in any case it depends on an external source of light. A more limited claim might be made on behalf of sociology that it is at least able to see better from the outside the way in which the individual panes of glass have been put together and can thus study the formal structure without deing distracted by a total effect which is difficult to depict in formal or statistical terms. But we can go further than this and claim that sociology provides us with a number of theoretical insights and methodological techniques by means of which we can study the history of the group, employ its own definitions in a process of *verstehen*, and can often participate in its activities—all of which are the equivalent of introducing an internal source of illumination which *does* allow us to look at the window from the outside. As long as we make clear where we are standing this is a legitimate and productive exercise, and it obviates the necessity of engaging in the sociological equivalent of 'total immersion' before making statements about the religious group in question, though detachment is not always easy to maintain. [8]

A similar concern with extra-sociological judgements characterizes the orientation which lies at the opposite extreme. Here, the basic position adopted is that religious beliefs, far from being beyond human scrutiny and explanation, are so much a product of the social environment in which they are located that it is possible to give a comprehensive account of their meaning and significance which is composed entirely of socio-economic explanations. It is sometimes implied by this approach, and it is even explicitly incorporated into the work of some analysts, that religion can never be 'real' in the sense that it claims some non-empirical point of reference for its adherents which it is beyond the scope of the human sciences to explain. The corollary of this is the argument that what appear to be religious activities and goals can always be reduced to empirical statements about the social world.

This epiphenomenalist approach varies somewhat according to the writer who is using it, but all the variants of this position have one thing in common: they involve a basic judgement about the reality or unreality of religious explanations as such, and they thus preclude any analysis of non-empirical goals that is not preceded by a translation of those goals into entirely empirical terms. The questionable aspect of this procedure is the assumption that such a translation is possible without eliminating a meaningful part of the phenomenon being studied, and since religious adherents themselves regard certain kinds of non-empirical statement as meaningful, this would seem to indicate that a satisfactory explanation of their actions must at some point include—at least in part—this aspect of their definition of the situation. Any attempt to explain away religion in naturalistic terms presents the sociologist with an unnecessary and, I think, misguided task, but since this approach has a long pedigree in sociology it is worth studying at length. The early evolutionist writers—Comte, Tylor, Spencer and Frazer—are usually cast in the role of rationalists who could not find a place for religion in their categories except in positivistic, and therefore empirical terms, and it is worth looking closely at their contributions to the early development of the sociology of religion.

Much of the second chapter is concerned with these early theories of religion, and there it is suggested that some of the accounts given by the positivists are rather more subtle than is usually claimed. For the moment, we can highlight a more recent treatment of religion as an *epiphenomenon*—a shadow of some more substantial reality—in Werner Stark's treatment of sectarianism. While apparently setting the universal church in a position which is inaccessible to social influences, Stark adopts a thoroughgoing reductionist approach to sectarian phenomena. Thus, when he comes to study the origin of sects, Stark goes as far as to underwrite a Marxist interpretation: 'Marxists are, by and large, within their rights when they claim that sect movements are phenomena of an ongoing class struggle in societies within which the class conflict as such has not yet become conscious.' [18b:5] The sect is therefore held to represent a contra-culture of the economically or politically underprivileged, and even the fellowship of love within a sect is impure because it is only a reaction to the surrounding society's antagonism. The sectarian claim to direct inspiration is the result of a 'philosophy of sour grapes' [18b:130] of the educationally and culturally deprived.

In other words, having depicted the universal church—what we are led to believe is 'real' Christianity—as above the social environment, Stark then goes on to argue that sectarian Christianity takes its form almost completely from strains existing in the social environment. In doing so he reduces the phenomenon of sectarianism to a secondary, almost disreputable form of religious expression. Bryan Wilson—a sociologist who has made a number of studies of sects—has rightly pointed out that Stark's views represent 'an extraordinary, extra-sociological judgement'. [23] Equally extraordinary is the way in which Stark manipulates his categories so as to support the central argument that sects only arise in protest against established churches. For example, he follows the interpretation of the Catholic writer Ronald Knox that medieval sects were not 'really' Christian manifestations at all (and thus had little to do with Roman Catholicism) but were Eastern imports. In a similar way, the apparent emergence of sectarianism and caesaropapism within French Catholicism are accounted for by the claim that this was not 'really' Catholicism but Gallicanism. As a result, the categories of established church and sect are shown to be contaminated by their too close contact with the society in which they emerge, while the category of the universal Church—rather like the island of Laputa in *Gulliver's Travels*—floats serenely in the air.

The third attitude to the observation of religious phenomena occupies an intermediate position between the two extremes, and it has been an important source of the demand by sociologists to have a legitimate interest in the study of religion. On the one hand it rejects the argument that religion is not amenable to scrutiny by the empirical techniques of sociology on the grounds that religious beliefs are held and expressed by men, and that the 'outward and visible sign' of this commitment most often takes a social form (even when it does not, as in the case of an isolated hermit, it may well have important implications for the rest of a society). Since sociology lays claim to a body of theoretical knowledge and systematic insights on social activity and organization, then there is no apparent reason why these should not be applied to this *aspect* of religious institutions. On the other hand, although the specialized orientation of sociology necessarily involves the observer in making judgements about what constitute the most appropriate aspects of a phenomenon for the purposes of his own research, this need not imply that he adopts the basic assumption that a complete explanation can in every case be expressed in a set of statements about the social activity of those involved. What is regarded as meaningful by the actors concerned will not always be couched in terms of goals which are empirically 'visible', and if we restrict our perspective to include only those activities which can be measured and tested on the criterion of their conformity with 'visible' reality, we are likely to omit or misunderstand much of what is meaningful to the actors.

It is worth elaborating this point, because it is a fundamental issue in the sociology of religion—and one over which there has been a considerable amount of argument. Basically, the position proposed is that we regard the sociological approach to religion as one among a number of possible approaches, each of which is valid within its own sphere of reference and using its own techniques. If the sociologist appears to ignore certain approaches and techniques of evaluation—for instance, if he refuses to commit himself on the question of what constitutes a valid 'revelation'— this is not because he necessarily denies the possibility of making this kind of judgement, but because *as a sociologist* he would not feel qualified to make it. A theologian or a committed believer, of course, might well consider himself qualified to make such judgements, but in doing so he would be claiming qualifications which are outside sociology. To say this is not, however, to imply that sociologists are unconcerned with theological claims: they may regard it as a vital part of their investigations to study the competing claims to a valid source of revelation that are often made by different religious groups within the same religious tradition. But sociologists can only take these claims as social facts, and cannot arbitrate between them. Sometimes this may be a source of controversy between sociologists and committed members of the religious group—there is always the possibility that a sociologist may misinterpret theological statements, as Weber has been accused of doing in his study of Calvinism and capitalism—but this would seem to me to be more a question of detailed interpretation then of basic objectives.

The criticisms made of Werner Stark and of *sociologie religieuse* should not be taken to mean that it is impossible to be both a committed believer and a sociologist of religion. The mere fact that so many sociologists in this field also happen to be practising members of different faiths would make such an argument absurd. It would also cast doubt on the viability of sociology in general, since most sociologists apparently manage to be participating members of the societies they study. At the same time, the sociologist adopts a particular *role* in his investigations which is partly defined by the body of theory from which he draws his hypotheses and partly by the critical scrutiny of his work among other sociologists. Thus there are expected standards and procedures surrounding the sociologist's role, and these apply no less rigorously to the believer *qua* sociologist than they do to his uncommitted colleague. Stark can be criticized because he oversteps this role and becomes an apologist for one particular brand of Christianity: as an indication of this, Bryan Wilson's review of his volume on 'Established Religion' commented on how far from the central traditions of the subject this book stands. [23] Religious sociology is a form of empiricism, and it can validly be argued of its practitioners: 'They already have their own philosophical framework as it were and can therefore afford to look at religious facts outside the special spectacles provided by classical sociology.' [11 : 69] In so far as *sociologie religieuse* sees its 'problem-defining agency' and source of basic objectives as lying outside the competence of sociological debate, we can say that it has surrendered part of its role. For the sociologist to state that his own approach to the study of religion does not exhaust its meaning, but simply analyses one aspect of it, is a modest claim: it none the less imposes strict demands on his procedures.

In this chapter it has been argued that the observer of religious phenomena might adopt one of three distinct stances and that the sociology of religion is possible only if the two extremes of these are avoided. If religion is regarded as an autonomous, self-regulating segment of human experience and activity which is above the influences of the social environment then it would not provide material for the empirical techniques of sociology. On the other hand, the assumption that it is necessary to reduce religion to its *real* components, which can be seen to lie entirely in the economic and social environment of its devotees, means that sociology necessarily takes the form of a critique of religion. However, if the sociological interpretation of religion is regarded as no more than one *perspective* in which no fundamental judgement over the 'reality' or 'unreality' of religion is implied, then it has a valid claim within its own frame of reference. In particular, the sociological perspective is based on a recognition that the meaningful reality of the adherents to a particular set of religious beliefs forms an integral part of the field of study. A brief account of the early development of the sociology of religion—emphasizing the way in which beliefs of a non-empirical nature were dealt with by sociologists—is given in chapter 2.

REFERENCES

1 BERGER, PETER L. 'Sectarianism and religious sociation', *American Journal of Sociology* vol. LXIV, no. 1, July 1958, pp. 41–4.

2 BERGER, PETER L. 'Charisma and religious innovation: the social location of Israelite prophecy', *American Sociological Review* vol. 28, no. 6, December 1963, pp. 940–50.

3 BROTHERS, JOAN (ed.) *Readings in the Sociology of Religion* (Pergamon, Oxford 1967).

4 DEMERATH III, NICHOLAS J. *Social Class in American Protestantism* (Rand McNally, Chicago 1965).

5 DEMERATH III, NICHOLAS J., and HAMMOND, PHILLIP E. *Religion in Social Context: Tradition and Transition* (Random House, New York 1969).

6 GREELEY, ANDREW M. 'After secularity: the neo-Gemeinschaft society: a post-Christian postscript', *Sociological Analysis* vol. 27, no. 3, Fall 1966.

7 HILL, MICHAEL *The Religious Order in a Sociological Context: A Study of Virtuoso Religion and its Legitimation in the Nineteenth Century Church of England*, Ph.D. thesis (University of London 1971).

8 JOHNSON, WELDON T. 'The Religious Crusade: revival or ritual?', *American Journal of Sociology* vol. 76, no. 5, March 1971, pp. 873–80.

9 KNUDTEN, RICHARD D. (ed.) *The Sociology of Religion* (Appleton-Century-Crofts, New York 1967).

10 LE BRAS, GABRIEL 'Religious sociology and science of religions', in BROTHERS, JOAN, op. cit.

11 MARTIN, DAVID A. *The Religious and the Secular* (Routledge and Kegan Paul, London 1969).

12 MEANS, RICHARD L. 'Weber's thesis of the Protestant Ethic: the ambiguities of received doctrine', *Journal of Religion* vol. XLV, no. 1, 1965, pp. 1–11.

13 NELSON, BENJAMIN 'Is the sociology of religion possible? A reply to Robert Bellah', *Journal for the Scientific Study of Religion* vol. 9, no. 2, 1970, pp. 107–11.

14 POULAT, E. 'Religious sociology and its aims', in BROTHERS, JOAN, op. cit.

15 SHIPPEY, FREDERICK A. 'The relations of theology and the social sciences according to Gabriel le Bras', *Archives de Sociologie des Religions* no. 20, July–December 1965, pp. 79–93.

16 SIMEY, LORD 'Weber's sociological theory, and the modern dilemma of value and belief in the social sciences', in BROTHERS, JOAN, op. cit.

17 SISSONS, PETER L. 'Concepts of church membership', in HILL, MICHAEL (ed.) *A Sociological Yearbook of Religion in Britain—4* (SCM Press, London 1971).

18 STARK, WERNER *The Sociology of Religion. A Study of Christendom* (Routledge and Kegan Paul, London):
   (a) *Volume I. Established Religion* (1966);
   (b) *Volume II. Sectarian Religion* (1967);
   (c) *Volume III. The Universal Church* (1967);
   (d) *Volume IV. Types of Religious Man* (1969).

19 SWIFT, D. F. *The Sociology of Education* (Routledge and Kegan Paul, London 1969).

20 TROELTSCH, ERNST *The Social Teaching of the Christian Churches*, 2 vols., translated by Olive Wyon (George Allen and Unwin, London 1931).

21 VRIJHOF, P. H. 'What is the sociology of religion? in BROTHERS, JOAN, op. cit.

22 WILSON, BRYAN R. *Religion in Secular Society* (Watts, London 1966).

23 WILSON, BRYAN R. 'Review article: establishment, sectarianism and partisanship', *Sociological Review* vol. 15, no. 2, July 1967, pp. 213–20.

24 WINCH, PETER GUY *The Idea of a Social Science* (Routledge and Kegan Paul, London 1960).

25 YINGER, JOHN MILTON *The Scientific Study of Religion* (Collier–Macmillan, London 1970).

2

The Early Development of the Sociology of Religion

BEFORE DISCUSSING the categories which particular sociologists have devised to accommodate aspects of meaningful reality that do not fit into a rational-empirical framework, it is first necessary to consider the extent to which the earlier theories of religion can be seen as attempts to maintain a 'rational' interpretation, and hence as being involved in basic judgements about the reality or unreality of religion. The early evolutionist theories of religion are often cited as attempts to explain away those phenomena, including religious explanations, which could not be fitted within a positivist framework. The latter were exposed as 'primitive' modes of thought, which characterized cultures at a lower level of development than those in which scientific explanations came to predominate. At the same time, the religious type of explanation represented for some writers an advance on the more primitive, magical view of the world, which was seen to lie at the very origin of human intellectual development. But scientific explanations, since they were intellectually superior, would come to displace a religious world-view, and sociology was sometimes given an important role in this final process since it could—or so it was thought—suggest alternative bases for moral and social norms. The underlying judgement in these positivist schemata is that 'real' and 'scientific' are closely identified and therefore that in order to arrive at a true perception of man's place in the natural order it is necessary to discard the imperfect representations of religion.

This approach to religion is best seen in the work of four of the most prominent exponents of nineteenth-century positivism—

Comte, Tylor, Spencer and Frazer: of these (together with Durkheim) Scharf notes that they 'all begin from the assumption that men do not, in their religion, apprehend a reality outside themselves, but rather come to imagine, because of certain mysterious aspects of human existence, spirits, gods and supernatural forces. [Men's] thinking is immature, uncontrolled by pragmatic tests, and perhaps goes awry under the influence of powerful emotions.' [60:14] In other words, religion is a 'mistake' and is brought in to explain events and phenomena whose 'real' significance can be more accurately accounted for in empirical terms. With this apparently unequivocal rejection of religion it is somewhat paradoxical that two of these theorists are noted for their highly religious conception of human society and that two more, while not adopting quite such a canonical mould, at least have a soft underbelly to the extent that they regard religion and similar non-empirical systems as providing in some ways valid meanings for their adherents.

Of the French sociologist Auguste Comte, Nisbet has written: 'it is often hard to remember that we are reading the works not of a theologian but of a self-proclaimed scientist' [47:228]. The strength of religious conceptions in Comte's writings, especially in his later writings, has often been remarked on: this appears contradictory in view of his avowed goal of replacing existing religious beliefs, but since he also wished to introduce in their place the new religion of Positivism the whole exercise clearly becomes one of transposition rather than of demolition. Above all, steady change and the avoidance of discontinuity are the main features of Comte's doctrine of progress—'at most he was a gradual reformer of whom Burke might have approved' [65:36]— and it is possible to suggest that the search for continuity in a period of rapid social and cultural change such as that which confronted Comte may often be serviced by religious institutions and beliefs. At all events, Comte's Law of the Three Stages, which at first sight appears to be a theory of secularization, turns out instead to be a programme of religious retrenchment, a counter-reformation with the clear purpose of reintroducing the social cohesion of medieval Catholicism in the name of the Religion of Humanity. Even the task which Comte undertook was in some ways similar to that of the Council of Trent, as the summary phrase of one writer suggests: 'Il faut terminer la Révolution et réorganiser la société.' [5:13]

The Law of the Three Stages postulated a gradual but inevitable tendency in human intellectual development—and Comte was interested in 'the progressive course of the human mind, regarded as a whole' [14:27] rather than in specific types of society—moving from an original state in which every branch of knowledge was characterized by a Theological, or fictitious theoretical basis, through a Metaphysical, or abstract stage which provided a transition to the third and final scientific stage, in which every branch of knowledge was characterized by its positivistic theoretical basis. This final stage was 'fixed and definitive' [14:28] rather than being a point of departure or a phase of transition. Between the first and second stages Comte speaks of a reorientation which is strongly reminiscent of 'the death of God', for instead of supposing all phenomena to be 'produced by the immediate action of supernatural beings' [14:28] there is a modification of man's thought so that explanations are given in terms of abstract forces, and the real world is interpreted by reference to these abstract entities.

Beyond the abstractions of stage two, however, lies the abandonment of the search for abstract notions and the attempt of positivism to explain phenomena in terms of the laws governing their operation—'that is their invariable relations of succession and resemblance'. [14:28] Comte gives a clear idea of the ultimate aim of positivism when he indicates how each of the three stages reaches a final point of development, after which in the case of the first two stages there is a transition to the succeeding stage: thus the ultimate point of the theological stage is arrived at with the development of strict monotheism; in the metaphysical stage the corresponding point is provided by the notion of one great entity, Nature, as the cause of all phenomena. In the positive stage we can anticipate that all particular phenomena will be subsumed under some general fact, 'such as Gravitation, for instance'. [14:28] Thus Almighty God gives way to the Ground of our Being and is eventually revealed as the Great Architect.

We find in Comte's work not a sociological interpretation of religion, but a religious interpretation of society. This draws attention to a major distinction between Comte and Durkheim, in that the latter proposed to interpret religion sociologically whereas the former was very much 'encapsulated' [59:197] in a religious position. Hence for Comte, if there was to be any firm basis for social groupings it must be located in religion. With this basic assumption, Comte was then in a position to make judgements between the various religious systems on the criterion of their contribution to social cohesiveness. He thought that the thing which reconciled men to the 'intellectually unsatisfactory' conceptions of God was the practical value these conceptions held for extending and strengthening of the social bond: this implies a 'reduction' of the non-empirical aspects of religion to statements about their social effectiveness. Polytheism was in this sense superior to Fetishism because it lent itself to the formation of a wider community, the State, whereas Fetishism tended rather to confine men's sympathies to the narrower limits of the family. Monotheism was the necessary basis of a still wider social unit in which men were bound together simply as men and not because of any special ties of blood or language: this was the case as long as the truth of the unity of humanity had not yet been verified scientifically and still needed external support. Once the science of sociology had revealed this unity there would no longer be any need for such external scaffolding (an argument which closely parallels the 'global optimism' of some contemporary theologians who see 'the world becoming one' and 'the world coming of age').

At this point, Comte makes one of those characteristic and in many ways contradictory judgements about religion which quite unmistakably puts him in the same camp as writers like Edward Gibbon, David Hume and later Freud and Marx: indeed, Comte's remarks are very similar to Marx's on alienation. He argues that an increasing generality of theological belief was a necessary precondition for the establishment of social unity on a broader and broader basis, but that, by directing men's eyes not to each other but to supernatural beings and by making the major focus of life turn on the favour or disfavour of such beings rather than on the social interaction of men with each other—in other words by reducing the concerns of this world and subordinating them to those of another—the theological orientation of monotheism tended to dissolve rather than knit closer the bonds of society. The relation of an individual to God tended to isolate him from his fellow-men and created an unparalleled selfishness which dissolved public life: the logical extreme of this was the life of the hermit.

Comte's religious interpretation of society—when set against the background of the views of Hume and Gibbon—gives us such a clear idea of the way in which *religious* preferences lay behind an apparently sociological interpretation, that it is useful to consider the different theories of these writers. In one sense, all three thinkers are agreed: religion is to be judged according to the criterion of social cohesion, or 'civic virtue', and religion is most to be castigated when it substitutes for social solidarity the selfish, individualistic pursuit of the supernatural. Comte's view of the hermit's life is exactly the same as that of Gibbon, who used the analogy of the cowls worn by monks almost in the sense of 'supernatural blinkers' when he wrote in one passage: 'Recluse fanatics have few ideas or sentiments to communicate; a special license of the abbot regulated the time and duration of their familiar visits; and, at their silent meals, they were enveloped in their cowls, inaccessible, and almost invisible, to each other. . . .' [28, vol. iv:71] Elsewhere Gibbon refers to hermits, 'who indulged their unsocial, independent fanaticism'. [28, vol. iv:72] Catholicism, with its strong component of monasticism, thus represents for Gibbon the most socially disruptive form of religion. Hume shared Gibbon's antipathy towards Catholicism, but this seems to have led him into a fundamentally contradictory position. To explain this, it is necessary to trace the 'oscillation' theory of polytheism and monotheism which Hume put forward in *The Natural History of Religion*. [34]

Hume's theory can be summarized in his own words: 'The feeble apprehensions of men cannot be satisfied with conceiving their deity as a pure Spirit and perfect intelligence; and yet their natural terrors keep them from imputing to him the least shadow of limitation and imperfection. They fluctuate betwixt these opposite sentiments.' [34:37] Polytheism, thinks Hume, was the first and most ancient religion of mankind: the multitude had a 'grovelling and familiar notion' of the supernatural powers, and since the natural progress of thought involves a movement from the inferior to the superior we can suppose that monotheism

B

developed out of this primitive state of idolatry. However, this rational progression was not typical of the 'vulgar' movement towards monotheism, which happened as a result of men's flattery of one god among many. One God would be singled out from a range of gods as being more powerful than the rest, and he would be elevated to a supreme position while the rest dropped out of significance—this is the situation in monotheism. However, having elevated this being so far, a vacuum is created between God and men which has to be filled by subordinate agents and mediators who maintain the channels of communication. This brings the pendulum back to the polytheistic position. Not only the primitive world but also the world of medieval Catholicism is depicted as falling into the polytheistic category. The saints and angels of Catholicism were in many ways analogous to the heroes and gods of the Greeks. But having drawn up his examples of polytheism, Hume then goes on to show the relevance of the oscillation theory for the cohesion of society.

Hume shares with Gibbon and Comte the idea that the higher are the obligations to God, the lower will be man's obligations to his fellow-men. (This negative correlation was perhaps most vividly portrayed by Nietzsche when he argued that with the rise of the Christian God, 'the record god up to this time', [46:109] there arose also the maximum feelings of guilt—and by guilt he meant a feeling of having broken one's debt to the community.) In line with these general conceptions of divine transcendence, Hume thought that where the gods were seen as only slightly superior to mankind, people were more at ease in their addresses to them, with the result that activity, spirit, courage, magnanimity, a love of liberty and all the other virtues that aggrandize a people would pervade the society. There were of course disadvantages in the case of polytheism because it did permit corrupt and barbarous practices, but in the main it was tolerant of other forms of belief, and the pagan heroes were thought of as defending the native country. Medieval Catholicism, on the other hand, shared none of the benefits of polytheism since its saints received their celestial honours by means of flagellation, cowardice, humility and slavish obedience. Thus there is the seeming paradox that Hume's view of monotheism, in which a deity who is infinitely superior to mankind produces a form of submission and

abasement best represented by the 'monkish virtues' of mortifi-
cation, penance, humility and passive suffering, is carried over into
precisely that form of Christianity—namely, medieval Catholicism
—which for Hume best represented an example of polytheism.

Against this background, Comte's argument attempts an
ingenious rescue of Catholicism before going on to give details
of the new form it will take under the guise of Positivism. He
agrees that it is a tendency of Christianity to break down social
solidarity by directing attention on an infinite Being, but points
out that the theological priesthood has continually sought to
counteract the natural influences of its doctrine by making
additions which were inconsistent with its 'absolute' principle but
which rendered it better fitted for the purpose of binding men
together. This form of counter-action was especially necessary in a
monotheistic religion. Comte saw the process in terms of the
elaboration of a whole series of supplementary doctrines that
generally tended to connect God with men and men with each
other. Saint Paul, the 'real founder of Catholicism', [16:212] had
taken the first step in reducing monotheism to a shape in which it
could operate as an 'organic' doctrine. While the omnipotence of
God tended to raise him above all human sympathy and to destroy
the collective feelings of his worshippers, the doctrines of the
Trinity and the Incarnation again brought God near to men and
taught them to reverence in themselves a humanity which was
raised into unity with God, a doctrine that was symbolized in the
celebration of the Eucharist. As a result of the further development of the same influence, Comte pointed to the adoration of
the saints and above all of the Virgin Mary, when devotion was
really directed towards Humanity through the simplest and ten-
derest affections. The struggle between egoism and altruism was
symbolized by the doctrines of the Fall and Redemption.

Because Comte regarded these additions to or corrections of the
original doctrine as inconsistent or imperfect in themselves, and
furthermore inadequate for the social purpose they were designed
to serve, he also thought that they would naturally disappear
whenever monotheism was able to break loose from the bounds in
which the church had confined it. Protestantism was the first
indication of this change, 'for Protestantism is but an organized
anarchy, and the only elements of order in it are derived from an

instinctive conservatism, clinging to the fragments of a past doctrinal system which, in principle, has been abandoned'. [16:213–14] The Comtean version of progress amply demonstrates the way in which Comte was involved in making very fundamental judgements about the extent to which the content of religious beliefs was explicable in other than theological terms. With the partial exception of Fetishism, every past religion is seen as an amalgam of two radically inconsistent elements, only one of which could be traced to the theological principle itself. The other was due partly to the practical instinct of the priests, which led them to modify the logical results of that principle in conformity with men's social requirements, and partly to the fact that the priests found themselves in a subordinate position where they had to use spiritual means of conviction and persuasion rather than the cruder weapons of material force. To Comte, the conscious manipulation of religious symbols which was necessary if they were to provide a solid basis for social cohesiveness accounted for a considerable part of any religious belief system. Perhaps this helps to explain why Comte found it relatively easy to devise a detailed blueprint for the new religion of Positivism and to give an account of its 'liturgy, the sacraments, the rituals, and even the vestments to be worn by the priests of Positivism who are, at one and the same time, the scientists'. [47:229]

Another writer who took an intellectualist perspective when dealing with religious phenomena, and hence tended to regard them as primitive interpretations which were logically imperfect and mistaken when compared with scientific explanations, was Edward Tylor. In the course of a discussion of animism in his work *Primitive Culture*, he made a direct statement to 'those who have been accustomed to find theological subjects dealt with on a dogmatic, emotional, and ethical, rather than an ethnographic scheme'. [70, vol. ii:358] He expressed disagreement with the accounts given by travellers 'and especially by missionaries' [70, vol. ii:358] because these were often controversial and written from the viewpoint of an infallible orthodoxy. Although his own account is of a very different kind it does become involved in questions about the truth or falsity of religious beliefs: as Tylor notes, 'the doctrines here examined bear not only on the develop-

ment but the actual truth of religious systems'. [70, vol. ii:358]
The reason that these judgements could be made was because
Tylor had a broadly rationalistic conception of what we might
call *homo sociologus*, and this provided a basis for his methodological position. If man is for analytical purposes seen as a reasoning,
scientifically calculating being, then it makes sense to study his
religious behaviour as being conducted along similar lines.
Presumably Tylor, along with the other evolutionists, saw
himself as a scientifically calculating observer and applied this
culturally derived image to the people he was studying.

Nevertheless, Tylor shows considerable awareness of the
emotional as against the intellectual aspects of religion, which do
not figure very prominently in his discussion, and he justifies
their omission on the grounds that strict adherence to a particular
perspective is often a valuable source of scientific progress. His
argument is worth quoting at this point: 'Those to whom religion
means above all things religious feeling, may say to my argument
that I have written soullessly of the soul, and unspiritually of
spiritual things. Be it so: I accept the phrase not as needing an
apology, but as expressing a plan. Scientific progress is at times
most furthered by working along a distinct intellectual line,
without being tempted to diverge from the main object to what
lies beyond, in however intimate connexion.' [70, vol. ii:359]
Though the solutions adopted by more recent sociologists in their
studies of religion may be different from the perspective of Tylor,
the basic problem of inclusion and exclusion is just as relevant
now as it was then, and one of the tasks of this chapter is to try
and suggest how the problem might be dealt with.

Herbert Spencer's evolutionary theory adopted a similar
intellectualist approach to the study of religious phenomena, but
behind it lay a rather more subtle view of the significance of
religious beliefs and an almost mystical belief in the force which
propelled social development. He began by considering primitive
man's attitude to the phenomena of sleep, dreaming and death,
and he argued that the primitive explanation of these events was to
postulate a soul which was distinct from, though contained within,
man's body and could become detached for a time during sleep
and permanently at death. Thus a man's 'other-self' was supposed
to exist at least for a certain period after death and had to be given

the same respect as the living man had been given. Spencer's idea of social development in the sphere of religious beliefs was based on this primary notion about the propitiation of the ghosts of the dead. All human societies had a belief in an other-self after death, and most practised a form of ghost-propitiation at funerals and for some time after.

At a more advanced level of development can be found those societies in which a belief in the permanent existence of ghosts is coupled with a persistent form of ancestor-worship. Even more advanced are those societies in which there is a supernatural 'pecking order'—in which the 'worship of distinguished ancestors partially subordinates that of the undistinguished'. [14:50] Such subordination is more marked where the distinguished ancestor was a leader of a conquering race. On this framework Spencer is able to reveal the higher religions, including Judaism and Christianity, as being particular developments of a once-general belief in the spirits of the dead. Of Christianity he says: 'Even in our own day the kinship is traceable. The statement that God is a spirit, shows the application of a term which, otherwise applied, signifies a human soul. Only by its qualifying epithet is the meaning of Holy Ghost distinguished from the meaning of ghost in general'. [14:50] There can be no mistaking the fact that Spencer intended his concept of the 'elementary form' of ancestor-worship to be applied to every example of religion which could be identified: 'there is no exception then. Using the phrase ancestor-worship in its broadest sense as comprehending all worship of the dead, be they of the same blood or not, we conclude that ancestor-worship is the root of every religion. . . .' [14:51]

Hence, when he came to consider the function of ecclesiastical systems and institutions in a societal setting, it was to the basis of these more developed forms in the rudimentary form of ancestor-worship that Spencer directed attention. Spencer was particularly concerned, in the proof of his argument, with the consequences for social cohesion of death, and it is interesting to note that Durkheim gave it a parallel treatment. [3:40] Three things took place at a funeral, Spencer argued: firstly, it is the occasion for a family gathering and a strengthening of the bonds of kinship; secondly, the existence of a shared respect for the dead serves to neutralize antagonisms between family members and thus to heal some of the divisions between them; thirdly, when the wishes of the deceased are made known this tends to unite the descendants in the attempt to carry them out (though Spencer was prepared to acknowledge that disposal of the deceased's property might cause some conflict). Because all religion is in the last analysis derived from ancestor-worship, we may expect to find ecclesiastical institutions performing entirely analogous functions.

Out of this parallel emerges Spencer's functionalist theory of religion as a source of social cohesion: 'In several ways they [Ecclesiastical Institutions] maintain and strengthen social bonds and so conserve the social aggregate; and they do this in large measure by conserving beliefs, sentiments, and usages which evolved during earlier stages of the society, are shown by it, survival to have had an approximate fitness to the requirements, and are likely still to have it in great measure.' [14:127] Ecclesiastical institutions thus stand for social continuity and social cohesion, and because they embody the primitive notion of the rule of the dead over the living their function is to preserve the product of earlier experience in the face of the modifying influence of more recent experience. They are above all else bearers of tradition, and agents of social stability.

Despite his rationalistic approach, Spencer was notably prepared to admit that religious beliefs always had some basis in an ultimate fact. Because he took a relativist position on the validity of different systems of thought it was difficult to apply a thoroughgoing objective critique to religious phenomena. Both religion and science, Spencer thought, were agreed in admitting that there was an Unknowable area which lay beyond the phenomena of which we have knowledge: the particular value of religion was that it had always served the function of preventing men from becoming 'wholly absorbed in the relative or immediate, and of awakening them to a consciousness of something beyond it'. [51:130] The difficulty which this argument encounters is one which will reappear in chapter 10 when the problem of how to explain primitive religious beliefs will be set against the different interpretations of 'rationality'. Briefly, if it is possible to affirm that a thing exists then it cannot be completely unknowable. Spencer's belief in the relativity of knowledge was anchored in the notion that there could be 'a positive though vague consciousness' of some unconditioned reality *in addition* to the definite but relative knowledge we have. What Spencer saw as a barrier against scepticism, his critics have seen as merely a logical device. 'The fact is that Spencer's unknowable is neither unknowable nor wholly unknown, but merely serves as the postulated substratum of phenomena.' [54:301]

The work of James Frazer is usually included with that of Tylor and Spencer as an illustration of nineteenth-century evolutionism: once again, although he broadly fits into the role of an intellectualist critic of religion, some of his views were decidedly paradoxical, and he was certainly prepared to argue that science might not be the final level of evolutionary development. He began with a three-stage schema which is based on the same fundamental conception as that of Comte and Spencer—the gradual development of the human mind—but which differs from Comte's plan by postulating a movement from magic, through religion to science. Magic was obviously seen as an 'elementary form' because in its attempt to manipulate the forces of nature it bore a strong resemblance to modern science: '. . . its fundamental conception is identical with that of modern science; underlying the whole system is a faith, implicit but real and firm, in the order and uniformity of nature'. [14:32] The similarity is confirmed by the magical techniques used by primitive man, which rest on a notion of causal links. There are two main types of magic—imitative and sympathetic; the first derives from the principle that since an effect resembles its cause, or like produces like, it is possible to produce an effect by imitating it; and the second is based on the principle that things which have once been in contact but which are no longer so, still continue to influence each other, with the result that any fragment of an object or person may be used to influence the object or person. Having set out the basic patterns of magical thought, Frazer gives his primitive men a certain degree of approval for being perceptive enough to observe correlations: 'The principles of association are excellent in themselves, and indeed absolutely essential to the working of the human mind.' [14:32] However, as we are no doubt aware, a correlation does not demonstrate a causal relationship, and here primitive men made an obvious mistake: 'Legitimately applied, they [the principles of association] yield science; illegitimately applied they yield magic, the bastard sister of science.' [14:32] Hence magic is always false, and if it is true it is not magic but science.

However, primitive man is also credited with having gradually realized his mistake. First of all, religion is defined as 'a propitiation or conciliation of powers superior to man which are believed to direct and control the course of nature and of human life'. [14:33] So when man realizes he cannot rely on his own powers to manipulate the forces of nature for his own ends, a process of projection occurs which in significant ways resembles the process of alienation. Frazer depicts the decline of magic thus: 'When he discovers his mistake, when he recognizes sadly that both the order of nature which he had assumed and the control which he had believed himself to exercise over it were purely imaginary, he ceases to rely on his own intelligence and his own unaided efforts, and throws himself humbly on the mercy of certain great invisible beings behind the veil of nature, to whom he now ascribes all those far-reachings powers which he once arrogated to himself. Thus in the acuter minds magic is gradually superseded by religion. . . .' [22, vol. i:679]

Frazer's definition of magic leads him to postulate what might be termed a 'u curve' in the development from magic to science, since the systems of thought at either end of the continuum 'take for granted that the course of nature is determined, not by the passions or caprice of personal beings, but by the operation of immutable laws acting mechanically'. [14:34] The most important difference between magic and science is that in the former the notion of a fixed order of nature is implicit, while science makes it explicit. Religion, on the other hand, stands in complete contrast to magic and science because it presupposes a certain elasticity in the natural world, which can be deflected by propitiating certain super-natural beings who have the power to bring about changes in the course of events. Frazer is careful to emphasize that it is difficult to agree on a definition of religion, [14:33] but the one he selects places a major emphasis on the intervention of supernatural beings in the course of natural events. [14:33] Belief and practice are given as the two permanent elements of all religion, and the key notion of conscious and personal forces governing the world is contrasted with the view common to both magic and science that the forces governing the world are unconscious and impersonal.

This contrast explained for Frazer the hostility which he thought had often existed between priests and magicians. All the same, this was something which was relatively late in appearing, since in an earlier period of the history of religion the functions of priest and sorcerer were often combined—'or, to speak perhaps more correctly, were not yet differentiated from each other'. [14:35] In this situation man made sure of his double indemnity by on the one hand seeking the good-will of gods and spirits while simultaneously short-circuiting this process by going through magical formulae in pursuit of similar goals. At this point, Frazer very characteristically gives his primitive man a lesson in logic: 'In short, he [man] performed religious and magical rites simultaneously; he uttered prayers and incantations almost in the same breath, knowing or recking little of the *theoretical inconsistency of his behaviour*, so long as by hook or by crook he contrived to get what he wanted.' [14:35—my italics] This phrase gives us an immensely valuable insight into the intellectual perspective of the nineteenth-century evolutionists. Adopting as they did an image of man as a rational, calculating being, they could not resist the temptation to make judgements about the kinds of explanations that primitive man gave of natural events—thus magic, to Frazer, is 'an error into which the mind falls almost spontaneously'. [14:36]

And yet Frazer is much more sophisticated in his treatment than the prevailing view might suggest. For one thing, he was fully aware of some of the pitfalls involved in making judgements about the beliefs of other men. As an example of this, we can point to the passage in which he remarks on the mixture of magic and religion in Egypt: such a combination was theoretically inconsistent, but 'though we can perceive the union of discrepant elements in the faith and practice of the ancient Egyptians, it would be rash to assume that the people themselves did so'. [49:1082] An underlying notion of coercion of supernatural agents was identified in modern European Catholicism, which permitted Frazer to argue that the popular versions of established religious creeds might well contain magical elements: this is very much the same kind of approach as the one adopted by Keith Thomas. [69] Above all, Frazer is very careful to stress the coexistence and interpenetration of the three systems of thought. Even the origin of magical thought is not given as an absolutely fixed starting point. We are told that there are 'some grounds for thinking' [49 : 1083] that magic on its own was once a self-sufficient basis for man's explanations of the natural order, and such evidence as we have may 'incline us to surmise' [49: 1083] that magic antedates religion.

The analogy he uses to portray the idea of interpenetration is of a fabric woven from three different coloured threads—black representing magic, red representing religion, and white for science. If we look back through history, he argues, we see its beginning as a chequer of black and white—'a patchwork of true and false notions' [24:713]—but further along, though the black and white motif persists, there appears in the middle of the fabric a red tint which increasingly shades off into white. Having set out this complex and gradual transformation, Frazer refuses to commit himself to a naïve view of progress: science is a possible source of progress, and for this reason should be encouraged, but it is by no means certain that the scientific theory of the world is the best that can be formulated—nor is its future assured. One cannot but be struck by the remarkable parallel between Frazer's uncertain vision of the future and the pessimistic vision which was to haunt Weber shortly afterwards; indeed, it is worth putting the two together. Frazer writes: 'Will the great movement which for centuries has been slowly altering the complexion of thought be continued in the near future? Or will a reaction set in which may arrest progress and even undo much that has been done?' [24:713] Frazer is clearly intent on enlisting his readers' support in the task of assisting the progress of science, but Weber's pessimism in the face of the rationalization he depicts in *The Protestant Ethic and the Spirit of Capitalism* is unmistakable: 'No one knows who will live in this cage in the future, or whether at the end of this tremendous development entirely new prophets will arise, or there will be a great rebirth of old ideas and ideals, or, if neither, mechanized petrification, embellished with a sort of convulsive self-importance.' [71:182]

The difference, of course, is in the attitude adopted towards a perceived growth in scientific rationality. Frazer sees the only hope of future progress in the continued development of science, and this fits well with his frequently expressed attitude towards magic and superstition. Looking at modern Europe, for instance, he thought the continued existence of a substratum of magical thought cold not fail to be 'a standing menace to civilization. We seem to move on a thin crust which may at any moment be rent by the subterranean forces slumbering below'. [49:1085] In a later work, subtitled *A Plea for Superstition*, Frazer was prepared to acknowledge that for certain men at certain levels of development superstition had performed highly positive functions—it had preserved respect for government (especially monarchy), private property, marriage and human life—and he was very careful to insist that, as the simple societies crumbled under the impact of European civilization, they should be very carefully documented. [23:174–6] But his basic attitude was quite unequivocal: superstition was a threat, and as such should be eradicated. Perhaps the best way of portraying the difference between Frazer and Weber is by saying that, while the former proclaimed 'the disenchantment of the world', the latter regarded it with a kind of agonized fatalism. We will shortly be considering what H. Stuart Hughes has called 'the revolt against positivism' [33:33] and its impact on the sociological study of religion, especially in the work of Max Weber. It is worth noting that the two quotations that were introduced might almost serve to epitomize the important watershed in European thought that occurred at the turn of the century.

Frazer also reveals another preoccupation of the nineteenth-century rationalists, which is perhaps most explicitly represented in the later writings of Freud but which forms a continuous theme in theories of progress. If the traditional belief-system of Christianity must inevitably be exposed by science as an inadequate and mythical body of thought, then what is to become of the moral basis of society which has previously rested on this false premiss? In other words, does not religious decline of necessity imply moral decline? Frazer's haunting image of a 'thin crust of civilization' and his almost missionary zeal in proclaiming a rational basis for society exemplifies this persistent theme. In a different form, Comte's religion of positivism with its traditional religious framework and its edict of social cohesion is yet another variation on this theme.

The early evolutionists in different degrees maintained a positivistic framework and were consequently drawn into the type of judgement about the 'reality' or 'unreality' of religious and magical beliefs which, it has been argued, sociology is not well equipped to handle. There are several examples of the 'revolt against positivism' through which religion was given a much more comprehensive and less evaluative analytical treatment. Talcott Parsons has provided an extremely useful account of this development in the work of Pareto, Malinowski, Durkheim and Weber: [48] by following his argument it is possible to trace the links between 'rationalistic positivism' and the more recent development of the sociology of religion in which the incorporation of beliefs that cannot be tested by the methods of the empirical sciences is an important part of the attempt to account for perceptions of meaningful reality that the actor regards as authentic and which cannot simply be dismissed as mistaken.

Pareto began with a very similar schema to that of the positivists. Patterns of social action, he contended, could in many cases be explained in terms of what he called their 'logico-experimental' standard. By this he meant that the goals pursued and the means adopted could be expressed in terms of their empirical scientific validity. However, he found it necessary to introduce the idea of two types of deviation from this criterion. One was the type of deviation familiar to evolutionists such as Frazer, which consisted in the failure to solve a problem that was intrinsically capable of being solved in a scientific way. The cause of such failure might be ignorance of available techniques, mistakes, or the acceptance as facts of things which could be empirically disproved as such. This type of deviation Pareto called 'pseudo-scientific', and he was careful to state that the awareness of error was governed by the *observer's* knowledge and understanding. Pareto was quite unambiguous on the question of absolute truth, whether in the form of a strongly-held religious belief or in the form of dogmatic positivism (which he explicitly labelled 'religious'): 'The man who believes he possesses the absolute truth cannot concede that there are any other truths in the world. Hence the fervent christian and the pugnacious "free-thinker" are, and must be, equally intolerant.' [21:171]

The other type of deviation was even more important for the sociological study of religion, and Pareto referred to it under the collective heading of 'the theories which surpass experience'. In order to give this concept greater clarity, it should be noted that the Italian word *esperienza* refers both to 'experience' and 'experiment', and thus denotes 'that which can be observed'. Thus Pareto included among such theories propositions which were intrinsically incapable of being tested by scientific procedures, such as the attributes of God.

Pareto's contribution to the study of religious phenomena is complex and does not easily lend itself to a brief summary. Its governing principle was the *relative* nature of sociological knowledge, and he demanded that in front of every proposition which was affirmed in his work there should be placed the conditional clause *'within the limits of time and experience as known to us'*. [21:173, original italics] In his attitude to religious phenomena he quite definitely fits the third of the perspectives set out in chapter 1:

> We do not propose to concern ourselves at all with the intrinsic 'truth' of any religion, faith, metaphysical or moral belief whatever—not because of any scornful disregard for these things, but simply because they are outside the limits in which we choose to work. Religions, beliefs and the like will only be considered externally in as much as they are social facts, and entirely apart from their intrinsic merits. A proposition like 'A *must* equal B by grace of some principle superior to experience' will therefore not come within our examination. But we shall examine how such a belief originates and grows and what its relations are with other social facts. [21:172]

Malinowski likewise took as his base-line of analysis the way in which men adapted to practical situations by using rational knowledge and techniques, but his way out of the positivistic framework was to show that such knowledge and techniques were on their own inadequate, since there was always an area of uncertainty in their application which was beyond man's control, and it was in this area that magic was brought in as a complementary mechanism. Hence magic, rather than God, fills the gaps left by science.

From his studies of the Trobriand Islands, Malinowski concluded that the natives possessed an impressive amount of valuable empirical knowledge about gardening, which was their main source of subsistence. Although they used fairly rudimentary implements they were able to provide enough food to support a dense population and at times to produce a surplus which they had begun to export. Yet combined with all their activities was magic,

> a series of rites performed every year over the gardens in rigorous sequence and order. Since the leadership in garden work is in the hands of the magician, and since ritual and practical work are intimately associated, a superficial observer might be led to assume that the mystic and the rational behaviour are mixed up, that their effects are not distinguished by the natives and not distinguishable in scientific analysis. Is this so really? [38:11]

Malinowski decides not: there is a clear-cut distinction in the natives' view between what can be achieved by scientific techniques and what remains to be accounted for by magical beliefs and ritual. Primitive man works with two domains of reality, the practical and the magical. The latter can be seen as coming into play when the emotional investment in the successful outcome of some activity is so strong that reliance cannot be placed on empirical techniques alone: 'Both magic and religion open up escapes from such situations and such impasses as offer no empirical way out except by ritual and belief into the domain of the supernatural.' [38:67]

For Malinowski, the way out of the positivist schema was to show how for various reasons rational knowledge and techniques did not provide a completely adequate way of coping with the environment: to this extent his explanation resembles Spencer's 'Unknowable'. Consequently, magical and religious beliefs and rituals are not 'mistakes' or misguided science—as Frazer maintained—but are responses of a different kind and are recognized as such by those who engage in them. There are a number of difficulties in this view, especially in the idea that men consciously 'change their wavelength' and are aware of the demarcation between instrumental actions and expressive rituals. This attribution of 'intellectual role-segregation' ('now I am logicking, now I am magicking') is as much a product of Malinowski's cultural standpoint as are Frazer's lessons in logic for primitive pseudoscientists. [50] This theme will be taken up again in the discussion on rationality, but it is sufficient for the present purpose to note that Malinowski thought that neither magical nor religious ritual practices and beliefs were to be regarded merely as inadequate rational techniques or mistaken scientific knowledge. They had quite different functions and must be placed in a separate category.

Durkheim was similarly concerned with the distinctive characteristics of the religious and the non-religious spheres of beliefs and activities, and in his distinction between the sacred and the profane he placed religious beliefs and practices in an even more clearly demarcated category. Rather than concentrating on the actions that were appropriate in different situations, Durkheim took as his key point of reference the *attitudes* which were exhibited towards the supernatural, and on this basis he argued that the sacred could be clearly marked off from the profane by the attitude of respect and awe that was exhibited towards it:

> Directly contrasting the attitudes appropriate in a ritual context with those towards objects of utilitarian significance and their use in fields of rational technique, he found one fundamental feature of the sacred to be its radical dissociation from any utilitarian context. [48:205]

Furthermore, the attitude of respect towards sacred things was for Durkheim identical with that shown towards moral obligations and authority. Since sacred objects could not have any intrinsic quality of 'sacredness' (because one society's sacred object is another's everyday article) they must be symbols of something else: 'The circle of sacred objects cannot be determined, then, once and for all. Its extent varies infinitely, according to the different religions.' [19:3] The equation now only lacks its final equivalent. If sacred objects and entities are symbols of something else, and that something else can command moral respect, then the sacred things of any religion are symbols of the *society* that practices that religion. Religious ritual can thus be seen as a mechanism for reinforcing social integration.

One effect of Durkheim's definition of religion is to create a radical distinction between magic and religion. On the face of it, magic and religion are similar, since they are both made up of beliefs and rites and each has its myths and dogmas, but in the case of magic 'they are more elementary, undoubtedly because, seeking technical and utilitarian ends, it does not waste its time in pure speculation'. [19:42] But in Durkheim's view it cannot be maintained that magic is hardly distinguishable from religion, because the two are mutually hostile:

> Magic takes a sort of professional pleasure in profaning holy things; in its rites, it performs the contrary of the religious ceremony. On its side, religion, when it has not condemned and prohibited magic rites has always looked upon them with disfavour. [19:43]

More crucial is the argument that the 'really religious beliefs' are always common to a group and serve to unite the group, so that: 'In all history, we do not find a single religion without a Church.' [19:44] With magic it is quite different. Magical beliefs may be widespread, and magical beliefs may claim as many adherents as those of a society's 'real religion', but magic does not serve to unite those who believe in it into a group:

> *There is no Church of magic.* Between the magician and the individuals who consult him, as between these individuals themselves, there are no lasting bonds which make them members of the same moral community . . . The magician has a clientele and not a Church, and it is very possible that his clients have no other relations between each other, or even do not know each other . . . [19:44, original italics]

The phrases 'really religious beliefs' and 'real religion'—which in each case refer to the *social* context—are taken straight from the text of *The Elementary Forms of the Religious Life,* and they indicate a problem which lies at the heart of Durkheim's theory of religion.

Parsons has noted the circular reasoning in Durkheim's thinking which tends to treat religious patterns as a symbolic manifestation of 'society', but at the same time to define the most fundamental aspect of society as a set of patterns of moral and religious sentiment. The dilemma can be expressed in the question, is 'society' real or is it ideal? If, as Durkheim appears to say, the society which is the object of its members' worship is real (society with a small 's') then Durkheim is in a position of 'explaining away' religion in terms of some natural object in the tangible world. If, on the other hand, Durkheim has in mind some 'ideal' society (society with a large 'S') which is the object of worship, then the notion of the sacred cannot be accounted for by referring to Society, since it is precisely 'the notion of the sacred, occurring spontaneously to the human mind', [6, vol. ii: 57] which transfigures society into Society. In other words, Durkheim looks for his explanation of the sacred to a phenomenon which is already defined in terms of its sacredness.

His position can be identified—referring back to the three perspectives outlined at the beginning of the chapter—as having one foot in each extreme and straddling rather than standing in the intermediate position. If society (small 's') is the object of worship, he is putting forward an epiphenomenalist explanation: if Society (large 'S') is the object, then religion, rather than being influenced by, itself transforms and defines the social environment. Recently, Durkheim's ideas have been developed in the work of Thomas Luckmann—whose synthesis of Durkheim's and Webers' theories in *The Invisible Religion* will be treated in the final chapter of this book. For the moment, it is sufficient to note that Peter Berger, Luckmann's co-author in *The Social Construction of Reality*, questions precisely the perspective in Luckmann's work which is closest to Durkheim's epistemological theory. [10: 177-8]

Although the present treatment of Durkheim will be short, it is important to place his work in the broader context not of a theory of religion but of a theory of knowledge, the implications of which will be developed more fully in chapter 12. Durkheim's philosophical starting point was essentially similar to that of Kant, for he began by noting the *obligatory* nature of moral rules. Kant had had traced the source of moral obligation to its divine origin and regarded the existence of God as a necessary condition of moral authority. The obverse of Kant's theory of morals was that of the empiricists, who argued that a perception of moral rules could be gained intuitively. For Durkheim, both of these theories were unsatisfactory: Kant's theory involved postulating an unprovable metaphysical foundation for ethics (and like the other writers whose theories have been discussed, he regarded this as an insecure basis). On the other hand, the theory of moral intuition could not readily account for the fact of moral obligation. Durkheim's solution was to argue that *society* was the source both of categories of thought and of morality, since society was conceived by its members to be superior to individuals and could thus exercise moral authority. Society, as has been shown, was also the object of religious worship and thus all knowledge and moral rules had their origin in religion, which was a permanent feature of social life and carried with it an obligatory character.

The permanent place which Durkheim gave to religion in social life has important implications for the theory of secularization, as we shall find in chapter 12. If religion as the basis of moral consensus and social cohesion is a necessary component of any society, then does secularization become impossible by definition? Durkheim clearly saw that some forms of religious institution in modern society—Roman Catholicism, for example— were no longer capable of maintaining their hold over adherents. However, some form of religious symbolization was a permanent feature of social life, and we will need to take up this theme in the later context of secularization.

The fourth sociologist considered by Parsons to have 'revolted against positivism', and thus to have prepared the ground for the theoretical development of the sociology of religion, is Max Weber. In particular, Weber's comparative studies of the religion and social structure of China, India, and Ancient Judea are seen as demonstrating that

it was not possible to reduce the striking variations of pattern on the level of religious ideas in these cases to any features of an independently existent social structure or economic situation, though he continually insisted on the very great importance of situational factors in a number of different connections. [48 : 208]

Religious ideas were therefore viewed as having—at least to some extent—independent causal significance in any system of social action or process of social change. Precisely how Weber developed this argument in his studies of the rise of Western capitalism and of charismatic authority is the subject of subsequent chapters.

Reference to Weber is a reminder that the term 'religion' has yet to be defined in the present context, for as Berger points out:

Max Weber . . . took the position that a definition of religion, if possible at all, can come only at the end, not at the beginning, of the kind of task he had set for himself. Not surprisingly, he never came to such an end, so that the reader of Weber's opus waits in vain for the promised definitional pay off. I am not at all convinced by Weber's position on the proper sequence of definition and substantive research, since the latter can only proceed within a frame of reference that *defines* what is relevant and what is irrelevant in terms of the research. [10:176]

Some of the implications of various definitions have already been indicated in this chapter, and it is clear that what we choose to include as 'religious' beliefs and explanations depends very much on how we define the term. Definitions couched in terms of 'ultimate problems', for example, are difficult to pin down with accuracy because there are no very clear criteria of what to include or exclude from this area. Similarly, the related notion of 'supreme values' in any social system is open to criticism because, firstly, it assumes the existence of such values, and secondly, it provides no criterion on which to distinguish between 'supreme values' which we might want to define as, for example, political, and those we might prefer to treat as religious.

A useful clue to the formulation of a definition is the term 'bifurcation', and the analogy which gives it content is that of an iceberg. Religion is characterized by the fact that it draws a distinction between a real, tangible world, which can be ascertained through the senses, and a postulated invisible world, which is equally real but not to be ascertained in the same way; and, moreover, this invisible world is of immense importance in the understanding and maintenance of the tangible world. Both are part of the same inseparable cosmos and the affairs of each part have ramifications in the other. The analogy breaks down in two ways, of course: firstly, we *know* that icebergs have underwater projections and we might not wish to prejudge the equivalent religious assertion; secondly, the unseen part of an iceberg is beneath, not above, the visible part and this creates difficulties with the imagery of terms like 'super-empirical' (though 'sub-empirical' seems a neat paraphrase for 'the ground of our being'). Nevertheless, bearing this analogy broadly in mind, religion can be defined as 'the set of beliefs which postulate and seek to regulate the distinction between an empirical reality and a related and significant supra-empirical segment of reality; the language and symbols which are used in relation to this distinction; and the activities and institutions which are concerned with its regulation'. Such a definition should be sufficiently catholic *and* agnostic for present purposes.

REFERENCES

1 ABSALOM, FRANCIS 'The historical development of the study of the sociology of religion', *Expository Times* vol. LXXXII, no. 4, January 1971, pp. 105–9.

2 ACTON, H. B. 'The Marxist–Leninist theory of religion', *Ratio* vol. 1, no. 2, December 1958, pp. 136–49.

3 ALPERT, HARRY 'Durkheim's functional theory of ritual', in NISBET, ROBERT A. *Émile Durkheim* (Spectrum Books, Prentice-Hall, Englewood Cliffs 1965).

4 ARBOUSSE-BASTIDE, PAUL 'Auguste Comte et la sociologie religieuse', *Archives de Sociologie des Religions* no. 22, July–December 1966, pp. 3–57.

5 ARBOUSSE-BASTIDE, PAUL 'De la religion comme sociologie dans l'oeuvre de Comte', *Archives de Sociologie des Religions* no. 25, January–June 1968, pp. 13–21.

6 ARON, RAYMOND *Main Currents in Sociological Thought*, 2 vols. (Weidenfeld and Nicolson, London 1968).

7 BELLAH, ROBERT N. 'Christianity and symbolic realism', *Journal for the Scientific Study of Religion* vol. 9, no. 2, 1970, pp. 89–96.

8 BELLAH, ROBERT N. 'Religion. The sociology of religion', *International Encyclopaedia of the Social Sciences* pp. 406–13.

9 BENOIT-SMULLYAN, ÉMILE 'The sociologism of Émile Durkheim and his school', in BARNES, HARRY ELMER, *An Introduction to the History of Sociology* (University of Chicago Press, Chicago and London 1948).

10 BERGER, PETER L. *The Sacred Canopy* (Doubleday, New York, 1967).

11 BERGER, PETER L., and LUCKMANN, THOMAS 'Sociology of religion and sociology of knowledge', *Sociology and Social Research* vol. 47, July 1963, no. 4, pp. 417–27.

12 BERNARD, L. L. 'The sociological interpretation of religion', *Journal of Religion* vol. XVIII, no. 1, January 1938, pp. 1–18.

13 BIERSTEDT, ROBERT *Émile Durkheim* (Weidenfeld and Nicolson, London 1966).

14 BIRNBAUM, NORMAN, and LENZER, GERTRUD (eds.) *Sociology and Religion* (Prentice-Hall, Englewood Cliffs 1969).

15 BOTTOMORE, T. B., and RUBEL, MAXIMILIEN *Karl Marx: Selected Writings in Sociology and Social Philosophy* (Penguin Books, Harmondsworth, Middlesex, 1963).

16 CAIRD, EDWARD *The Social Philosophy and Religion of Comte* (James Maclehose and Sons, Glasgow 1885).

17 DAUTRY, JEAN 'Nouveau Christianisme ou nouvelle théophilanthropie? Contribution à une sociologie religieuse de Saint-Simon', *Archives de Sociologie des Religions* no. 20, July–December 1965, pp. 7–29.

18 DOBBELAERE, K. 'Trend report of the state of the sociology of religion: 1965–1966', *Social Compass* vol. XV/5, 1968, pp. 329–65.

19 DURKHEIM, ÉMILE *The Elementary Forms of the Religious Life* (George Allen and Unwin, London 1954).

20 EISTER, ALLAN W. 'Values, sociology and the sociologists', *Sociological Analysis* vol. 25, no. 2, Summer 1964, pp. 108–12.

21 FINER, S. E. (ed.) *Vilfredo Pareto. Sociological Writings* (Pall Mall Press, London 1966).

22 FLETCHER, RONALD *The Making of Sociology. A Study of Sociological Theory: Volume 1. Beginnings and Foundations; Volume 2. Developments* (Michael Joseph, London 1970).

23 FRAZER, JAMES GEORGE *The Devil's Advocate. A Plea for Superstition* (Macmillan and Co. London 1927).

24 FRAZER, JAMES GEORGE *The Golden Bough* (abridged edition) (Macmillan, London 1933).

25 FREUD, SIGMUND *Civilization and its Discontents* (Hogarth Press, London, 1930).

26 FREUD, SIGMUND *The Future of an Illusion* (Hogarth Press, London 1962).

27 FROMM, ERICH *Psychoanalysis and Religion* (Yale University Press, New Haven 1950).

28 GIBBON, EDWARD *The History of the Decline and Fall of the Roman Empire*, 7 vols., 3rd edn. (Methuen and Co., London 1909–14).

29 GIVENS, R. DALE, and GARZA, JOE 'The treatment of religion in introductory sociology texts', *Journal for the Scientific Study of Religion* vol. V, no. 1, 1966, pp. 59–63.

30 HECKER, JULIUS F. *Religion and Communism* (Chapman and Hall, London 1933).

31 HEIMANN, EDUARD 'Christian foundations of the social sciences', in KNUDTEN, RICHARD D., op. cit.

32 HONIGSHEIM, PAUL 'The influence of Durkheim and his school on the study of religion', in WOLFF, KURT H. (ed.) *Émile Durkheim* (Ohio State University Press, Columbus 1960).

33 HUGHES, H. STUART *Consciousness and Society* (Vintage Books, New York 1958).

34 HUME, DAVID *The Natural History of Religion* (Freethought Publishing Co., London 1889).

35 KNUDTEN, RICHARD D. (ed.) *The Sociology of Religion* (Appleton-Century-Crofts, New York 1967).

36 KOLB, WILLIAM L. 'Values, positivism, and the functional theory of religion: the growth of a moral dilemma', *Social Forces* vol. 31, no. 4, May 1953, pp. 305–11.

37 LENSKI, GERHARD 'The sociology of religion in the United States', *Social Compass* vol. IX/4, 1962, pp. 307–37.

38 MALINOWSKI, BRONISLAW *Magic, Science and Religion and Other Essays* (The Free Press, Glencoe 1948).

39 MARTIN, DAVID A. *The Religious and the Secular* (Routledge and Kegan Paul, London 1969).

40 MARX, KARL, and ENGELS, F. *On Religion* (Foreign Languages Publishing House, Moscow 1957).

41 MEANS, RICHARD L. 'Textbooks in the sociology of religion: a review article', *Sociological Analysis* vol. 27, no. 2, Summer 1966, pp. 101–5.

42 MOBERG, DAVID O. 'The sociology of religion in Western Europe and America', *Social Compass* vol. XIII/3, 1966, pp. 193–204.

43 MOBERG, DAVID O. 'Some trends in the sociology of religion in the U.S.A.', *Social Compass* vol. XIII/3, 1966, pp. 237–43.

44 MOBERG, DAVID O. 'The encounter of scientific and religious values pertinent to man's spiritual nature', *Sociological Analysis* vol. 28, no. 1, Spring 1967, pp. 22–33.

45 MORRIS, RUDOLPH 'The concept of the spiritual and the dilemma of sociology', *Sociological Analysis* vol. 25, no. 3, Fall 1964, pp. 167–73.

46 NIETZSCHE, FRIEDRICH *The Genealogy of Morals* (T. N. Foulis, Edinburgh 1910).

47 NISBET, ROBERT A. *The Sociological Tradition* (Heinemann, London 1967).

48 PARSONS, TALCOTT 'The theoretical development of the sociology of religion', in *Essays in Sociological Theory* (revised edition) (Free Press, Glencoe 1954).

49 PARSONS, TALCOTT; SHILS, EDWARD; NAEGELE, KASPAR D., and PITTS, JESSE R. (eds.) *Theories of Society* (The Free Press, New York 1965).

50 PEEL, J. D. Y. 'Understanding alien belief-systems', *British Journal of Sociology* vol. XX, no. 1, March 1969, pp. 69–84.

51 PEEL, J. D. Y. *Herbert Spencer: the Evolution of a Sociologist* (Heinemann, London 1971).

52 PEMBERTON, PRENTISS L. 'An examination of some criticisms of Talcott Parsons' sociology of religion', *Journal of Religion* vol. XXXVI, no. 4, October 1956, pp. 241–56.

53 PHILP, H. L. *Freud and Religious Belief* (Rockliff, London 1956).

54 REARDON, BERNARD M. G. *From Coleridge to Gore* (Longman, London 1971).

55 REX, JOHN *Key Problems of Sociological Theory* (Routledge and Kegan Paul, London 1961).

56 RICOEUR, PAUL *Freud and Philosophy* (Yale University Press, New Haven 1970).

57 RIEFF, PHILIP *Freud: The Mind of the Moralist* (Victor Gollancz, London 1960).

58 ROBERTSON, ROLAND (ed.) *Sociology of Religion* (Penguin Books, Harmondsworth, Middlesex 1969).

59 ROBERTSON, ROLAND *The Sociological Interpretation of Religion* (Basil Blackwell, Oxford 1970).

60 SCHARF, BETTY R. *The Sociological Study of Religion* (Hutchinson, London 1970).

61 SCHARF, BETTY R. 'Durkheimian and Freudian theories of religion: the case of Judaism', *British Journal of Sociology* vol. XXI, no. 2, June 1970, pp. 151–63.

62 SCHNEIDER, LOUIS 'Problems in the sociology of religion', in FARIS, ROBERT E. L. (ed.) *Handbook of Modern Sociology* (Rand McNally and Co., Chicago 1964).

63 SIMMEL, GEORG 'A contribution to the sociology of religion', *American Journal of Sociology* vol. LX, no. 6, May 1955 (supplement), pp. 1–18.

64 SISSONS, PETER L. 'The sociological definition of religion', *Expository Times* vol. LXXXII, no. 5, February 1971, pp. 132–7.

65 SKLAIR, LESLIE *The Sociology of Progress* (Routledge and Kegan Paul, London 1970).

66 STARK, WERNER 'Max Weber's sociology of religious belief', *Sociological Analysis* vol. 25, no. 1, Spring 1964, pp. 41–9.

67 STARK, WERNER 'The place of Catholicism in Max Weber's sociology of religion', *Sociological Analysis* vol. 29, no. 4, Winter 1968, pp. 202–10.

68 STEEMAN, THEODORE M. 'Max Weber's sociology of religion', *Sociological Analysis* vol. 25, no. 1, Spring 1964, pp. 50–8.

69 THOMAS, KEITH *Religion and the Decline of Magic* (Weidenfeld and Nicolson, London 1971).

70 TYLOR, EDWARD B. *Primitive Culture*, 2 vols. (John Murray, London 1913).

71 WEBER, MAX *The Protestant Ethic and the Spirit of Capitalism* (Unwin University Books, London 1930).

72 WEBER, MAX *The Sociology of Religion*, translated by Ephraim Fischoff, introduced by Talcott Parsons (Methuen, London 1965).

73 WILSON, BRYAN R. 'Religious Organization', in *International Encyclopaedia of the Social Sciences* pp. 428–36.

74 YINGER, JOHN MILTON *Religion, Society and the Individual* (Macmillan, New York 1957).

75 YINGER, JOHN MILTON 'A structural examination of religion', *Journal for the Scientific Study of Religion* vol. viii, no. 1, 1969, pp. 88–99.

76 YINGER, JOHN MILTON 'The present status of the sociology of religion', in KNUDTEN, RICHARD D., op. cit.

3

Church and Sect

ONE OF THE most fruitful attempts to devise a set of categories for the analysis of religious organizations has been the church–sect typology which was first put forward by Max Weber and Ernst Troeltsch. It is important to note that these categories were devised specifically in the context of Christianity; their applicability for the analysis of other religious traditions is a problem which will be raised later in the present discussion. More fundamental perhaps is the way in which the elaboration of organizational typologies throws light on the general problem surrounding the use of ideal types in sociology. As a broad interpretation it can be argued that typological analysis in many branches of the subject has begun with the initial construction of large and inclusive type-forms on an apparently high level of generality; that the work of later sociologists has shown this apparent generality to be, at least to some extent, spurious in that it is derived from analysis of a rather more restricted cultural setting; and that the result has been the elaboration of more sophisticated sub-types. Viewed in these terms, the development of the church–sect typology has owed a great deal to the dialectic between insights derived from a European context and those derived from an American.

The dichotomy between church and sect was first noted by Weber in *The Protestant Ethic and the Spirit of Capitalism*. [43:144–154] There he indicated the basic difference between a church, which was 'a sort of trust foundation for supernatural ends, an institution, necessarily including both the just and the unjust...' [43:144] and the 'believer's church', which saw itself 'solely as a community of personal believers of the reborn, and only these. In other words, not as a Church but as a sect.' [43:145] Since this

47

distinction was made in a discussion of the Baptists, Mennonites and Quakers it is clear that Weber attached crucial importance to the membership principle as a key characteristic of sects, and he emphasized the sectarian provision that 'only adults who have personally gained their own faith should be baptized'. [43:145] Much of the later debate about sect development has centred on this feature; and some of the other characteristics that Weber attributed to sects in contrast to churches have also been employed in subsequent research. The observation, for example, that separation from the State characterizes some churches as well as sects, and cannot thus be termed a distinguishing characteristic of sects, seems closely allied to the approach of a number of later sociologists. [2; 38] Similarly, the shared though differently interpreted concept of *extra ecclesiam nulla salus* held by both the church and the sect, which Weber indicated, has been effectively adopted by David Martin in order to contrast the denomination, which has a somewhat less exclusive ethos. [24] The separation from the world which Weber noted in sectarian groups has likewise been given a more extensive analysis in the work of Bryan Wilson. [47]

In Weber's later elaborations, which were based on this initial groundwork, some further characteristics were noted which provide rather more specific hypotheses about the way in which sects may emerge and their likely course of development. In 'The Protestant Sects and the Spirit of Capitalism', for instance, Weber considered the two possible forms which a theological emphasis on voluntarism and adult commitment might take. Either 'the conventicle of the exemplary Christians' could be accommodated within the church, as in the case of Pietism, or it could emerge as a community of religious 'full citizens'. [10:314] There are important implications in this passing reference by Weber to the notion of an *ecclesiola in ecclesia*: some of these have been greatly expanded by Joachim Wach [41] and have later been employed by Martin to draw attention to the non-sectarian origins of denominations in the English context. Personal as against office charisma was included in Weber's concept of the sect, and this was incorporated in the argument that early Christianity showed clear sectarian characteristics: anti-authoritarianism was thus often associated with sectarianism. Next to the qualified membership principle one of the most important features of sects was seen to be the principle of sovereignty of the local community of believers. Clearly, Wilson regards this characteristic as an important mark of sectarian organization, and has associated the tendency of sectarian groups to evolve a professionalized and centralized organization with the process of denominationalization. [46] Weber further argued that the necessity of judging whether a sect member was fully qualified demanded some form of personal acquaintance and investigation: this, he thought, could only be achieved if the total number of members was small.

The criterion of size was also applied to sects by Georg Simmel in a brief passage in a work published in 1908 in which he was considering 'The Significance of Numbers for Social Life'. [48:89–90] The sociological structure of religious sects, he argued, made it impossible for them to support a large membership since the community of believers insisted on regulating the members' relationship with the rest of society, often to the extent of meticulous restriction of personal behaviour. In some sects this even involved the wearing of special dress as a form of insulation against normal social intercourse and a symbol of membership of the community. Simmel argued that 'in such situations, extension to large groups would evidently break the tie of solidarity which consists to a large degree precisely in the position of being singled out of larger groups and being in contrast with them'. [48:90] To this extent he thought that sectarian groups could with some justification claim to represent the original structure of Christianity, and it was notable that when Christianity ceased to be a minority religion and spread through society at large its organization as well as its beliefs substantially changed.

Weber noted that within each self-governing congregation of a sect an extraordinarily strict moral discipline was practised in maintaining the purity of the whole community. This would seem to be equivalent to Wilson's contention that sects have a totalitarian hold over their members, [46:4] but Weber was concerned to draw a parallel with a different type of religious organization. Having pointed out that the discipline of an asceticist sect is far more rigorous than that of any church, he continues: 'In this respect, the sect resembles the monastic order.' [10:317] Furthermore, sects also tend to require some form of probationary period, which can be interpreted as analogous to the monastic order's novitiate. Some sects, moreover, have two layers of membership, which parallels that of orders. Expulsion followed by ostracism is another sectarian characteristic which is not typical of churches, and the dominance of the lay element in a sect contrasts strongly with the professional ministry of a church —this emphasis is related to the different definition of charisma put forward by each organization. The requirement that sect members should practise brotherliness in their dealings with each other is similarly a logical extension of the observation that every sect is based on the primacy of a local community of committed believers.

In a later version of the original 1906 article—translated as 'Sect, Church and Democracy' [45, vol. iii: 1204]—Weber briefly broadened his perspective to include religions other than Christianity, among them Judaism and Brahminism, which were seen as 'churches'. He also distinguished various ways in which an individual might be judged 'qualified' to become a sect member: this is a very interesting line of investigation in view of the importance which has been attached, especially by contemporary research on sect development, to the way in which a rigorous definition of the criteria on which membership is accorded may operate so as to preserve the sectarian characteristics of a religious group. [46] In one form or another, all the 'qualifications' which Weber listed involve 'given or acquired charisma', [45, vol. iii: 1204] and by contrast he emphasized the importance of *office* charisma for church organization. Having argued that sects characteristically demand freedom of conscience, Weber appears to suggest a solution to one of the more involved problems that have re-emerged in recent research, particularly in that of Johnson [14] and Millett. [27] The problem can be stated as: how does one analyse a religious organization which has many of the organizational features of a church but which fundamentally rejects the norms of the surrounding society, a situation which some would regard as highly relevant to the situation of Roman Catholicism in America. The solution suggested by Millett is to adopt a subtype which he terms the 'minority church', and this—or some similar notion of a *Diaspora* church—is very much what Weber seems to have had in mind, for he argued: 'A fully developed church—advancing universalist claims—cannot concede freedom

of conscience; wherever it pleads for this freedom, it is because it
finds itself in a minority position and demands something which,
in principle, it cannot grant to others'. [45 vol. iii: 1209]

Like most of Weber's statements on the distinction between
church and sect, a possible line of interpretation is put forward
but a detailed treatment is not given. In most of his references to
internal processes within sects he made use of more general
categories of development which were analysed in greater depth
elsewhere in his work. For instance, the observation that sectarian
groups emphasize personal charisma, together with the emphasis
in 'The Social Psychology of the World Religions' on virtuoso
qualifications for sect members, implies that Weber conceived of
the development of sectarian groups towards a more church-
based type of organization. This implication can be drawn from
Weber's insistence on the routinization of charisma and on the
emergence of a mass style of religion, and it highlights a different
interpretation from that of Troeltsch, who envisaged a dialectical
resolution of the church–sect opposition and the development of
a third type of religious organization in the form of mysticism. It
is of great interest, however, that many of Weber's tentative or
hypothetical suggestions were later—consciously or unconsciously
—to be taken up and to emerge as fruitful pieces of research. Thus,
Weber's contribution to the typology of church and sect was
largely confined to the sociological reformulation of a distinction
which had previously been the preserve of theological controversy
and to the identification of a number of important processes within
these organizations.

The most extensive treatment of the different types of religious
organization in the context of Christianity was undoubtedly that
of his pupil, Ernst Troeltsch. Troeltsch shared with Weber the
basic belief that, in its origin, a religious movement frequently
revealed predominantly religious characteristics—in other words,
such a movement could not be entirely explained by reference to
economic or social interests. 'The primitive Christian movement
was, Troeltsch declared, a purely religious upsurge, conditioned,
to be sure, by the social crises of the time but focused not on the
demand for reform and justice in this world but on equality before
God.' [50: 311] This explains why Troeltsch adopted the particular approach found in *The Social Teaching of the Christian Churches*,

which was to treat the Gospel ethic as the source of all subsequent development in Christianity and to trace how this purely religious ethic was realized in terms of social organization.

Within the Gospel ethic itself Troeltsch identified 'a free personal piety, with a strong impulse towards profound intimacy and spiritual fellowship and communion, but without any tendency towards the organization of a cult, or towards the creation of a religious community'. [39, vol. ii:993] However, as soon as the mystical faith in Jesus as the Risen Lord and Messiah who was to be approached through the sacramental means of Baptism and the Eucharist arose among the loosely knit group of Christian believers waiting in Jerusalem, it became possible to identify the emergence of a new religious community: indeed, the account in Acts 2:41 of 3,000 baptisms on the first day quite clearly signals the inception of a new phase of development. Simultaneously, while the main elements of the Gospel ethic were preserved, they began to receive a new shade of meaning as the ethics of a new religious community. With the development of the Pauline ethic it became necessary for Christianity to search for a more positive relationship with society, though initially this involved 'merely a search for points of contact which offer themselves naturally'. [39, vol. i:80] Even so, the basis had been laid for two complementary and coexistent tendencies within Christianity: on the one hand there existed an idealistic anarchism and love-communism which combined 'radical indifference or hostility towards the rest of the social order with the effort to actualize this ideal of love in a small group'. [39, vol. i:82] On the other hand there occurred a development along social-conservative lines in which submission to God's will was combined with 'a strong independence of an organized community which manages its own affairs, which, as its range of influence increases, finds that it cannot ignore secular institutions, but that it must do its utmost to utilize them for its own purposes'. [39, vol i:82] It ought to be made clear that Troeltsch, far from regarding the conservative stream as an accidental development due to the personal attitude of Paul and to the exigencies of the primitive church, saw it as a logical component of the spirit and meaning of the gospel. Both radical and conservative elements had a legitimate place within the framework of Christianity, albeit in a state of tension.

Troeltsch saw the gradual accommodation of both elements in the history of the early church. While social and political life were accepted by the church and the anarchic communism contained in the gospel had been hidden and silenced, the primitive ideal lived on in various forms. One way in which it survived in the church was 'in the ideas of sanctification and of brotherly love, which were bound up with sacerdotal and sacramental ideas, and yet were always capable of a vital release'. [39, vol. i:61] This is an immensely useful insight, which will be discussed in chapter 8 in the context of charismatic authority: the implication of Troeltsch's statement is that any routinized charismatic role should be seen as retaining a latent potential for personal charismatic reinterpretation. Another embodiment of the primitive ideal can be found in the theory of a primitive happy state which was partly derived from Stoic thought and which gave rise to the goal of religious communism. [3] Finally, and perhaps most significantly, the Gospel ideal was maintained in the form of monasticism, which attempted to realize the goal of a small, intimate group on the model of the early disciples by withdrawing from the church into a segregated community but at the same time providing specialized services for the church. It is clear from statements which Troeltsch made in other contexts that he regarded the radical tendency within Christianity either as being contained within the more universalistic form of church organization or as emerging in a distinct type of religious organization (as did Weber), for he referred to the 'two sociological forms of the sect-type, the Religious Order and the voluntary association'. [39, vol. ii:723] This is not the same thing as saying that the two types are in any strict sense functional equivalents, but it does suggest some form of analogous relationship between the sect and the religious order.

At this point, the initial dichotomy of church and sect which Troeltsch elaborated may be outlined. The church, he suggests, is overwhelmingly conservative, accepts the social order and dominates the masses; hence, in principle, it is universalistic. Sects, on the other hand, are comparatively small. They aim at direct personal fellowship between members and renounce the idea of dominating the world. Their attitude to the surrounding society is one of avoidance, and may be characterized by aggression or indifference. While churches utilize the state and the ruling classes and become part of the existing social order, sects are connected with the lower classes and the disaffected. In a church, asceticism is a means of acquiring virtue and of demonstrating a high level of religious achievement, whereas in a sect it constitutes merely the principle of detachment from the world and opposition to established social institutions. This brief summary of some of the main features of Troeltsch's dichotomy is sufficient to demonstrate that the features he selected as characteristic of the church-type and the sect-type are a combination of elements which have been logically abstracted from his basic theoretical distinction—for example, the distinction between two types of asceticism—and of empirically clustered components, such as the identification of the church with the ruling class. The reason for this lies partly in the specific period of church history with which he was concerned.

It is significant that Troeltsch put forward these contrasting types of organization in the course of his treatment of late medieval Catholicism, since it was only at this stage, he thought, that a clear and permanent fission between the two types emerged. Although there had been sectarian eruptions before the twelfth and thirteenth centuries, these had not been so obvious because the major tradition of Christianity had itself fluctuated somewhat between these two types. However, the main stream of Christian development settled into the form of organization characterized by the church-type since this represented the clearest means towards attaining a universal, all-embracing control over civilization. Troeltsch argued that when the Catholic church came closest to attaining this universalistic goal and the relationship between the church and society had been most fully articulated in the work of St Thomas Aquinas, the radical individualism of the gospel which was represented in the sect-type had been given a secondary place or had even been completely abandoned. This must necessarily create a vacuum, since 'both types are a logical result of the gospel, and only conjointly do they exhaust the whole range of its sociological influence, and thus also indirectly of its social results. . . .' [39, vol. i: 341] In this sense, only when the church had pushed its claim to be the objective dispenser of sacramental grace to an extreme did the sectarian tendency reassert itself.

One of the important influences on the origin of medieval sectarianism is seen to be the twelfth-century Gregorian reform within the Catholic church. The basis of this reform was the establishment of a powerful and universal papacy and the removal of power from territorially based ecclesiastical administration, which was very much in the control of the feudal aristocracy. In order to achieve this, Gregory VII utilized popular agitation, especially in the newer urban centres, against ecclesiastical abuses, but the eventual outcome, according to Troeltsch, was to radicalize the urban laity, many of whom found themselves in a situation of rapid social change, and to encourage the spread of sectarian movements such as the Cathari, the Waldensians and —a group which only after a period of considerable conflict was fully incorporated into the church—the Franciscans.

Having postulated a dialectical opposition between the church and the sect, which is first readily identifiable in these new urban centres in the form of lay sectarian protest against the ecclesiastical hierarchy, it is also in the late medieval towns that Troeltsch identifies the third (if we treat the sect and the religious order as belonging to a basically similar type) of his categories of religious organization, which he terms mysticism. The way it is depicted—'a foreshadowing of coming developments in the interplay of church and sect' [39, vol. i:381]—suggests that we are justified in treating the concept as a synthesis of the polar type-concepts around which most of Troeltsch's analysis is organized. Mysticism is depicted in terms of a growing individualism, in which there is little desire for organized fellowship and in which emphasis is placed on the importance of freedom for the interchange of ideas. The isolated individual becomes paramount. Although originating in the late medieval towns, this process of individualization only emerges with universal significance in the thought of the later Protestant Dissenters, but in contrast to other forms of religious group the emergent organization has neither the concrete sanctity of the church-type institution nor the radicalism of the sect. Its ideology derives in large part from syncretism with modern ideas—especially with science—and there is some difficulty in formulating a clear social programme. Gradually, thinks Troeltsch, 'the third type has come to predominate. This means, then, that all that is left is voluntary association

c

with like-minded people, which is equally remote from Church and Sect'. [39, vol. i: 381] The end product is 'simply a parallelism of spontaneous religious personalities'. [39, vol. ii: 744]

> It is neither Church nor sect, and has neither the concrete sanctity of the institution nor the radical connection with the Bible. Combining Christian ideas with a wealth of modern views, deducing social institutions, not from the Fall but from a process of natural development, it has not the fixed limit for concessions and the social power which the Church possesses, but also it does not possess the radicalism and the exclusiveness with which the sect can set aside the State and economics, art and science. [39, vol. i: 381]

Mysticism, furthermore, tends to be the religious form of expression of more privileged social groups. It is of some interest to analyse closely this emergent type of Christian individualism because different writers tend to see the 'end point' of Christianity in different ways. The original concept of 'mysticism' has been converted by subsequent writers into the category of the 'cult', and it is quite clear that one interpretation of the development of cults may be that they mark a final stage in Christianity. David Martin, for example, finds the increasing individualism of Christianity a most important analytical perspective and traces the process from the subjectivism in a social context of Luther, through Methodism with its stress on a personal saviour and a congregational context, to the practitioner–client relationship of Christian Science in the individual mysticism of a small spontaneous group. [25] Looked at in this context, however, it seems that Troeltsch has missed a stage by suggesting that mystical cults emerge directly out of the church–sect dialectic, and thus ignoring the intermediate level of individualistic organization which seems to be most adequately incorporated in the denomination. And indeed, Troeltsch's detailed discussion of mysticism as a form of Christianity does seem to hover between the extreme individualism of the mystical cult and the fluid, pragmatic organization coupled with a lack of dogmatic orthodoxy characteristic of the denomination.

The initial model-building of Weber and Troeltsch was in many ways incomplete and in need of refinement, but they undoubtedly provided a rich vein of insights and hypotheses which have subsequently been explored in a more comparative and empirically tested way. As a result, more sophisticated sub-types and categories have been developed. Even so, the impression is often given that the original concepts of church and sect are deficient in the sense that they provide only static and polar models against which a range of empirical cases have to be studied. This is certainly a shaky criticism. Already in the work of Weber and Troeltsch we find the notion of an incipient source of change *within* the organization of religious groups: Weber suggested a sect-to-church development in which the routinization of originally charismatic aspects of organization and the formulation of spontaneous features resulted in a different kind of structure, and Troeltsch envisaged a dialectical opposition between church and sect emerging as a third type of Christian organization, which he termed mysticism. Weber noted that separation from the State was characteristic of some churches as well as sects, and both he and Troeltsch saw the religious order as in some ways analogous to the sect. Above all, Weber, Troeltsch and their contemporary, Simmel, attached great importance to the principle on which membership of a sect was accorded and to the significance of size for the sect's organization and stability. It was this idea which was to form the basis of the next development in the typology and to spark off a quite considerable amount of further research.

H. Richard Niebuhr, whose perceptive account of the origin of denominations was to form the basis of a long debate, expressed his underlying orientation in a formula to which Weber would have given substantial assent. He thought that

theological opinions have their roots in the relationship of the religious life to the cultural and political conditions prevailing in any group of Christians. This does not mean that an economic or purely political interpretation of theology is justified, but it does mean that the religious life is so interwoven with social circumstances that the formulation of theology is necessarily conditioned by these. [29:16]

His purpose was to understand how a basic set of theological premisses were incorporated in a religious organization through their interaction with the social and economic environment in which the organization found itself.

Particular attention should be given, he argued, to the important distinction made on this basis by Weber and Troeltsch between the church and the sect. Having briefly summarized this distinction, Niebuhr noted that the sociological character of sectarianism was 'almost always' [29:19] modified in the course of time by the processes of birth and death, and that as a result of structural changes, concomitant changes would inevitably occur in the area of doctrine and ethics. This interpretation, while viewing the process of sectarian transformation as typical, leaves open the possibility that sectarian groups may remain such, and it also sets no time limit on the change. In his next sentence, by contrast, he very precisely delineated the features of this change:

Niebuhr's Theory.

By its very nature the sectarian type of organization is valid only for one generation. The children born to the voluntary members of the first generation begin to make the sect a church long before they have arrived at the years of discretion. For with their coming the sect must take on the character of an educational and disciplinary institution, with the purpose of bringing the new generation into conformity with ideals and customs which have become traditional. Rarely does a second generation hold the convictions it has inherited with a fervor equal to that of its fathers, who fashioned these convictions in the heat of conflict and at the risk of martyrdom. [29:19–20]

As a result, with each succeeding generation it becomes increasingly difficult to maintain the sectarian community's isolation from the outside world, a difficulty often increased by the unintended consequence of a disciplined, ascetic way of life—the accumulation of wealth. Ethical compromise means that the sect begins to approach a more churchly conception of morals, and coupled with this is the growth of a specialized ministry where there had previously been only lay leadership. 'So', concluded Niebuhr, 'the sect becomes a church.' [29:20]

There is some inconsistency in Niebuhr's use of terminology which at times becomes confusing, though it need not obscure or detract from the impact of his argument. Principally, the confusion springs from the different meanings intended by his use of the word 'church', which is sometimes employed in its strict sociological sense, following the content given it by Weber and Troeltsch, sometimes as a loose synonym for 'institutionalized religious organisation' (as I think he intends it to mean when he speaks of a sect becoming a church) and sometimes in a purely theological sense—he was, after all, a theologian in background —as, for example, when he refers to sects as 'revolutionary churches'. [29:54] At all events, his major interest was in the origin of denominationalism, and the key observation which has been credited to him by later sociologists is the way it was possible to understand the emergence out of sects of denominations, a process he attributed mainly to the increasing prosperity of sect members: '. . . most important among the causes of the decline of revolutionary churches into denominations is the influence of economic success. The churches of the poor all become middle-class churches sooner or later and, with their need, lose much of the idealism which grew out of their necessities.' [29:54]

Thus for Niebuhr the principal characteristic of a denomination was that, unlike a church, it was not universalistic and was restricted in its appeal to a respectable middle-class style of religious expression. Unlike a sect, though, it had already differentiated the specialized role of minister—a step in the direction of the church's sacerdotal organization—and had a more relaxed, world-compromising ethic. The denomination was most fully attuned to the needs of the bourgeoisie, and thus exhibited the main features of an intensely personal definition of salvation, a concern with activism and a doctrine of reassurance concerning the individual member's worth. Individualism and personal responsibility are highly valued goals, and there is an ethic of coexistence between different religious groups.

Niebuhr's elaboration of a process of sect-to-church development which had been hinted at by Weber (who had observed at first hand the religious situation in the United States) and had been given a somewhat different interpretation by Troeltsch as a result of his emphasis on the growth of religious individualism, is the first sign of the fruitful exchange of ideas derived from a European and an American context respectively. The religious situation of post-Reformation and even of pre-Reformation Europe had been broadly characterized by the existence of established or institutionalized churches against which the protest of small, élitist sectarian groups was a frequently observed phenomenon. Coupled with the occurrence of substantial social inequality, which was often manifested in religious cleavages, the resulting social structure can be described as polarized and undifferentiated. [32:117] The society with which Niebuhr was mostly concerned was that of twentieth-century America—although it should be pointed out that he did trace the development of some denominations, such as Methodism, through their English origins. The predominant characteristics of the American religious situation were the absence of any formally established Christian church and a relatively higher level of differentiation between the different institutional sectors, together with the absence of any rigidly crystallized lines of social inequality and a situation of rapid social change. While the context in which Troeltsch worked out his dichotomy was specific to Europe, it might also be argued that the early twentieth-century American context of Niebuhr was in some respects just as specific, and later elaborations of the typology have taken this as their starting point.

The next step in the development of a typology came with Howard Becker's conscious attempt to systematize the range of Christian organizations into a comprehensive set of sociological sub-types. The point of departure he adopted was basically the same as that of Niebuhr, for he considered 'the dilemma of the church' as the clash of two irreconcilable sets of values. On the one hand there was a constellation of values which derived from a religious source, but once these formed the basis for a social collectivity there arose the constellation of values which derived from the social sphere. These two sets of values were 'wholly alien to each other and often directly opposed'. [2:617] Using the word 'church' in its broadest meaning, as 'any group of Christians', Becker summarized the dilemma by saying, 'The church combines after a fashion, the water of the religious and the oil of the social.' [2:617] The tension between these two sets of values could never be resolved and thus no one type of organization could completely neutralize the opposition.

A considerable range of religious collectivities resulted from this situation, ranging from a social group at one extreme to a shrine where a deity is worshipped at the other. This is a valuable contrast because it points to one of the few forms of observance within Christianity which is not based on a local, more or less stable community. The shrine and the cult—and it is interesting to note that the highly specific religious observances linked with some saintly figure or geographical location which often characterize a shrine are referred to in the Roman Catholic church as a 'cult'—both represent extremes of religious individualism in which the personal encounter with the transcendental is of prime importance. Even here, however, there may arise some additional social institutions, such as a collective pilgrimage or a permanent religious community whose function it is to tend the shrine and accommodate visitors to it.

Once a religious collectivity came into existence, Becker thought that it became involved in a process of compromise since it would be forced to regulate and organize the otherwise centrifugal tendencies of members. A particularly significant means of strengthening social bonds was the articulation of the principle *extra collectivum nulla spes salutis*—salvation is only attainable through the collectivity. The tension involved in realizing religious values through a social organization could be seen throughout the whole history of Christianity, but the historical period beginning with the break-up of the medieval unity of Catholicism and ending in what, for Becker, was the last great Christian religious movement—the rise and consolidation of Methodism—was most instructive since it revealed most clearly the different tendencies. Like Troeltsch, Becker tended to regard the history of Protestantism as a form of experimental laboratory in which the elements always present within Christianity could be separated and distilled. Thus he broke down Christian organization into four sub-types: '(1) the ecclesia, (2) the sect, (3) the denomination, and (4) the cult'. [2:624] These he went on to depict in greater detail.

The ecclesia he saw as predominantly conservative, not in open conflict with the secular aspects of society, and professedly universalistic. Its goal of dominating the whole of a society, which was pursued in amalgamation with the state and the ruling class, was neatly drawn by Becker: 'The phrase "Come out from among them and be ye separate" has no place in the ideology of the genuine ecclesiastic; "Force them to come in" is likely to characterize his thinking.' [2:624] Membership was by birth rather than by conscious adult choice and thus the ecclesia was both an educational institution and a dispenser of grace through an official priesthood and by the administration of sacraments. There were two main varieties of the ecclesia: international and national. Catholicism was the clearest example of an international ecclesia, while Lutheranism and Anglicanism were two varieties of the national ecclesia. However (a qualification which seems to have been neglected by some subsequent treatments) 'It should not be supposed . . . that a sharp line can be drawn between the two'. [2:625] Catholicism, for example in the case of France, showed considerable evidence of being 'pervaded' by nationalistic rivalries.

The sect, by complete contrast, was a small separatist group with a voluntary membership and an exclusive character. Religious qualifications had to be shown before membership was accorded and there was a 'priesthood of all believers'. Furthermore, as in the work of Troeltsch, the origin of sects was traced to pre-Reformation Christianity. The third sub-type, the denomination, is a rather simplistic version of Niebuhr's concept: 'Denominations are simply sects in an advanced stage of development and adjustment to each other and the secular world.' [2:626] Becker gives a brief account of the 'cooling' process involved in the change from sect to denomination which is summarized as 'age inevitably brings compromise'. [2:626] An additional factor which Becker saw as mitigating the mutually exclusive tendency of Christian sects was the common opposition of all Protestant bodies to Roman Catholicism. Although in the early phases of the Reformation the members of the rival Protestant sects had detested each other just as much as they detested Rome —as epitomized by Calvin's burning of Michael Servetus in 1553 for his anti-Trinitarian doctrines—with the passage of time their attitudes to each other mellowed and they perceived in Catholicism a common enemy. Becker noted that this was especially true of evangelical sects, an insight which has later been found useful in distinguishing sects that experienced a denominationalizing tendency from those that retained fundamentally sectarian characteristics. Becker himself was quite unequivocal about the origin of denominations: 'It should not be forgotten, however, that any denomination is a sect in historical origin and doctrine, and only failure or unwillingness on the part of the clergy to emphasize the grounds of division can obscure this fundamental fact.' [2:627]

Finally, his definition of the category of cult to some extent follows Troeltsch in viewing the emergence of this type of Christian organization as the final outcome of the individualistic tendencies observable in the sect. Adherents of this highly amorphous and loosely knit type of social structure were little concerned with the maintenance of the structure itself in the way that church and sect members would attempt to protect their organization, but were seeking 'purely personal ecstatic experience salvation, comfort, and mental or physical healing'. [2:627] Instead of *joining* a cult, which implied that the consent of other members was necessary, the individual adherent simply chose to believe particular theories or follow certain practices: thus the cult came near to being merely an abstract crowd, and only the unifying force of its ideology provided it with a recognizable structure—though Becker considered the term 'structure' almost a misnomer. The source of emotional satisfaction for the cult believer was purely personal; 'I' became the centre of the believer's cosmos, and thus only a highly atomistic and secular social order could give rise to cults. Almost as though anticipating some of the later conceptual debate, Becker noted that cults were much like sects, so that it was extremely difficult to draw a line between the two, just as it was difficult to mark the boundary between the sect and the denomination. Those cults which were thought sufficiently well delineated to cite as examples were: Spiritualism, Theosophy, New Thought, Christian Science, Unity, Buchmanism and a variety of 'pseudo-Hinduisms' associated with (and here Becker is pungently topical) 'Swamis and Yogis who consent, for a consideration, to carry their messages to the materialistic Western World'. [2:628]

Having constructed this typology, Becker went on to apply it to the history of Christianity since the immediate pre-Reformation period. His treatment owes much to Weber and Niebuhr—the latter especially in so far as nationalism is regarded as an important source of religious fission—and there is a useful development of the concepts of inner- and other-wordly asceticism. This is especially well applied to the change in emphasis which can be seen in the Reformation, and Becker symbolizes the change in the words of the sixteenth-century German humanist, Sebastian Franck: 'You think you have escaped from the monastery, but everyone must now be a monk throughout his life.' [2:634] Becker's typology, with important modifications, represents the earliest and most frequently used systematic attempt to provide abstract conceptual models for the analysis of the whole range of Christian organizations. It incorporates much of the earlier work of Weber, Troeltsch and Niebuhr and it provides broad hypotheses about the origins and internal processes of development of the different types. The cult is seen as a progression out of tendencies clearly visible in the sect, and denominations are merely mature sects. This last interpretation was later to be increasingly questioned in the light of empirical studies both of sectarian and denominational groups, as was the tendency to disregard the opposite movement from denominational to sectarian ideology and organization.

One of the ways in which broad hypotheses in these typologies have stimulated further research has been in the attempt to operationalize the processes involved by separating them out into quantifiable factors. This was precisely what Liston Pope, who made the next major contribution to the discussion, tried to do. Niebuhr's contention that the denominationalization of sects was predominantly a response to the changing class-composition of such groups was challenged by Pope, whose own study of the religious situation of a textile area in North Carolina in the late 1930s did not lend support to the social-class explanation as a major factor. Instead, he seems to have found more useful the kind of explanation which has been attributed to Simmel, namely that an increase in size—which would normally be the goal of an evangelical sect—reorientates the organization towards a more compromising attitude to the world. 'A sect, as it gains adherents and the promise of success, begins to reach out toward greater influence in society, whatever the roots of its ambition may be—evangelistic fervour, denominational rivalry, ministerial desire for greater income and influence, the cultural vindication of its peculiar faith, or what not.' [30:119] In the process of doing this, it gradually becomes accommodated to the surrounding culture and thus loses its influence over those who are relatively estranged from it: at the same time it attracts a more privileged clientele.

While not altogether rejecting the proposition that sectarian practices such as frugality and industry cause sect members to become more wealthy, Pope found little evidence in his own study that 'rising sects' carried their original economic group of membership with them. Furthermore, sectarian teachings seemed to operate so as to maintain the previous socio-economic position of workers: 'Emphasis on personal virtues produces more efficient workers; it does not necessarily produce owners and managers of the economic system.' [30:119] A few members of any sect were likely to prosper, sometimes as a result of personal qualities but more often by chance, and as they became more 'responsible' they would either desert their sect or reshape it in keeping with their new position; not a difficult thing to do if a sect is in need of the funds which these members can provide. The process thus engendered is referred to as movement along the sect-to-church continuum—or 'scale of transition' [30:120]—and results in the formation of denominations, which are thus either mature sects or 'emergent Churches', [30:120] depending on the perspective adopted. In order to operationalize the elements involved, Pope formulated a set of twenty-one indices by which the movement from sect to church could be measured: some of them, it will be apparent, are more capable of quantitative measurement than others, but this represents the first attempt to identify comprehensively the detailed distinctions between sect and church.

Pope described the various components of the sect-to-church transition as being: (1) from membership of the propertyless to membership of property owners; (2) from economic poverty to economic wealth, as shown by the value of church property and ministerial salaries; (3) from the cultural periphery to the cultural centre of the community; (4) from renunciation of or indifference to the prevailing culture and society to affirmation of it; (5) from personal to institutional religion; (6) from non-co-operation with or ridicule of established religious institutions to co-operation with them; (7) from suspicion of rival sects to disdain and pity for all sects; (8) from a moral community excluding unworthy members to a social institution embracing all who are socially compatible within it; (9) from an unprofessionalized, part-time ministry to a professional, full-time ministry; (10) from a psychology of persecution to a psychology of success and dominance; (11) from voluntary, confessional membership to ritualized membership (such as previous membership of another acceptable denomination or socialization by the denomination itself); (12) from being predominantly concerned with adult members to equal concern with children; (13) from emphasis on evangelism and conversion to emphasis on religious education; (14) from emphasis on death and a future in the next world to emphasis on life and a future in this world; (15) from adherence to strict biblical standards such as tithing and non-resistance to acceptance of general cultural standards of religious obligation; (16) from a high degree of congregational participation in services to delegation of responsibility to a small minority; (17) from fervour and activity in worship to restraint and passivity; (18) from a comparatively large number of religious services to a programme of regular services at stated intervals (evidence of the compartmentalization and institutionalization of the religious style); (19) from reliance on spontaneity in worship and administration to a fixed order of service and administrative procedure; (20) from use of hymns derived from folk music to slower, more stately hymns derived from a remote liturgical tradition; (21) from emphasis on religion in the home to delegation of responsibility to church officials and organizations.

This catalogue of characteristics was then very briefly used by Pope to rank different Christian groups on a continuum, with Free-Will Baptist Holiness, Pentecostal Holiness and Church of God groups at the 'sect' end, Methodist, Baptist and Presbyterian groups occupying the 'denomination' band in the centre and Protestant Episcopal and Roman Catholic groups at the 'church' end. No sophisticated techniques of measurement were used, and it is more than likely that modern techniques of statistical analysis, together with the need to incorporate the more sophisticated sub-types which have resulted from cross-cultural comparisons, would considerably modify these indices. Pope's analysis, however, remains as the earliest and indeed one of the only attempts to isolate a complete range of factors that are precise enough to form the basis for a programme of quantitative research.

In this chapter we have traced the origins of the church–sect typology in the work of Max Weber and its elaboration in the study of late medieval and Reformation Christianity by Ernst Troeltsch. It has been shown that these early formulations contained the idea of an internal dynamic which, in Weber's view, represented a process of institutionalization of sectarian forms of religious grouping in the direction of a church-type organization. Troeltsch on the other hand tended to view the process as a dialectic between church and sect with the emergent category of mysticism as a postulated line of development. Although Weber was interested in American forms of religious organization, and made his first contributions to the discussion of church and sect in this societal context, both his and Troeltsch's cultural perspectives were based on a European situation in which the polar opposition of established churches and radical sects was the prevailing pattern. H. Richard Niebuhr broke out of this conceptual framework by arguing that in the more fluid context of American religion it was more typical for sects to develop denominational characteristics. These three contributions were systematized by Howard Becker into a typology containing a number of sub-types and translating the category of mysticism into that of 'cult'. Finally, Liston Pope offered a number of empirical criteria on which the transformation of sects into churches might be measured. What is perhaps most interesting about the early literature on church and sect is that it provided a number of important hypotheses which were later to be taken up in research, and this observation provides a link with chapter 4, where subsequent theoretical developments are discussed.

REFERENCES

1 BARNES, HARRY ELMER (ed.) *An Introduction to the History of Sociology* (University of Chicago Press, Chicago and London 1948).

2 BECKER, HOWARD *Systematic Sociology* ... *of Leopold von Wiese* (John Wiley, New York 1932).

3 BOAS, GEORGE *Essays on Primitivism and Related Ideas in the Middle Ages* (The John Hopkins Press, Baltimore 1948).

4 BUTLER, EDWARD CUTHBERT *Religions of Authority and the Religion of the Spirit* (Sheed and Ward, London 1930).

5 CLARK, ELMER T. *The Small Sects in America* (Abingdon-Cokesbury Press, New York 1937).

6 CLARK, S. D. *Church and Sect in Canada* (University of Toronto Press, Toronto 1948).

7 COLEMAN, JOHN A. 'Church–sect typology and organizational precariousness', *Sociological Analysis* vol. 29, no. 2, Summer 1968, pp. 55–66.

8 EISTER, ALLAN W. 'Religious institutions in complex societies: difficulties in the theoretic specification of functions', *American Sociological Review* vol. 22, no. 4, August 1957, pp. 387–91.

9 GAGARIN, IU. V. 'The abandonment of sectarianism in the Komi ASSR', *Soviet Sociology* vol. VIII, no. 3–4, Winter–Spring 1969/70, pp. 358–81.

10 GERTH, H. H., and MILLS, C. WRIGHT *From Max Weber: Essays in Sociology* (Routledge and Kegan Paul, London 1948).

11 GOLDSCHMIDT, WALTER R. 'Class denominationalism in rural California churches', *American Journal of Sociology* vol. XLIX, no. 4, January 1944, pp. 348–55.

12 GOODE, ERICH 'Class styles of religious sociation', *British Journal of Sociology* vol. XIX, no. 1, March 1968, pp. 1–16.

13 GOODE, ERICH 'Another look at social class and church participation: reply to Estus and Overington', *American Journal of Sociology* vol. 75, no. 5, March 1970, pp. 779–81.

14 JOHNSON, BENTON 'A critical appraisal of the church–sect typology'. *American Sociological Review* vol. 22, no. 1, February 1957, pp. 88–92.

15 JOHNSON, BENTON 'Do holiness sects socialize in dominant values?', *Social Forces* vol. 39, no. 4, May 1961, pp. 309–16.

16 JOHNSON, BENTON 'On church and sect', *American Sociological Review* vol. 28, no. 4, August 1963, pp. 539–49.

17 JOHNSON, BENTON 'Church and sect revisited', *Journal for the Scientific Study of Religion* vol. 10, no. 2, Summer 1971, pp. 124–37.

18 JONES, R. K. 'Sectarian characteristics of Alcoholics Anonymous', *Sociology* vol. 4, no. 2, May 1970, pp. 181–95.

19 KLIBANOV, A. I. 'Fifty years of scientific study of religious sectarianism', *Soviet Sociology* vol. VIII, no. 3–4, Winter–Spring 1969/70, pp. 239–78.

20 KLIBANOV, A. I. 'Sectarianism and the socialist reconstruction of the countryside', *Soviet Sociology* vol. VIII, no. 3–4, Winter–Spring 1969/70, pp. 383–411.

21 LIEBMAN, CHARLES S. 'Some theoretical elaborations of the church–sect typology', *Review of Religious Research* vol. 7, no. 3, Spring 1966, pp. 157–60.

22 MCKINNEY, JOHN C. 'The polar variables of type construction', *Social Forces* vol. 35, no. 4, May 1957, pp. 300–6.

23 MCKINNEY, JOHN C. *Constructive Typology and Social Theory* (Appleton-Century-Crofts, New York 1966).

24 MARTIN, DAVID A. 'The denomination', *British Journal of Sociology* vol. XII, no. 1, March 1962, pp. 1–14.

25 MARTIN, DAVID A. *Pacifism* (Routledge and Kegan Paul, London 1965).

26 MARTINDALE, DON 'Sociological Theory and the Ideal Type', in GROSS, LLEWELLYN (ed.) *Symposium on Sociological Theory* (Harper and Row, New York 1959).

27 MILLETT, DAVID 'A typology of religious organizations suggested by

the Canadian Census', *Sociological Analysis* vol. 30, no. 2, Summer 1969, pp. 108–19.

28 MUELDER, WALTER 'From sect to church' in YINGER, JOHN MILTON, *Religion, Society and the Individual* (Macmillan, New York 1957), pp. 480–8.

29 NIEBUHR, H. RICHARD *The Social Sources of Denominationalism* (Henry Holt and Co., New York 1929).

30 POPE, LISTON *Millhands and Preachers* (Yale University Press, New Haven 1942).

31 POPE, LISTON 'Religion and the class structure', *Annals of the American Academy of Political and Social Science* vol. 256, March 1948, pp. 84–91.

32 ROBERTSON, ROLAND *The Sociological Interpretation of Religion* (Basil Blackwell, Oxford 1970).

33 ROGERS, ROLF E. *Max Weber's Ideal Type Theory* (Philosophical Library, New York 1969).

34 SCANZONI, JOHN 'A note on method for the church–sect typology', *Sociological Analysis* vol. 26, no. 4, Winter 1965, pp. 189–202.

35 SÉGUY, JEAN 'Ernst Troeltsch. Ou de l'essence de la religion à la typologie des christianismes', *Archives de Sociologie des Religions* no. 25, January–June 1968, pp. 3–11.

36 STARK, RODNEY 'Class, radicalism, and religious involvement in Great Britain', *American Sociological Review* vol. 29, no. 5, October 1964, pp. 698–706.

37 STARK, RODNEY 'Social contexts and religious experience', *Review of Religious Research* vol. 7, no. 1, Fall 1965, pp. 17–28.

38 STARK, WERNER *The Sociology of Religion. A Study of Christendom* (Routledge and Kegan Paul, London):
   (a) *Volume I. Established Religion* (1966);
   (b) *Volume II. Sectarian Religion* (1967);
   (c) *Volume III. The Universal Church* (1967);
   (d) *Volume IV. Types of Religious Man* (1969).

39 TROELTSCH, ERNST *The Social Teaching of the Christian Churches*, 2 vols., translated by Olive Wyon (George Allen and Unwin, London 1931).

40 VOLLMER, HOWARD M. 'Member commitment and organizational competence in religious orders', *Berkeley Publications in Society and Institutions* vol. 3, no. 1, Spring 1957, pp. 13–26.

41 WACH, JOACHIM *Sociology of Religion* (Chicago University Press, Chicago 1944; Phoenix edition 1962).

42 WATKINS, J. W. N. 'Ideal types and historical explanation', in FEIGL, HERBERT, and BRODBECK, MAY, *Readings in the Philosophy of Science* (Appleton-Century-Crofts, New York 1953).

43 WEBER, MAX *The Protestant Ethic and the Spirit of Capitalism* (Unwin University Books, London 1930).

44 WEBER, MAX ' "Objectivity" in Social Science and Social Policy', in *The Methodology of the Social Sciences*, translated and edited by Edward A. Shils and Henry A. Finch (Free Press, New York, 1949).

45 WEBER, MAX *Economy and Society*, 3 vols., ed. by Guenther Roth and Claus Wittich (Bedminster Press, New York, 1968).

46 WILSON, BRYAN R. 'An analysis of sect development', *American Sociological Review* vol. 24, no. 1, February 1959, pp. 3–15.

47 WILSON, BRYAN R. *Sects and Society* (William Heinemann, London 1961).

48 WOLFF, KURT H. *The Sociology of Georg Simmel* (Free Press, New York 1950).

49 YINGER, JOHN MILTON 'A structural examination of religion', *Journal for the Scientific Study of Religion* vol. viii, no. 1, 1969, pp. 88–99.

50 YINGER, JOHN MILTON 'The sociology of religion of Ernst Troeltsch' in BARNES, HARRY ELMER, *An Introduction to the History of Sociology*, op. cit.

4

Typologies of Religious Organization

ONE OF the most influential of the subsequent attempts to formulate a comprehensive typology of Christian groups has been that of the American sociologist J. M. Yinger, which was first put forward in 1946 and 1957, and in a considerably modified form—which will be considered later—in 1970. [59; 60; 61] There has been some modification in the basic structure of his typology —in the 1946 version there are four sub-types, in the 1957 version there are six with three subdivisions of sect, and in the 1970 version six main sub-types with a further subdivision into two species of universal churches and three of sects. The fact that Yinger prefaces his original discussion and punctuates his later versions with very helpful statements about the heuristic value of ideal-type concepts in general makes his work one of the clearest and most accessible approaches to the problem.

The first formulation accepts as its basis the broad distinction between church and sect, and is presented in terms of Troeltsch's discussion of these categories. In order to achieve greater analytical precision it is found necessary to break down the ideal type of the church into two sub-types, distinguished by the extent to which universality is achieved. On the one hand is the church which manages to achieve a high degree of universality—exemplified by the thirteenth-century Catholic Church—and for this Yinger adopts the term 'universal church'. It is universal both in the sense of incorporating a wide range of social groups and also in accommodating a variety of religious tendencies, including the radical stream that finds expression in monasticism.

The other sub-type of the church is the *ecclesia* (a term taken from Becker), which fails to achieve universality because of geographical and class boundaries. Lutheranism is seen as being nearest to the modal type of the *ecclesia*, the Church of England lying somewhere in between this and the universal church. Since the inclusion of sect tendencies is one mark of universalism, Yinger sees contemporary Methodism as nearer a universal church than even the Church of England. But among more recent churches, early Calvinism is seen as the only church with a comparable degree of universality to that of late medieval Catholicism —an insight which Werner Stark seems to have used in his contention that Calvinism was 'an attempt' at a universal church which largely failed to materialize. [46, vol. iii: 410] The *ecclesia* tends to be 'respectable' and to push its compromise with the established social order to a considerable extent, mainly because the revolutionary religious element has been hived off and is catered for by the sect.

A similar division can be made within the sect type of organization. At one extreme is a fluid, non-institutionalized group which is unified only by the common beliefs and religious experience of its members: in its original form this is what Becker refers to as a cult (a reminder that the analytical boundary between sect and cult has always been regarded as somewhat tenuous) and only a higher level of organization and of self-consciousness distinguishes a sect from a cult. At this level, Yinger refers to the organization as simply a *sect*. If, however, a second or third-generation sect takes on certain of the characteristics of a church while still being typified by fairly stable social divisions, it can be referred to as an *established sect*. The fact that this group is still seen as a group apart means that it remains a sect.

To summarize, Yinger originally conceived of four basic types of religious organization within Christianity: (1) the *universal church*, (2) the *ecclesia*, (3) the *sect*, and (4) the *established sect*. In the 1957 version this has been expanded to six, though the starting point for the discussion is still the fundamental dichotomy of church and sect. The *universal church* is pointed up in rather clearer detail, and the interesting observation is made—derived from Troeltsch but subsequently obscured by the tendency to regard church and sect as *alternative* organizations—that this type of religious organization combines both church and sect tendencies: this perspective has recently been used in empirical research ta demonstrate that church-type and sect-type orientations may exist among different members of the same religious organization. The *ecclesia* remains as the second sub-type of church, and is shown to occur in societies in which there are, as a result of this religious group's reinforcement of the existing social order, 'widespread indifference, sectarian protests, and secular opposition'. [60:149] To this extent the *ecclesia* is a universal church in a state of rigidification. A new sub-type of the church is elaborated in the form of the 'class church' or *denomination*. This type is in substantial, though not perfect harmony with the secular power-structure but tends to incorporate more of the less privileged members of society and more sectarian elements, mainly because 'many denominations started out as sects and have not completely escaped their origins'. [60:149] An important feature of this type is the enormous range of empirical examples it reveals in the United States, though its predominant style is a conventional and respectable form of religious observance.

Next to the denomination in terms of position on the church–sect continuum—which Yinger sees in relation to the degree of universalism coupled with the degree of emphasis on social integration as against personal needs, which these groups emphasize—comes the *established sect* which is to be seen as a development from the sect end of the continuum and, therefore, not a later stage in the development of a denomination. The best way of exemplifying an established sect in Yinger's account is to compare Methodism, which, he argues, originated as a sect and developed into a denomination (an interpretation that we will later question) with contemporary Quakerism, where sectarian features have been maintained. One of the important ways of distinguishing sects that are likely to denominationalize from those that they may become established is by looking at the nature of the original protest: those sects that place a major emphasis on individual anxiety and sin are most likely to become denominations, whereas those that originally stress the evils of society seem to have an inbuilt resistance to this process. Yinger, like Pope, finds that the social class of the members is not a key precipitating factor.

The fifth type, which is called simply the *sect*, can be subdivided into:

(a) Acceptance sects. These are individualistic and often middle class. Their concern is with personal rather than societal failure, and a good example is the Oxford Group Movement;

(b) Aggressive sects. Here Yinger adopts one of the little-used notions of Troeltsch, which he thinks typifies those lower-class sects that are most clearly associated with poverty and powerlessness. Society is viewed as intrinsically evil and in need of reform, and hence the teachings of Jesus are interpreted in radical-ethical terms. Since sects with this orientation—a notable example of which is the Anabaptist movement—are likely to meet strong opposition and in most cases failure, they are likely to turn into

(c) Avoidance sects. This is a common form of sectarian reaction, and consists in a devaluation of the existing social order and an emphasis on a new life hereafter. Because its protest is symbolic it does not run the risk of such obvious defeat as does the aggressive sect, and its outlook reflects the pessimism of despair.

Yinger's final category, the *cult*, is elaborated in response to 'the need for a term that will describe groups that are similar to sects, but represent a sharper break, in religious terms, from the dominant religious tradition of a society'. [60:154] Thus a cult is small, short-lived, often local and built around a single dominant leader in contrast to the more typical sectarian feature of widespread lay participation. Beliefs and observances tend to deviate quite widely from those that are typical in a society. There is almost complete concern with individual adjustment and little questioning of the social order: Spiritualism is one of the examples given—the other, American Negro 'Moslem' movements, may well have been valid in 1957, but would seem to have become less so in more recent years, as Yinger indeed recognizes in his 1970 discussion.

Yinger's contribution represents the most comprehensive attempt in the post-war growth of the sociology of religion to provide a full range of organizational models for the analysis of

Christianity on the basis of models discussed in chapter 3. More recently, Yinger has provided a comparative framework, which will be included in the section on typological reformulations. Before turning to this, however, mention must be made of an entirely distinct typology of religious organizations. Wach's contribution to the sociology of religion is genuinely comparative, wide-ranging and sadly ignored, but this may provide a valuable clue to the limitation of the church–sect typology. Because the latter is based so very solidly in the doctrinal blueprint of Christianity as seen through a specifically Western (and within that, basically a European and North American) perspective, it may well be that the sub-types and hypotheses derived from them may only be applicable within this context. Nor need this unduly worry us as long as the concepts provide us with fruitful lines of research and valuable insights into the relationship between religious and other institutions within these limits, which I think the church–sect dichotomy and its later elaborations into a formal typology certainly do. It has always been necessary to distinguish between general ideal types, of which the Weberian typology of legitimate authority provides an excellent example, and more specific ideal types. The church–sect typology is just such an instance of the elaboration of relative ideal-type concepts, and part of its value lies precisely in the fact that its 'nearness' to empirical reality makes it possible to develop detailed, testable hypotheses. For this reason too, Wach's attempt to provide genuinely comparative categories for the analysis of religious institutions has stimulated very little empirical research.

But there is one segment of Wach's work that does provide a useful adjunct to the church–sect typology and, I think, obviates much of the involved argument about the origin of sects and denominations: this is his treatment of the *ecclesiola in ecclesia*. This concept is delineated in the course of Wach's treatment of the 'specifically religious organization' of society, which includes a wide range of organizational types from secret societies and mystery societies to churches and sects. Apart from the criticisms that his categories tend to be descriptive, to consist of empirically clustered features, and to lack the requirement of typological analysis that analytical concepts should be part of some clearly articulated theoretical scheme, some of Wach's comments are

highly relevant to the church–sect typology already set out above.
Wach makes a basic distinction between two forms of religious
protest: secession, and 'protest within'. In the latter case there is a
characteristic pattern of the formation of an *ecclesiola in ecclesia*, a
term derived from Spener's late seventeenth-century *collegia
pietatis*. The range of forms that such a group might take can be
ranked in terms of the degree of protest. Thus the first type of
protest within is the *collegium pietatis*. This is an intermediate
step between individual protest and complete separation, and
characterizes groups that do not see themselves as the ideal
community or try to form special units but simply propound a
distinctive attitude or form of devotion. 'In other words, there
is a loosely organized group, limited in numbers and united in a
common enthusiasm, peculiar convictions, intense devotion, and
rigid discipline, which is striving to attain higher spiritual and
moral perfection than can be realized under prevailing conditions.
. . . The "meeting" is the typical sociological expression of the
piety of these *collegia*.' [48:75] Two examples given are early
Methodism and the Oxford Tractarian movement—inclusion of
the latter suggests that we might loosely paraphrase the *collegium*
as a 'ginger group'. Implicit and explicit criticism of the main
body of the church is a characteristic feature of *collegia*, as is the
use of new and intensified devotional practices, such as the love
feast and the washing of feet.

The second form of 'protest within' is the *fraternitas*, which
develops when the initial 'parallelism of religious spontaneity' no
longer sufficiently serves to unite a protest group against the
status quo. There is a fairly broad range within which such a
brotherhood may develop its minimal organization, but there is
usually an egalitarian conception of fellowship, though often
stratification and specialization of functions emerge. The Brethren
of the Common Life represent a good example of a *fraternitas*
which eventually formalized its position within the wider church
by organizing themselves as 'Augustinian Canons': the Methodist
groups, which Wach also cites as examples, adopted an alternative
strategy by forming a religious organization distinctly separate
from the parent church.

Finally, the third form of 'protest within' is demonstrated by
the *order*. In this type of *ecclesiola* there is a more formal and

segregated expression of the more loosely based withdrawal found in the *fraternitas*, and there is an insistence on permanent loyalty. 'Absolute obediance, fixed residence, peculiar garb, meals in common, special devotions, and common labor bind the members of the convent and the order together'. [48:182] The relationship between the order and the church of which it forms part is seen as being complex and dynamic. Elsewhere I have analysed this relationship in detail, [23] and there will be only brief mention later in this chapter of the place of the order in a typology of Christian organizations. In so far as Wach regards the crystalliz-ation and self-conscious definition of internal protest as the dimen-sion on which these three types of *ecclesiola in ecclesia* can be ranked, his contribution is extremely apposite and can help to remove some of the conceptual confusion that surrounds the early stages of movements like Methodism.

More recent developments of the conceptual models and typol-ogies which were outlined in the first part of this chapter can be summarized under five headings. These do not refer to discrete, isolated lines of enquiry but they provide a useful context for the subsequent discussion. The five points of concern are: (1) the circumstances under which certain types of sect may *retain* their sectarian characteristics or may *revert* to them after a process of denominationalization; (2) the process whereby denominations may originate not as sects but as *ecclesiolae in ecclesia*, and the usefulness of this model in analysing 'protest' movements within more universalistic religious institutions; (3) the way in which different religious orientations may *interpenetrate* so that within a single institution there may exist distinct and sometimes com-peting definitions of its structure; (4) the reformulation of organizational typologies in the light of empirical data and theo-retical principles that challenge existing assumptions; (5) the difficulty of using the concepts of 'church' and 'sect' in a wider comparative contest than that of Christianity. It will be apparent that some of these headings do not exclude approaches that are listed in others, and in a number of studies two or more lines are pursued: these we will indicate.

The most extensive research on the extent to which sects *retain* their sectarian characteristics has been that of Bryan Wilson. [50; 51; 53] He typifies a sect as follows: (a) it is a voluntary association; (b) membership is by proof to the sect authorities of some special merit, such as knowledge of doctrine or conversion experience; (c) exclusiveness is emphasized and expulsion of deviants exercised; (d) the self-conception is of an elect, gathered remnant with special enlightenment; (e) personal perfection—however defined—is the expected level of aspiration; (f) there is ideally a priesthood of all believers; (g) there is a high level of lay participation; (h) the member is allowed to express his commitment spontaneously; (i) the sect is hostile or indifferent to the secular society and state. Pointing out that this list is more general than those of Becker, Pope and Yinger—since it omits features such as subjectivism, informality, the expression of fervour, and poverty—Wilson maintains that these characteristics appear only in certain sub-types of sect. He then adds two further general features of sects: (j) the commitment of the sectarian is always more total and more clearly defined than that of the member of other religious organizations; (k) sects have a totalitarian rather than a segmental hold over their members, and their ideology tends to keep the sectarian apart from 'the world'. The ideological orientation to secular society is *dictated* by the sect, or member behaviour is strictly specified.

Taking religious organizations with these general characteristics, a number of sub-types of sect may be identified. In his 1959 article, Wilson identified four. The *Conversionist* sect centres its activity on evangelism, and in contemporary Christianity it takes the form of an orthodox fundamentalist or pentecostal sect. Literal belief in the Bible, conversion experience and distrust of more 'lukewarm' religious organizations are common features of this sub-type, examples of which are the Salvation Army and Pentecostal sects. The second sub-type, the *Adventist* or *Revolutionist* sect, is focused on the coming overthrow of the present order. Biblical exegesis and allegory are used as evidence of the second coming of Christ, the resurrection of the dead is conceived to be a major eschatological event, and admission is based on knowledge of such doctrines, not on conversion experience. The established church is seen as Antichrist and the wider society is viewed with hostility. Examples are the Jehovah's Witnesses and the Christadelphians. The third sub-type—the *Introversionist* or *Pietist* sect—directs its members' attention away from the world to the community of believers, which is seen as an enlightened elect that possesses the true Spirit. There is no evangelism and no formal ministry, strong ingroup morality and indifference to other religious movements. Some Holiness movements follow this pattern, as do the Quakers and the Amana Society. Finally, the *Gnostic* sect emphasizes some special body of teaching of an esoteric kind, and offers a new interpretation of Christian teaching. Christ is portrayed more as a way-shower than a personal saviour, and the sect usually puts forward an exclusive set of mystical beliefs, which the adherent can expect to penetrate only gradually. Secular scientific theories are replaced, and a new means to everyday success and self-realization is offered: ministers are usually regarded as teachers, and the cultural standards of the surrounding society are accepted. These characteristics are found in the examples of Christian Science, New Thought sects and the Order of the Cross.

One of the principal sources of tension within sects is the coexistence of an ethic of separation from the world with the injunction that many sects accept to go out and preach the gospel. Evangelism means exposure to the world and the risk that the standards of admission originally maintained by the group will be compromised. However, Introversionist and Gnostic sects typically do not engage in a programme of proselytism, since they admit new members through formalized procedures. Adventist sects see it as their function to forewarn the world of the coming cataclysm and to gather a remnant, but their evangelists are put through rigorous doctrinal training and their new admissions are similarly examined. This leaves Conversionist sects as those most likely to experience the tension between insulation and evangelization. The emotional form of conversion characteristic of fundamentalist revivals is not the best-designed 'sifting' mechanism, and since the Conversionist sect's doctrine is often not very clearly marked off from that of other religious groups it is more difficult to make knowledge of doctrine a test of entry. The second-generation problem is most important in Conversionist sects, since Gnostic sects (having an individualist appeal) are less likely to attract the children of existing members, and Pietist and Adventist sects tend to have exacting standards of entry, and can thus hold their second generation without damage to sect identity. Thus, on the criteria of distinctive sectarian values and rigorous standards of entry, Conversionist sects 'are most likely to fulfil the conditions which transform sects into denominations and are least likely to enjoy the circumstances preventing this process'. [50:14]

Some reference should be made to the sub-type of Gnostic sect, because by incorporating this into his schema, Wilson has obliterated the cult as a separate category. This is clearly intentional, for in subsequent discussions he has given as examples of Gnostic or Manipulationist sects groups that have elsewhere been labelled cults—Scientology and Theosophy are notable examples. [57] The concept of cult, taken from Troeltsch's 'mysticism' by Becker and refined by Yinger, has had a precarious status in most discussions of Christian organization. At best, it has occupied a position on the fringe of what can meaningfully be called organization: Marty, for example, considers both sects and cults to be a residual 'third force', though he does make the important observation that sects have a negative orientation towards the values of the surrounding society, while cults are positively oriented. [31:129] In an analysis of contemporary cults, Jackson and Jobling distinguish between the 'mystic-religious cult where certain esoteric practices are pursued in order to maximize the votary's religious experience' and a form of cult which is world-affirming and in which 'esoteric practices are . . . adopted as manipulative techniques which will be instrumental in enhancing the success, prestige, and power of the votary in the world'. [27:97]

In more recent articles, Wilson has added to his four sub-types three further categories of sect, one of which bears directly on the distinction made by Jackson and Jobling. The Gnostic/Manipulationist sub-type is retained for groups like Christian Science and Scientology, but *Thaumaturgical* sects are added to take account of 'mystic-religious' responses that are found in Spiritualist groups. [41:368–9] Also added is the category of *Reformist* sects, which 'seem to constitute a case apart' [41:369] and which study the world in order to involve themselves in it by good deeds, adopting the role of social conscience. This is a marginal category, and the only distinction between groups of this sort and denominations is seen to be their retention of a sectarian structure:

English Quakerism is one of the few firm examples given. The third additional category is that of *Utopian* sects, which withdraw from the world in order to remake the world to a better pattern, beginning within their own communities. The Oneida and the Brüderhof are examples of this type.

It seems that there are two significant criteria on which cults can still be distinguished from sects. The first, which David Martin regards as the 'fundamental' criterion of the cult, [30:194] is its individualism. Troeltsch's original claim that mysticism was a distinct form of religious expression was based on this, and there does seem to be a strong contrast between the totalitarian hold of sectarian groups and the more amorphous, free-floating membership principle of groups such as Theosophy and Spiritualism. The second criterion, put forward by Becker and elaborated more recently by Geoffrey Nelson, is the way that cults represent a fundamental break with the religious tradition of the society in which they originate. [35; 36; 37] Especially important in this respect are the syncretistic imports of Eastern mysticism (for example, in Theosophy) and of quasi-scientific techniques and terminology (an instance of which is provided by Scientology). Troeltsch, it will be recalled, traced the premisses of both the church and the sect to complementary aspects of Christianity that could be deduced perfectly legitimately from the New Testament. Although cults might well draw on biblical sources in constructing their belief systems—as the founder of Christian Science did to a considerable extent—they are more concerned to *use* insights drawn from them than to attempt, as both church and sect-type groups do, to derive from them an authentic and complete basis of legitimacy. The whole problem of defining a religious organization by its *lack* of organization might be solved by referring to a *cultic milieu*. [7]

Roland Robertson has given another account of organizational development which runs counter to the sect-to-denomination process, and suggests that an originally denominational movement may *revert* to a sectarian form. [42:127–8] The Salvation Army originated in the revivalist preaching of William Booth, who had begun his career as a Methodist but became alienated from the Methodist New Connexion because of its lack of enthusiasm for revivalist campaigns among the poor. Booth attributed the

No. He was refused permission to at an explain.

previous failures of other religious bodies to their reluctance to use uncompromising methods, and advocated a return to the original techniques of John Wesley. Very rapidly, the incipient movement gravitated from a denominational position, as one evangelical movement among others, to the position of a conversionist sect with a tight-knit, authoritarian 'military' structure. What prevented it from being drawn into the developmental sequence which Wilson suggests as being most typical of conversionist sects was this very distinctive form of organization. The Salvation Army, Robertson suggests, is better viewed as an established or institutionalized sect than as a denomination. This is because, while it has retained most of its sectarian characteristics, it has achieved a solid *modus vivendi* with the surrounding society. Interestingly, this is not seen as a one-way process of compromise on the part of the religious organization but as a process of convergence in which the surrounding society has become more tolerant of deviant forms of religious expression: the Salvation Army has become 'respectable' from without as well as from within.

The second line of research has been on the origin of denominations as *ecclesiolae in ecclesia*, and the main proponent of this interpretation has been Martin. [29] To set this approach in its context, it is clear that from Niebuhr onwards, denominations have tended to be seen as mature sects rather than as originating *sui generis*. In addition, there have been several attempts to apply the polar concepts of church and sect as opposite ends of a continuum, so that groups originate as sects and develop into churches—Methodism in particular has been interpreted in this framework. [6; 9] Against this, Martin contends that the emergence of denominations out of sects is not so much incorrect (for it might well apply to the Quakers) as atypical. If one looks at the major denominations—the Methodists, Congregationalists and Baptists—it is evident that their early history is almost completely devoid of sectarian characteristics. To some extent they all originated as *ecclesiolae in ecclesia*, which developed into denominations, but they were never sects. The denomination can be distinguished from both the church and the sect because it formally maintains that it has no institutional monopoly of salvation, and thus it maintains a fairly tolerant position. Its organizational principles are more fluid and pragmatic than those of the church (they are especially well represented in Wesley's own 'innovations'), and its separate ministry—which is maintained in contrast to the more typically sectarian rejection of it—is seen more as a matter of convenience than of divine institution. Sacraments are given a subjective interpretation, in contrast to the church's objective doctrine of sacraments and the sect's rejection of them. In its attitude to the existing social order the denomination is neither conservative (as is the church) nor revolutionary/indifferent (as is the sect), but *reformist*: hence 'The sociological idea of the denomination is the idea of Her Majesty's Opposition, of disagreement within consensus, except that the opposition is permanently out of office'. [29:13]

The use of Wach's notion of *ecclesiola in ecclesia* to depict the initial crystallization of denominations is especially fruitful, since it opens up the possibility of considering the different 'strategies' facing potentially schismatic groups within more universalistic religious institutions. One option—the option considered by Martin—is to hive off and form a denomination. A second, which would seem to be more characteristic of societies in which the identification of established religious institutions with the political élite is more complete and monolithic, is to hive off and form a sectarian protest group. O'Dea, for instance, speaks of 'two important "choices" confronting sectarian protest groups' [38:68] in a church, one of which is secession. Care is needed in using concepts of this kind. In the first place, it cannot be assumed that all sectarian movements begin within a church and thus have a 'choice'. Perhaps more important is the idea conveyed by the word 'choice' that if a protest group within a church does 'decide' to secede, then it has somehow missed the opportunity to engage in internal reform and has 'rocked the boat'. In other words, this is a 'churchy' interpretation. Nevertheless, *some* sects and denominations do originally emerge as protest movements within churches, and *some* protest movements do crystallize into the third of Wach's types of *ecclesiola in ecclesia*, the religious order. There are interesting parallels, as well as distinct contrasts, between religious orders and sects, some of which may be outlined here.

Referring back to the typical features of sects listed by Wilson

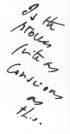

Order

(see page 78), the parallel features of religious orders can be summarized as follows: [22] (a) religious orders, being in their most fully developed form celibate, cannot bestow birthright membership, and to this extent at least are voluntary organizations; (b) special merit in the form of a high level commitment and stringent tests of entry are usually demanded; (c) a special dress is one way in which orders have emphasized exclusiveness, and provision is normally made in the Rule of an order for expulsion; (d) special enlightenment is certainly emphasized in the more contemplative religious orders, and although the concept of a 'remnant' is incompatible with Catholic dogma, a disproportionate number of saints have come from the ranks of hermits and monks; [45:157] (e) personal perfection, which in the more community-based religious orders may be given social concomitants (such as 'minimal disruption'), is a key goal in religious orders; (f); (g) although monasticism originated as a lay protest movement, by the twelfth century it had been 'clericalized': recently there have been moves towards the more pristine form by abolishing the 'choir' (ordained) and 'lay' (lay) distinction in some orders, and ritual participation has always been more sustained and more inclusive than in 'secular' churches; (h) spontaneity, being potentially disruptive in a tightly knit community, is not encouraged in the context of group activities, though it may be tolerated in exceptional cases; (i) orders adopt a 'reserved' rather than hostile/indifferent attitude to the world, but retain virtuoso values against compromise; (j) commitment is total, typically expressed in segregation, which in many instances is lifelong; (k) in some respects, orders resemble Goffman's concept of a 'total institution', though their voluntaristic basis distinguishes them from prisons and other asylums.

The major difference between religious orders and sects are two: firstly, orders, being part of a wider institutional church, rely on a source of authority that is ultimately external, though they may be permitted a considerable degree of organizational autonomy in their internal arrangements. Sects, on the other hand, are self-legitimating and rely on no external sanctions in regulating their beliefs and structure. A corollary of this is that orders often claim to perform mystical and sometimes practical services for the whole of society, while this is by no means true of all sects. Secondly, religious orders impose strict regulations on sexual activity and often seek to minimize the tensions that this might cause by geographical isolation. Sects are very rarely celibate, although they may impose rules of endogamy and other sexual regulations, which sometimes generate opposition, as the campaign against the Exclusive Brethren in 1964 illustrated, [54] but it is interesting to note that the Shakers—who began as a celibate sect—adopted a communitarian organization. [57:203–7]

There have been a number of studies in the third area of research on the *interpenetration* of different religious orientations in terms of the organizational typology. Isichei's studies of the history of English Quakerism, for example, suggest that competing groups within the overall membership of the Society of Friends had different beliefs about its basic structure and that these were more or less influential depending on both the relative strength of the groups internally and on changes in the external environment. [24; 25] Starting from Wilson's criticism of the Niebuhr thesis, Isichei notes that not only is it inapplicable to every type of sect, but that the very idea of a linear progression over time from sect to church is misleading, since the evidence of sects like the Exclusive Brethren suggests that the process may be thrown into reverse. The development of English Quakerism in particular was much more complex and paradoxical than Niebuhr's account suggests. On the one hand, some aspects of eighteenth-century Quakerism fit the sect-to-denomination process quite well. The proselytizing zeal in which the movement had originated soon faded, and the Society was replenished not by adult converts but by natural increase, a fact that was given official sanction in 1737 by the recognition of Quaker's children as birthright members. The income of the group rose, as did the status of its members, and there is much evidence to suggest that in the eighteenth and nineteenth centuries Quakers were coming to accept the prevailing values of their social environment and to respect worldly ranks and titles. On the other hand, there were strong sectarian characteristics in the organization until the middle of the nineteenth century: 'Its attitude was that of a select body isolated from a corrupting environment, and Quaker literature is full of references to "the world" in the pejorative (and scriptural) sense of the term. The group's refusal to obey certain of the State's laws was again typically sectarian.' [24:209]

Until the 1860s it seems that there were stringent Quaker embargoes on amusements like dancing, novel-reading and theatre-going, many of which could not be traced to the primitive period of the sect's origin because they were not amusements available to the artisan founders. The changing social environment of a sect, and especially the new consumption patterns it encounters, present serious challenges to its rigorous stance towards 'the world'. God may be the Ancient of Days, but Mammon is for ever launching new products, which must somehow be given the sect's seal of approval (or disapproval). Because Quaker embargoes on expenditure consisted in general conventions rather than detailed regulations, the pace of liberalization was uneven, but it had begun by the 1840s and was fairly complete by the 1880s. Coupled with the adoption by many Quakers of middle-class consumption patterns, there were other signs of a denominationalizing tendency. The growth of agitation for a trained ministry was one sign of this; and as nineteenth-century revivalism brought in converts, there were suggestions that the ministry should be paid.

The most important factor halting this development, and one that has received little attention in studies of sects, was the growth of historical studies in the group. The leaders of English Quakerism towards the end of the nineteenth century 'attempted to discover the true character of Quakerism by studying its historical origins. The result of this quest (which found its most important expression in the Rowntree Quaker histories) was to revive the older sectarian aspects of Quakerism. The trend towards a professional ministry was reversed, and the practice of recording ministers was abolished in 1924; at a later date, the birthright membership of children was replaced by the Temporary Membership list.' [24:213]

There thus coexisted within Quakerism for some considerable period of time both a sectarian and a denominational outlook. These came into sharp conflict during the 1880s, when the Yearly Meeting debated the issues of group endogamy and distinctive modes of dress and speech. Sectarian protagonists regarded these as insulating mechanisms which prevented religious decline, while the advocates of liberalization saw them as crippling restraints which were holding back converts, alienating the young and restricting religious liberty:

> Here we have many of the classic positions of the denomination in microcosm—a concern for the young, a desire to make entry into the group attractive and easy, an insistence on the liberty of the individual, and a self-conceptualization of the group as one of many churches, all pleasing to God. The reaction of the sectarian to those who complain that the rules of his group are too difficult is to expel the backsliders. He is indifferent to the effect which his rigorism has on membership statistics, for he sees the sect as a chosen élite of spiritual athletes. Often he will value the barriers around the sect so highly that he will identify them with the sect's continued existence, although he is unable to provide a rational explanation of his attitude. [24:215]

Thus the history of the Quakers in the nineteenth century represents an oscillation between denominational tendencies—associated with conversionism and the need to minister to new members—and sectarianism, represented by withdrawal and the re-emphasis of a unique mission based on the doctrinal 'discoveries' of Quaker historians. Isichei concludes that 'a sect is likely to move through successive phases of outward and inward orientation, which are closely associated with fortuitous external circumstances, and are unlikely to be subsumed in any widely accurate and meaningful statement of sectarian sociology'. [24:221] Despite the rejection of any concept of linear progression as an adequate framework for the study of sectarian development, the idea of oscillation conveys very clearly the element of structural and ideological strain and play-off in an organization with interpenetrating orientations. It has been used in a similar way by John Whitworth in the study of a Utopian sect, the Brüderhof, which went through successive stages of conversion/introversion (or, to use the sect's own terminology, 'outreach' and 'creative withdrawal') [49] in much the same way as the English Quakers.

A rather different use of the concept of interpenetration has been that of Russell Dynes and the later, more extensive, study by Nicholas Demerath. [10; 11; 13] Both of these pieces of research

D

acknowledge the initial groundwork done by Liston Pope, who, it was argued earlier, represents one of the first attempts to operationalize the dimensions of the church–sect typology in terms that could be quantified. Pope's characteristics of sect- and church-type organizations are translated by Dynes into statements of personal preference, which were then constructed into a Likert-type scale with twenty-four items. Examples of the statements included on the scale are: 'I think a minister should preach without expecting to get paid for it', 'I feel that a congregation should encourage the minister during his sermon by saying *amen*', 'I think being a success in one's job is one mark of being a good Christian', and 'Children should not become members of the church until they are old enough to understand about it'. Both sociological and theological judges were used to assess the validity of the scale, and a questionnaire was sent to a random sample of the adult population in Columbus, Ohio—*not* to church members alone.

Significant differences in church–sect scores were found using the three measures of educational level, Census occupational classifications and occupational prestige ratings. Dynes found that 'Churchness is associated with high socio-economic status and, conversely, that sectness is associated with low socio-economic status.' [13:559] Nor was this simply a function of denominational affiliation, since it could be hypothesized that by holding denominational affiliation constant, members of the same denomination who differed in occupational prestige would still show different orientations. This was found to be the case with two denominations which were sufficiently well represented in the sample to make possible a detailed breakdown (the Methodists and Presbyterians). The conclusion can thus be stated: 'Holding denominational affiliation constant ... the difference in the degree of Churchness and Sectness is still associated with socio-economic status.' [13:560]

Demerath comments that the church–sect dichotomy has been restricted to the study of religious organizations when it might usefully be applied to the delineation of types of religious *involvement* within the same organization. [10:43] Demerath found a consistent relationship between 'churchlike religiosity' and high status and between 'sectlike religiosity' and low status, and the relationship remained when denominational affiliation was held constant. In an interesting review of the implications of this finding, Demerath points out that although the existence of churchlike and sectlike orientations in the same institutions may lead to conflict and even dissolution, there is an immensely valuable consequence because the two strains balance each other and prevent 'unbridled bureaucratization' on the one hand and 'unfettered insularity' on the other. [10: 184–5] 'Not only is there a division of labour among religious groups but also within them. There may indeed be short-run friction and even rare cases of dissolution. But, in the long run, the coexistence is an asset for the organization's endurance, and this may be true even of the friction generated.' [10:184] Just as the monastic movement has often been interpreted as a source of organizational balance, it appears that this type of impulse can be found across a much broader spectrum of Christian organizations.

Two recent *typological reformulations* which are broadly based on the typologies discussed above but which attempt to provide a more comparative analytical framework in which evaluative labels are minimized have been suggested by Yinger and Robertson. [61:260; 42:123] Yinger bases his typology on two axes, the first of which is made up of two variables: inclusiveness of the religious structures (the extent to which all members of a society can be accommodated within the religious organization) and extent of alienation from societal values (the extent to which the religious organization 'rejects the world'). These are inversely correlated, argues Yinger, and can be ranked together on the same axis. The second axis represents the degree of organizational complexity and differentiation of the religious structures. Thus we have two extremes, the institutional ecclesia (high inclusiveness/low alienation on the first axis, high organizational complexity on the second) and the charismatic sect (low inclusiveness/high alienation on the first axis, low organizational complexity on the second). In varying intermediate positions are six other types of religious organizations, the 'diffused ecclesia', the 'institutional denomination', the 'diffused denomination', the 'established sect', the 'established lay sect' and the 'sect movement'. While Yinger's typology is firmly based on three fundamental criteria (inclusiveness, alienation and organization) and opens up the possibility of more precise comparative application, it does not exhaust all the dimensions which are involved in the eventual location of empirical cases. Thus there is a further sub-specification of three types of sect in terms of 'attitude to the world'—acceptance, aggression and avoidance. In these circumstances, it would seem preferable to use a simple framework as a starting point and then to elaborate sub-types on a more detailed empirical level, especially if these are to be drawn from traditions outside Christianity. There comes a point when the proliferation of sub-types in a general typology begins to blunt the heuristic potential of ideal types.

Robertson's typology is constructed on two axes, both of which are concerned with the relationship between the religious organization and its environment. The first axis is concerned with the effective leadership's perception of the organization's legitimacy: whether it is 'pluralistically legitimate' (one of a set of acceptable religious vehicles) or 'uniquely legitimate' (holding some variant of *extra ecclesiam non salus*). The second axis concerns the organization's membership principle: whether it is 'inclusive' (accepting low standards of admission) or 'exclusive' (demanding rigorous tests of entry). Hence we have a four-part typology:

Self-conceived basis of legitimacy

		Pluralistically legitimate	Uniquely legitimate
Member-ship principle	Exclusive	Institutionalized sect	Sect
	Inclusive	Denomination	Church

Robertson emphasizes that these categories are to be used in a *societal context* (that is, we must speak of, for example, British Congregationalism rather than Congregationalism in general) and that they are intended to denote a relationship between the religious organization and the surrounding society. It seems to me that this solves the immediate problem of where to place the religious order. Its membership principle is certainly exclusive, but it does not maintain that salvation is only available to its members—which would put it alongside the institutionalized sect. However, since it derives its authority from a church which *does* maintain such a monopoly on legitimacy with regard to the surrounding society, it might be more appropriate to locate it between the sect and the church.

Both Yinger and Robertson are very much concerned with the extent to which the church–sect typology has a *comparative* use. It is worth ending on this topic because it brings the discussion back to Weber's original statement. Weber, it was pointed out, used the concepts of church and sect as potentially comparative tools, which could be related to the broader analysis of charisma and its routinization. Just as his limited analysis of the religious factors involved in the development of Western capitalism was taken up by Troeltsch and given a more comprehensive treatment *for Christianity*, so the church–sect dichotomy was similarly adopted by Troeltsch and given a much more substantial *Christian* content. However, while Weber later returned to a comparative treatment of religion and capitalism in the context of China and India, his treatise on *Religionssoziologie* contains virtually nothing on the comparative use of 'church' and 'sect'. It seems highly probable that Weber would have disclaimed any identification of the sect with 'real' religiosity and the church with an implicitly disreputable form of compromise. What is beyond doubt, however, is that Weber distinguished the two types of religious organization above all on their principle of membership: membership of a church was in theory compulsory and was not based on the religious 'qualifications' of its members; while membership of a sect was voluntary and based on the acceptance of duly qualified members. In a sect, charisma attached to the leader whereas in a church it attached to an office.

Peter Berger, in an early and often neglected article, has shifted the emphasis from the membership principle to the charismatic component as the key characteristic of sects. [3;4] Since this is an attempt to develop Weber's ideas on a comparative level, his argument is worth following, though in several respects it conflicts quite sharply with recent studies of sectarianism. Referring to Weber's emphasis on the principle of membership as a major distinguishing feature, Berger uses an almost Aristotelian notion of 'Accident': 'It seems to me that in Weber's definition a sectarian characteristic has been made decisive which, though widespread, is logically accidental to the phenomenon as such. . . . Weber's most valuable contribution is not his definition of the sect but his discovery of the process of "routinization" in the development of the sect.' [3:470] Niebuhr's contention that sects are 'churches of the disinherited' is argued to be true of the United States to a large extent, but falls down completely in the case of Islamic sects. [41:130–1] Using the phenomenological perspective of the inner meaning of religious phenomena to the participants involved in them, Berger suggests that the sect 'may be defined as a religious grouping based on the belief that *the spirit is immediately present*. And the church, on the other hand, may be defined as a religious grouping based on the belief that *the spirit is remote*. [3:474] On this definition, it becomes possible to relate the inner meanings of belief systems in terms of their quasi-geographical location of the spirit.

This, says Berger, turns the sociology of religion into an 'ecology of the sacred', and we are close to a Durkheimian inter-pretation of the primitive equation of the sacred with a geo-graphical area. On this basis too we may study the spatial sym-bolism of traditional church architecture, with its railings barring access to the sanctuary in which the sacred is 'reserved'. Graphic-ally represented, the sacred can be seen as the centre of a set of concentric circles: immediately surrounding it is the sectarian circle, further out is the church circle and beyond that the world. From the point of view of the sect, the church merges with the world, while from the point of view of the church the sect makes an irreverent and illicit claim on forbidden territory. Added to this image is the idea that the centre may shift at any moment, since the spirit blows where it wills, and a new manifestation may appear in the middle of what was previously 'the world'—an 'epicentre', to push Berger's analogy.

The parallel he seems to have in mind is a pool into which stones are dropped and cause ripples. If the ripples from the centre are strong enough, then a stone dropped further out will make little impression—hence, of sectarian phenomena *within* churches, Berger claims: 'If the church is strong these will be transitory.' [3:477] As an image of charismatic manifestation and routinization this is extremely useful because it conveys the idea (discussed more fully in chapter 8) that routinization can be 'broken through' at any point in an institutional structure.

There are in Berger's schema three major orientations of sectarian movements, with seven specific types of sect: (1) Enthusiastic (subtypes—Revivalist/Pentecostalist; Pietist/Holiness), (2) Prophetic (subtypes—Chiliastic; Legalistic), (3) Gnostic subtypes—Oriental; New Thought; Spiritist). The major orientations, but not their detailed examples, are presented as comparative types, possibly existing in non-Christian contexts. Furthermore, to speak of routinization means to suggest that the initial influence on a sect's development is its religious impulse, but as time goes on the influence of social factors is felt more and more—though one would want to add that the option is always open for a new breakthrough. As distance from the spirit widens, so does social distance in the religious group:

In the sect, facing the immediate presence of the spirit, the members form a compact, unified group. When there is strong organization it is usually motivated by the sect's mission in the world; the bonds between the members themselves are immediate, without the need for institutional formalization. The religious experience itself is the unifying force. In the church, however, where the spirit is remote and can be brought nearer only by formalized means, the bonds between the members weaken, and the unity of the structure require the establishment of legalistic bonds to replace the religious ones. As Bacon has put it, '*religio praecipuum humanae societatis vinculum*', when this bond weakens, the bonds of the world—the area away from the spirit—have to be reestablished. [3:480]

Whether *all* new sectarian movements could be attributed to a charismatic breakthrough (using 'charisma' as a type of authority rather than in the diffuse sense of 'proximity to the sacred') is questionable. Nevertheless, it *has* been one important source of new religious movements as well as of revivals in more institutionalized ones, and the central problem of maintaining a specifically *religious* form of sociation, represented by the sect's belief in close contact with the source of its experience, is well analysed in Berger's two accounts. They represent one of the few attempts to analyse sectarian phenomena in terms of Weber's original observations about them, and they also suggest that the category of *ecclesiola in ecclesia* is a valuable device for analysing sectarian 'island formations' which interpenetrate church organizations. [4:43] Some of the interpretations that Berger suggests for the study of sectarianism will later be developed in the section on charisma.

REFERENCES

1 APTEKMAN, D. M. 'A preliminary characterization of the contemporary status of the religious temperance movement', *Soviet Sociology* vol. VIII, no. 3-4, Winter–Spring 1969/70, pp. 329–42.

2 BENSON, J. KENNETH and DORSETT, JAMES H. 'Toward a theory of religious organizations', *Journal for the Scientific Study of Religion* vol. 10, no. 2, Summer 1971, pp. 138–51.

3 BERGER, PETER L. 'The sociological study of sectarianism', *Social Research* vol. 21, no. 4, Winter 1954, pp. 467–85.

4 BERGER, PETER L. 'Sectarianism and religious sociation', *American Journal of Sociology* vol. LXIV, no. 1, July 1958, pp. 41–4.

5 BRADEN, CHARLES S. 'The sects', *Annals of the American Academy of Political and Social Science* vol. 256, March 1948, pp. 53–62.

6 BREWER, EARL D. C. 'Sect and church in Methodism', *Social Forces* vol. 30, no. 4, May 1952, pp. 400–8.

7 CAMPBELL, COLIN 'The cult, the cultic milieu and secularization', in HILL, MICHAEL (ed.) *A Sociological Yearbook of Religion in Britain—5* (SCM Press, London 1972).

8 CATTON, WILLIAM R. JR. 'What kind of people does a religious cult attract?', *American Sociological Review* vol. 22, no. 5, October 1957, pp. 561–6.

9 CHAMBERLAYNE, JOHN H. 'From *sect* to *church* in British Methodism', *British Journal of Sociology* vol. XV, no. 2, June 1964, pp. 139–49.

10 DEMERATH III, NICHOLAS J. *Social Class in American Protestantism* (Rand McNally, Chicago 1965).

11 DEMERATH III, NICHOLAS J. 'In a sow's ear: a reply to Goode', *Journal for the Scientific Study of Religion* vol. VI, no. 1, 1967, pp. 77–84.

12 DEMERATH III, NICHOLAS J. 'Irreligion, a-religion, and the rise of the religion-less church: two case studies in organizational convergence', *Sociological Analysis* vol. 30, no. 4, Winter 1969, pp. 191–203.

13 DYNES, RUSSELL R. 'Church–sect typology and socio-economic status', *American Sociological Review* vol. 20, no. 5, October 1955, pp. 555–60.

14 EISTER, ALLAN W. 'Toward a radical critique of church–sect typologizing', *Journal for the Scientific Study of Religion* vol. VI, no. 1, 1967, pp. 85–90.

15 FARIS, ELLSWORTH 'The sect and the sectarian', *American Journal of Sociology* vol. LX, no. 6, May 1955 (supplement), pp. 75–90.

16 FRANCIS, E. K. 'Toward a typology of religious orders', *American Journal of Sociology* vol. LV, no. 5, March 1950, pp. 437–49.

17 GODDIJN, H. P. M. 'The sociology of religious orders and congregations', *Social Compass* vol. VII/5–6, 1960, pp. 431–47.

18 GOODE, ERICH 'Some critical observations on the church–sect dimension', *Journal for the Scientific Study of Religion* vol. VI, no. 1, 1967, pp. 69–77.

19 GUSTAFSON, PAUL, 'OU–US–PS–PO: a restatement of Troeltsch's church–sect typology', *Journal for the Scientific Study of Religion* vol. VI, no. 1, 1967, pp. 64–8.

20 HILL, MICHAEL (ed.) *A Sociological Yearbook of Religion in Britain—4* (SCM Press, London 1971).

21 HILL, MICHAEL, and TURNER, BRYAN S. 'John Wesley and the origin and decline of ascetic devotion', in HILL, MICHAEL (ed.) *A Sociological Yearbook of Religion in Britain—4*, op. cit.

22 HILL, MICHAEL 'Typologie sociologique de l'ordre religieux', *Social Compass* vol. XVIII/1, 1971, pp. 45–64.

23 HILL, MICHAEL *The Religious Order in a Sociological Context: A Study of Virtuoso Religion and its Legitimation in the Nineteenth Century Church of England*, Ph.D. thesis (University of London 1971).

24 ISICHEI, ELIZABETH ALLO 'From sect to denomination in English Quakerism, with special reference to the nineteenth century', *British Journal of Sociology* vol. XV, no. 3, September 1964, pp. 207–22.

25 ISICHEI, ELIZABETH ALLO 'Organisation and power in the Society of Friends (1852–1859)', *Archives de Sociologie des Religions* no. 19, January–June 1965, pp. 31–49.

26 JACKSON, JOHN A. 'Two contemporary cults', *Advancement of Science* vol. 23, no. 108, June 1966, pp. 60–4.

27 JACKSON, JOHN A., and JOBLING, RAY 'Towards an analysis of contemporary cults', in MARTIN, DAVID A. (ed.) *A Sociological Yearbook of Religion in Britain* (SCM Press, London 1968).

28 KANTER, ROSABETH MOSS 'Commitment and social organization: a study of commitment mechanisms in utopian communities', *American Sociological Review* vol. 33, no. 4, pp. 499–517.

29 MARTIN, DAVID A. 'The denomination', *British Journal of Sociology* vol. XII, no. 1, March 1962, pp. 1–14.

30 MARTIN, DAVID A. *Pacifism* (Routledge and Kegan Paul, London 1965).

31 MARTY, MARTIN E. 'Sects and cults', *Annals of the American Academy of Political and Social Science* vol. 332, November 1960, pp. 125–34.

32 MOBERG, DAVID O. 'Potential uses of the church–sect typology in comparative religious research', *International Journal of Comparative Sociology* vol. 2, no. 1, March 1961, pp. 47–58.

33 MOULIN, LÉO. 'Pour une sociologie des ordres religieux'. *Social Compass* vol. X/2, 1963, pp. 145–70.

34 MOULIN, LÉO 'Policy making in the religious orders', *Government and Opposition* vol. 1, no. 1, 1965, pp. 25–54.

35 NELSON, GEOFFREY K. 'The analysis of a cult: Spiritualism', *Social Compass* vol. XV/6, 1968, pp. 469–81.

36 NELSON, GEOFFREY K. *Spiritualism and Society* (Routledge and Kegan Paul, London 1969).

37 NELSON, GEOFFREY K. 'The Spiritualist movement and the need for a redefinition of cult', *Journal for the Scientific Study of Religion* vol. VIII, no. 1, 1969, pp. 152–60.

38 O'DEA, THOMAS F. *The Sociology of Religion* (Prentice-Hall, Englewood Cliffs 1966).

39 ROBERTS, BRYAN R. 'Protestant groups and coping with urban life in Guatemala City', *American Journal of Sociology* vol. 73, no. 6, May 1968, pp. 753–67.

40 ROBERTSON, ROLAND 'The Salvation Army: the persistence of sectarianism', in WILSON, BRYAN R. (ed.) *Patterns of Sectarianism*, op. cit.

41 ROBERTSON, ROLAND (ed.) *Sociology of Religion* (Penguin Books, Harmondsworth, Middlesex 1969).

42 ROBERTSON, ROLAND *The Sociological Interpretation of Religion* (Basil Blackwell, Oxford 1970).

43 ROGERS, ROLF E. *Max Weber's Ideal Type Theory* (Philosophical Library, New York 1969).

44 SÉGUY, JEAN 'Les problèmes de la typologie dans l'étude des sectes', *Social Compass* vol. XII/3, 1965, pp. 165–70.

45 SOROKIN, PITIRIM A. *Altruistic Love. A Study of American 'Good Neighbours' and Christian Saints* (The Beacon Press, Boston 1950).

46 STARK, WERNER *The Sociology of Religion. A Study of Christendom* (Routledge and Kegan Paul, London):
   (a) *Volume I. Established Religion* (1966);
   (b) *Volume II. Sectarian Religion* (1967);
   (c) *Volume III. The Universal Church* (1967);
   (d) *Volume IV. Types of Religious Man* (1969).

47 TURNER, BRYAN 'Virtuoso and Mass Religion. A comparative study of Wesleyan Methodism and Islamic Sufism', typescript of paper read at the Lancaster conference on Max Weber, summer 1970.

48 WACH, JOACHIM *Sociology of Religion* (Chicago University Press, Chicago 1944; Phoenix edition 1962).

49 WHITWORTH, JOHN 'The Brüderhof in England: a chapter in the history of a utopian sect', in HILL, MICHAEL (ed.) *A Sociological Yearbook of Religion in Britain—4*, op. cit.

50 WILSON, BRYAN R. 'An analysis of sect development', *American Sociological Review* vol. 24, no. 1, February 1959, pp. 3–15.

51 WILSON, BRYAN R. *Sects and Society* (William Heinemann, London 1961).

52 WILSON, BRYAN R. 'On the fringe of Christendom', *Rationalist Annua* 1963, pp. 40–50.

53 WILSON, BRYAN R. 'Typologie des sectes dans une perspective dynamique et comparative', *Archives de Sociologie des Religions* no. 16, July–December 1963, pp. 49–63.

54 WILSON, BRYAN R. 'The paradox of the Exclusive Brethren', *New Society* 20 August 1964, pp. 9–11.

55 WILSON, BRYAN R. 'The migrating sects', *British Journal of Sociology* vol. XVIII, no. 3, September 1967, pp. 303–17.

56 WILSON, BRYAN R. (ed.) *Patterns of Sectarianism* (William Heinemann, London, 1967).

57 WILSON, BRYAN R. *Religious Sects* (Weidenfeld and Nicolson, London 1970).

58 WILSON, JOHN 'British Israelism: a revitalization movement in con-

temporary culture', *Archives de Sociologie des Religions* no. 26, July–December 1968, pp. 73–80.

59 YINGER, JOHN MILTON *Religion in the Struggle for Power* (Duke University Press, Durham, North Carolina 1946).

60 YINGER, JOHN MILTON *Religion, Society and the Individual* (Macmillan, New York, 1957).

61 YINGER, JOHN MILTON *The Scientific Study of Religion* (Collier–Macmillan, London 1970).

5

The Theoretical Background to 'The Weber Thesis'

THE INTERPRETATION of a link between the rise of capitalism in the West and certain aspects of Protestantism in Europe and North America, which Max Weber put forward in *The Protestant Ethic and the Spirit of Capitalism*, expanded in 'The Protestant Sects and the Spirit of Capitalism' and set in a comparative framework in *The Religion of China*, *The Religion of India*, and his *General Economic History*, has generated more debate and empirical research than any other set of hypotheses in the sociology of religion. If we bear in mind that the original formulation of the church–sect dichotomy was presented in the first of these works, and that the debate about 'the religious factor' often begins from the methodological issues with which Weber was concerned, then the influence of his research can be plainly judged. What is remarkable, therefore, about much of the debate is its grotesquely polemical level and its frequent failure to understand basic ideas: indeed, the epithet that recurs again and again in accounts of 'the Weber thesis' is 'misunderstood'. [12; 21; 33; 57; 58] The fact that some of those who use this word then go on to make quite basic misunderstandings themselves is ample warning that we should treat with great care any contribution to what one writer has called (in many ways inappropriately) 'a scholarly controversy'. [22:vii] It seems that many writers work with a mythical version of what Weber actually said, an observation which has been recently incorporated in the label '"The Max Weber Thesis" Thesis'. [38:82]

The account given here of Weber's ideas and the debate which has surrounded them is based on the contention that, while some of the sources of misunderstanding and criticism can legitimately be attributed to vagueness or open-ended statements on Weber's part in the text of *The Protestant Ethic and the Spirit of Capitalism*, a major source of misunderstanding has been the failure to take into account the full context of Weber's work—both theoretical and comparative—within which the study of the Protestant ethic is centrally located. While this material may not have been familiar to the historians who have taken up different aspects of Weber's study—with the result that some of their criticisms reveal quite striking inadequacies—it ought properly to have received fuller treatment by sociologists.

To illustrate this remark: two of the most frequently made and interrelated criticisms of Weber's initial work are (a) that it did not investigate the influence of economic factors on religious beliefs, and (b) that the explanation given was consequently mono-causal. If we look at the account of Weber's work given by the historians F. H. Knight and R. H. Tawney we find the sort of misstatement inferred by these propositions. Knight had translated Weber's *General Economic History* in 1923 and published an article on Weber's study of capitalism in 1928, and Tawney contributed a 'Foreword' to Talcott Parsons' translation of *The Protestant Ethic and the Spirit of Capitalism* in 1930, which suggests a fairly close acquaintance with Weber's work by both writers. In the 1930 Foreword, Tawney asks: 'Why insist that causation can work in only one direction? Is it not a little artificial to suggest that capitalist enterprise had to wait, as Weber appears to imply, till religious changes had produced a capitalist spirit? Would it not be equally plausible, and equally one-sided, to argue that the religious changes were themselves merely the result of economic movements?' [62:8]

The concluding paragraph of Weber's work—in addition to other passages which will be considered later—deals with precisely this issue, and the footnotes explain why a particular approach was taken. Weber points out that he has only looked at one aspect of the relationship between economic development and religious ideas because it is the one most frequently overlooked, but 'it would also further be necessary to investigate how Protestant Asceticism was in turn influenced in its development and its character by the totality of social conditions, especially economic.' [62:183] He states in a footnote that he has investigated only those relationships where an influence of religious ideas on the material culture was 'really beyond doubt'. [62:283] The reasons why he had not followed up this programme of research were, he pointed out, partly fortuitous: the publication by Ernst Troeltsch of *The Social Teaching of the Christian Churches* had largely disposed of many of the things that would have needed investigation, and since Troeltsch was a theologian the task had been carried out in a way which, Weber admitted, he himself would have found impossible. The other reason was that 'in order to correct the isolation of this study and to place it in relation to the whole of cultural development' [62:284] he had embarked on comparative studies of the relationship between religion and society.

The implication of this is plain enough—that the early study should be understood in conjunction with his comparative work on religion—but F. H. Knight seems to be unaware of the significance of these other pieces of research. How else can we explain his statement in the 1928 article that: 'It seems to the writer that the question of the origin of capitalism would gain by being stated in negative form: why did capitalism *not* develop (in the sense in which it did not) in other times and places than modern Western Europe?' [32:134] The only note given of Weber's own discussion of this aspect of the subject is a reference to the sketchy account in the *General Economic History*—yet Weber defended his incomplete treatment of the wider manifestations of the European problem mainly in terms of his preoccupation with the comparative studies.

There is little justification for some of the grosser misreadings of Weber's argument. To take the final passage once more as an example, there is a concise rejection of the charge of idealism:

> But it is, of course, not my aim to substitute for a one-sided materialistic an equally one-sided spiritualistic causal interpretation of culture and of history. Each is equally possible, but each, if it does not serve as the preparation, but as the conclusion of an investigation, accomplishes equally little in the interest of historical truth. [62:183]

The accompanying footnote states: 'I should have thought that this sentence and the remarks and notes immediately preceding it would have sufficed to prevent any misunderstanding of what this study was meant to accomplish, and I find no occasion for adding anything.' [62:284] Since the polemical background to the debate is clearly of immense importance, we may best approach the controversy by considering some of the issues that have sustained it and some of the ideas that lay behind Weber's initial account.

One of the most significant elements in the development of the controversy has been the value-orientation of those involved in it. It is very largely true that the whole Weberian thesis has been 'bedeviled' [12:70] by extrascientific valuations and partisan contentions which depended on the economic orientation and religious affiliation of the writer: 'Thus most of the critics of Weber adjudged the influence of Protestantism on capitalism in the light of their attitude to capitalism.' [12:70] Those who were admirers of capitalism were inclined to claim that it had been engendered by their own religious tradition, while those who were hostile to it denied the connection between it and their religion. In particular, some of the Catholic treatments of the Weber thesis have sought to find in Catholicism the 'laudable' attributes that might culminate in the inner-worldly asceticism attributed to the Puritan, while disclaiming the influence of Catholicism for any of the less desirable effects of capitalism.

While this type of approach is helpful in putting the contributions of Weber's critics into context, it should not be overstated. In the first place, it is insufficient to reject an argument simply by demonstrating its possible links with and implications for religious or political belief. Secondly, it opens up the possibility of much the same category of statement about the origin of Weber's own insights. Freund, for example, suggests that although Weber had considerable sympathy for a socialist philosophy, he was never ashamed of belonging to the bourgeoisie; and he continues: 'Je pense aussi qu'il fallait être protestant, comme Max Weber, pour pouvoir manier avec autant d'autorité et de perspicacité la sociologique compréhensive en un domaine aussi délicat que celui des rapports entre le protestantisme et l'économie.' [16:5]

Weber's work has undoubtedly suffered from the tendency to regard it as 'a dramatic and radical thesis in historical interpretation'. [43:500] This does not only apply to the methodological concerns but to the basic idea behind the study—that of an association between Protestantism and capitalism. Just as Weber took the categories of church and sect out of the area of theological controversy and worked them into sociological concepts, and just as the concept of charisma originated in a theological treatment but was incorporated into a sociological theory, so there are numerous predecessors in the case of the 'Protestant Ethic', and the most significant contribution on Weber's part was to rigorously define and meticulously trace the relationship between a religious ethic and an economic ethos. Weber acknowledged the insights of Lavelye and Matthew Arnold, and expressed surprise (and perhaps we can also detect a note of annoyance) that the relationship between a religious ethic preaching frugality and the unintended accumulation of wealth which had previously been taken for granted had now become such a highly controversial issue. [62:191 and 280] Bendix has given a useful account of these earlier writers and it seems beyond question that Weber regarded the equation of industriousness and Protestant dissent as well founded and well documented: 'What is new, on the contrary, is the quite unfounded denial of it.' [62:191]

Robert Southey, whose two-volume work *Sir Thomas More: or, Colloquies on the progress and prospects of Society* published in 1829 seems to have prefigured a whole range of intellectual debates, can be credited with having also prefigured the present debate. His statement of the problem is very precise:

> In some things, and those essential ones, the Protestants brought back a corrupted faith to its primitive purity. But it is not less certain that the Reformation has, in its consequences, lowered the standard of devotion, lessened the influence of religion, not among the poor and ignorant alone, but among the classes [*sic*]; and prepared the way for the uncontrolled dominion of that worldly spirit which it is the tendency of the commercial spirit to produce and foster. [53:158]

Matthew Arnold, who apparently took the relationship so much for granted that he only refers to it incidentally, may well have stimulated Weber into using one of his most vivid images, for he spoke of the English middle class as having 'entered the prison of Puritanism' at the beginning of the seventeenth century and having 'had the key turned upon its spirit there for two hundred years'. [6:267] This brief discussion of the history of an idea is vital if we are to understand how Weber envisaged the task he undertook in *The Protestant Ethic and the Spirit of Capitalism*, and it demonstrates that Weber had every cause to argue that the burden of proof lay on those who wanted to deny this relationship.

There already existed the germ of a hypothesis when Weber began his study: it was widely accepted and clearly documented, and it appeared that little could be gained by accumulating more and more instances. What was needed, in Weber's view, and what his own work attempted to supply, was an interpretation of a correlation which had already been demonstrated. The technique he used—as we shall see—was that of 'filtering out' (by the technique of ideal types) those elements in a historical process which were not centrally relevant to the specific hypothesis but which would without question form part of a comprehensive account of the rise of Western capitalism, and to assess where possible the causal links within the correlation. In doing this he made two assumptions. The first was that the correlation, however weak, existed. This is immensely important, as Bendix notes: 'Even today students might read Weber's essay differently, if they were made aware that Weber assumed rather than tried to prove the existence of a positive relation between Protestant piety and economic growth.' [6:271] The second assumption was that the influence of material culture on the historical process, which was strictly speaking a side-issue as far as his specific formulation was concerned, could be taken for granted. He periodically reiterated this aspect of his work in the text, both when he was disclaiming a monocausal idealistic explanation and at specific points where he was pointed to the relationship between Calvinism and capitalism in different regions, and added a note, for example, that: 'This, of course, was true only when some possibility of capitalistic development in the area was present.' [62:190]

Another way of expressing this is by saying that Weber assumed Marx. Precisely how Weber reacted to Marx's interpretation of the development of capitalism (and, perhaps more pointedly, to the work of subsequent Marxists) is an issue which has provoked a large amount of controversy in itself. The belief that Weber represents a kind of anti-Marx has been widely accepted but needs to be closely examined. Talcott Parsons, for instance, prefaces his discussion of Weber's work by referring to his 'anti-Marxian interpretation', [43:503] but then goes on to show that there was a substantial measure of agreement between Marx and Weber on the main features of modern capitalism and that it was on the level of explanation that their views bifurcated: whether or not they were diametrically opposed is questionable. Others have depicted an apparent antithesis in the Marxian and Weberian explanations of capitalism. [28] Fischoff, however, regards it as fallacious to treat Weber as an anti-Marxist idealist, and he notes of Weber: 'Actually, he was an admirer of the Marxian hypothesis, only objecting that it should not be made absolute and universal, a summary philosophy; but then he rejected all absolutes and all monisms.' [12:75] It is better to see Weber more as making explicit what Marx had left implicit—namely, the psychological function of belief systems —and thus he can be viewed as testing and amending rather than supplanting Marx's ideas.

The concept which serves best to bridge the gap between Marx and Weber, to integrate the idealistic and materialistic strands in Weber's own work, and to eliminate much of the misunderstanding surrounding *The Protestant Ethic and the Spirit of Capitalism* is that of 'elective affinity'. The German equivalent of 'elective affinity', as Bendix indicates, appears in the English translation as 'certain *correlations* between forms of religious belief and practical ethics' [62:91, my italics] and this may explain why relatively little discussion has been devoted to it. Since the concept is crucial to both the present discussion of Protestantism and capitalism and the ensuing analysis of the concept of charisma/routinization, it is worth presenting in some depth. This discussion will also serve to introduce some of the concepts which will be expanded in chapter 7.

'Elective affinity' is intended to demonstrate a change in the relative contribution of 'ideas' and 'interests', and it contains almost an element of intellectual biography, since there was a change in the primary orientation of Weber's work from an emphasis on the autonomous generation and influence of ideas to an emphasis on the importance of the economic basis and the 'interests' of different social strata.

Throughout his life, Max Weber was engaged in a fruitful battle with historical materialism. In his last course of lectures in Munich at the time of the Revolution, he presented his course under the title, 'A Positive Critique of Historical Materialism'. Yet there is a definite drift of emphasis in his intellectual biography towards Marx. [19:63]

Marx had held that ideas 'express' interests, so that the way to explain the emergence of particular sets of ideas was to identify the material interests of those who held them: in doing this the location of these ideas in the economic basis of the social structure could be demonstrated. Looked at from this aspect the transcendent God of the Puritans might be seen to 'express' the irrationality and anonymity of the market. Weber held the view that there was very rarely a close relationship between the social location and material interests of the articulator(s) of a religious idea and its content *during its inception*. Religious ideas are generally derived from a purely religious source. In Weber's words:

> It is not our thesis that the specific nature of a religion is a simple 'function' of the social stratum which appears as its characteristic bearer, or that it represents the stratum's 'ideology', or that it is a 'reflection' of a stratum's material or ideal interest-situation. On the contrary, a more basic misunderstanding of the standpoint of these discussions would hardly be possible. However incisive the social influences, economically and politically determined, may have been upon a religious ethic in a particular case, it receives its stamp primarily from religious sources, and, first of all, from the content of its annunciation and its promise. [19:269–270]

The assertion made here that a religion is not just a reflection of a stratum's material *or ideal* interest-situation contains an insight which is very important to the present discussion but which is very rarely stated.

The argument that ideas, as well as material factors, can generate 'interests' means that when we study the beliefs of sixteenth- and seventeenth-century Puritans we are studying a set of beliefs which result from an *internal* dialectic as well as having a relationship with the interests derived from material culture. This puts the frequently encountered argument that Calvin himself provided little justification for capitalist activity into a clearer perspective. What Weber was interested in was Calvin's ethic 'at a distance', after it had been modified by later Calvinists. Thus, given a particular conception of the universe and man's place in it—such as, for example, the conception which Calvin put forward—this in itself will generate 'interests' as adherents of the particular ethic proceed to work out their strategy for salvation. As Parsons puts it:

> ... it is not the mere verbal injunction to certain kinds of conduct, delivered by representatives or leaders of religious bodies, to which these masses of men adhere, on which Weber's argument depends. It is, rather, the structure of the total system of religious ideas *in its relation* to men's religious interests. Both the injunctions of religious leaders and the practical attitudes of the masses are to be understood in relation to this system. [43:520-1]

If a practical analogy will serve to make this any clearer, we might put the religious leader in a similar position to that of a Chancellor of the Exchequer. The Chancellor puts forward his system of taxation with the intention of providing an overall framework in which certain broad goals are included—stopping inflation or preventing unemployment, for instance. There may well be an underlying logic in the system as far as its originator is concerned, but this does not necessarily have to coincide with the logic of the individuals who are required to contribute their taxes. Thus as soon as the system has been proposed, all those involved in it will begin to calculate their own strategies by adjusting their expenditure and, when possible, finding convenient loopholes. If certain loopholes are adopted by a sufficient number of people they become part of 'the structure of the total system'. It will usually be the case that some individuals will see their role as one of advising others on how best to secure their own interests within the system: these we call accountants (substitute for this, 'lay leaders'). It may also happen that recourse to one loophole becomes so frequent that it constitutes a threat to the whole tax system. In this case the Chancellor (substitute, 'religious leader') or the Commissioners of Inland Revenue (substitute, 'religious authorities' or 'ecclesiastical hierarchy') may step in and attempt to block the loophole in the light of their interpretation of the original legislation. The notion that this analogy is intended to imply is that within any system of religious ideas there will be a bargaining process between the original ethic and the 'interests' it generates among adherents. In the present context it will be argued that one of the crucial elements in the original ethic of Calvin was the doctrine of predestination, and Weber was most concerned to show how this particularly ruthless theological enactment was 'loopholed'.

Still on the level of ideas, we may add that Weber was not just interested in the logical outcome of the original system of religious ideas, and he was not only concerned with the directly expressed wishes of religious leaders for the practical conduct based on them. 'He is, rather, concerned with the *total consequences* of the religious system.' [43:521] This has two important implications: the first of them, which may have been understated in the preceding analogy, is that the relevant consequences are *psychological* rather than purely logical. The personal reaction of adherents to the original ethic and its significance for their human existence rather than any rigidly pursued casuistry is the centre of interest. The second implication takes us to the core of the concept of 'elective affinity' by its insistence that the influence of a set of religious ideas is a dynamic process, not a once-and-for-all logical deduction. While the original impetus to a religious movement will be given by religious ideas, its ethic will undergo change over time and may eventually gravitate to a position which is quite different from that of its point of origin. This, however, does not disprove the contention that the later attitudes are to a significant extent a consequence of the original ideas.

Weber used an important image to portray this relationship between original ideas and their gradual modification in practical action. He had a sufficiently strong element of historical determinism to see the course of history as being rather like a railway track—and it is useful here to recall Gellner's discussion of Marxism as a 'railroad theory' of history [17:100–1]—but the exceptional feature of Weber's railway is that it has points on it, and these are operated by ideas: 'Not ideas, but material and ideal interests, directly govern men's conduct. Yet very frequently the 'world images' that have been created by 'ideas' have, like switchmen, determined the tracks along which action has been pushed by the dynamic of interest.' [19:280] Both material and ideal interests have their own internal dynamic, but each depends on the other to maintain its historical momentum.

This *duel* orientation' rests on the notion that 'material without ideal interests are empty, but ideal without material interests are impotent'. [4:177] Both of these perspectives were, in Weber's view, legitimate as devices for narrowing down the elements in a particular historical process that need to be investigated; but, as his remarks at the end of *The Protestant Ethic and the Spirit of Capitalism* make clear, the attempt to generalize one or the other perspective into a complete explanation is altogether illegitimate. The two perspectives were reconciled in the concept of elective affinity by suggesting that as soon as a group of adherents is attracted to a particular idea or ethical system, which in origin is purely concerned with problems of salvation and ultimate meaning, they will begin to 'elect' those features of the original idea with which they have an 'affinity', or 'point of coincidence'. Thus there is the paradox that as soon as a new religious idea gets under way in the form of a religious movement, its members will have already begun the process of selection from the core of the message of those elements that are particularly relevant to the social location of those who have joined the movement.

Weber thought that there was no pre-established correspondence between the content of an idea and the material interests of those who were the first to become followers. Nevertheless, elements of the idea would be 'sifted, selected out and supplemented' [24:104] in the light of the material interests of the new recruits. As we have pointed out elsewhere in relation to Weber's discussion of the Protestant ethic: 'It is vital to stress that elective affinity is not intended to describe the permissive rationalization of questionable activities but rather the spontaneous and gradual convergence of a religious ethic and a materialistic spirit to produce a powerful motivation towards rational involvement in economic activities.' [24:104] The eventual outcome of this convergence brings Weber very close to a Marxian position, because he believed that 'ideas are discredited in the face of history unless they point in the direction of conduct that various interests promote'. [19:63] Ideas that have been selected and reinterpreted from the original doctrinal formulation eventually tend to establish an affinity with the material interests of particular social strata.

Furthermore, ideas that do not establish such an affinity are likely to be discarded. 'Both the ideas and their publics are seen as independent; by a selective process elements in both find their affinities.' [19:63]

A number of points can now be made on the way in which Weber incorporated this theory of 'elective affinity' into the specific historical treatment in *The Protestant Ethic and the Spirit of Capitalism*. The first of these is the observation made by Aron that what Weber is attempting to demonstrate is the *significant equivalence* between the spirit of capitalism and the Protestant ethic. [1, vol. ii: 216] It is perhaps worth noting that some critics have seen in Weber's definitions of the two elements a kind of tautology—arguing that the two orientations are defined as being so similar that it is almost impossible *not* to find a correlation between them. [44:172–3] The fact that Weber also manages to document in a very comprehensive way the internal dialectic which brought the religious ethic to a position in which it was able to exert such a profound influence on the development of capitalism (and such documentation was, after all, part of the primary task which he had undertaken) suggests that his definition of the Protestant ethic is not merely one of convenience. We will turn to the problem of defining the spirit of capitalism later in this chapter: in the meantime, Aron's phrase—'an amazing coincidence between certain requirements of Calvinist and capitalist logic' [1, vol. ii: 217]—is a suitable note on which to pitch the account.

Calvinist theology has been seen to rest on five central propositions, which do not logically imply each other but which were in fact combined in Calvinist doctrine. Each one could be separately fitted into another theological system, but they are mutually compatible and together they form a meaningful theological system which was, in the case of Calvinism, original and unique, and engendered important consequences. These propositions can be summarized as follows: (1) there is one transcendent God who created and governs the world and who is beyond the scope of man's intellect except through revelation; (2) for reasons unknown and unknowable to man, this God has irrevocably and eternally predestined every human soul either to everlasting salvation or to damnation; on this central tenet of Calvinism the Westminster Catechism of 1647 is unequivocal 'God, having out of his mere good pleasure from all eternity elected some to everlasting life did enter into a Covenant of grace to deliver them out of the estate of sin and misery, and to bring them into an estate of Salvation by a Redeemer'; (3) for his own reasons, God has created the world and set man in it for his own glory; (4) to attain the latter he has imposed on man—whether saved or damned—the duty of working under his laws for the establishment of God's kingdom on earth; and (5) on their own, earthly things, human nature and flesh are lost in 'sin and death' and can only be redeemed by divine grace. The logic of this theology is consistently to declare the problem of evil in history beyond human scrutiny by relegating it to the unchallengable will of God.

But this gives us little more than the original system as propounded by Calvin. We must now turn to the problem that Weber regarded as crucial—the way in which this system was incorporated by Calvinists in their practical conduct. Firstly, the system as constructed with its insistence on the transcendence and distance of the deity from the things of the world meant that mysticism—the attitude of unity with and absorption in the divine spirit—was eliminated. Coupled with this was the conception that man stood in complete submission to the divine will and must therefore become God's instrument on earth. The effect of these two ideas was to channel religious energies into an active ascetic direction rather than a passive mystical one. God is to be served, and since such service cannot consist in indulgence of or adaption to the things of the flesh, it must consist in their disciplined *control:* this is the meaning of 'inner-worldly asceticism'. Another vital consequence implied in this theology is that, since the natural world is also created by God and reveals his will, the best way to know God is to study his works. These, like man, are submitted to a preordained order. Belief in a natural order, it has been suggested, is an important factor in the growth of modern science: on this we might quote Whitehead's statement that 'The *basic* assumption in modern science "is a widespread, instinctive conviction in the existence of an *Order of Things*, and, in particular, of an Order of Nature".' [36:581]

The deity of Calvinism is *par excellence* a transcendental one; so much so in fact that he intervenes very little in the world, and then only in quite specific areas of activity. Since ritual is a means of

This is a contradiction of fact! Worth has ... of great importance.

linking the divine and the worldly it is of minimal importance for Calvinism, and in consequence the religious energies of its adherents are diverted from ritualistic expression to active control over the things of the world. They do this in the belief that it is God's will that man should act in accordance with his law in helping to establish his kingdom on earth. The conception of a totally transcendent God is one example of 'Hume's vacuum'—the argument that once the gap between man and his deity becomes so wide that it is a source of tension man will find it necessary to populate the no-man's-land in between with intermediaries who will maintain the flow of communications. The solution of medieval Catholicism, in Hume's version, was to line up its 'middle men' on the other-worldly side in the form of saints. This solution was strictly unavailable to the Calvinist since the other-worldly was entirely the preserve of God; therefore, what 'middle men' there were had to be lined up on the this-worldly side in the form of the predestined saints. As Michael Walzer has observed of these figures: 'The Calvinist saint seems to me now the first of those self-disciplined agents of social and political reconstruction who have appeared so frequently in modern history.' [59:ix]

Some aspects of the Calvinist doctrine of election are relevant for the later discussion of charismatic authority. It is important to note that German sociologists regarded Calvinist election as distinct from charismatic endowment but nevertheless as containing charismatic elements. There is in Calvin's political writing a further link with the theory of charisma. Since Calvin regarded the power of the monarch as an emanation of God's grace, it therefore became the duty of the Christian to submit to the secular power. Nevertheless, he conceived of one form of deliverance from oppressive burdens: 'God, Calvin says, may send a providential saviour to his people. God manifests his miraculous power, goodness, and providence by appointing one of his servants as a saviour and arming him so that he may punish an unjust ruler and deliver the people from oppression. However, people must not be too credulous when such a saviour appears.' [40:92] This indeed seems very close to the idea of a charismatic breakthrough.

So far, the original ethic of Calvinism has been shown to produce a positive impulse in the direction of this-worldly activity and a removal from the sphere of the this-worldly of magical and mystical 'incursions'. The central tenet of original Calvinism was in Weber's view responsible for the systematic and compulsive nature of the Calvinist's activity, and in this context his discussion of the process through which religious ideas generate religious interests can be used to show how the idea in question—that of predestination—galvanized the belief system of its adherents and set in motion the 'moral machinery' which was to produce the unique significance of the Protestant ethic. ?

The doctrine of predestination formulated by Calvin was un-equivocal and uncompromising: furthermore, it was widely perceived by sixteenth- and seventeenth-century contemporaries as the most characteristic dogma of Calvinism. Weber makes clear that he is going to concern himself with this doctrine 'in a state of full development', and thus 'we are not studying the per-sonal views of Calvin' [62:220]—which is why the evidence for the doctrine's importance is taken from late sixteenth-and seven-teenth-century doctrinal disputes and statements. Firstly, it is pointed out that there are two ways of arriving at the doctrine of predestination. On the one hand it can arrive as the outcome of religious experience, as in the case of Luther. Religious thinkers who arrive at the conviction through this process are typified by a

> powerful feeling of light-headed assurance, in which the tremen-
> dous pressure of their sense of sin is released, apparently breaks
> over them with elemental force and destroys every possibility
> of the belief that this overpowering gift of grace could owe
> anything to their own co-operation or could be connected
> with achievements or qualities of their own faith and will.
> [62:101-2]

Although Luther never formally abandoned his position of *sola fide*, Weber thought that it never had a central position in his thought, and that 'it receded more and more into the background, the more his position as responsible head of his Church forced him into practical politics'. [62:102] This potentially 'dark and danger-ous teaching' [62:102]—since it logically engenders and in fact precipitated antinomian movements—was moderated by the early authorities within Lutheranism.

In the case of Calvin, however, the process was the opposite: it actually increased in importance with the development of his doctrine, and only acquired its position of central prominence after his death. It was, in addition, the product not of religious experience but of logical necessity, and thus it is very much an integral part of a *systematic* theology: at this point Weber characterizes the elaboration of Calvinism itself in terms of the *rationalization* which it was later to endow with moral sanctions in the growth of modern capitalism. Only a part of humanity—Calvin thought a small part—is destined for salvation; the rest is damned, and nothing any man can do will alter this immutable fact.

In this chapter Weber's study of the relationship between Protestantism and capitalism has been placed in the context of his other studies of world religions, and against the background of previous writers who had noticed such a link. The important concept that 'ideal' as well as material interests are a significant source of social change was introduced, and finally the broad characteristics of Calvinist theology were elaborated. In the following chapter we will study the causal relationship that Weber tried to establish between later Calvinism and the growth of capitalism.

REFERENCES

1 ARON, RAYMOND *Main Currents in Sociological Thought*, 2 vols. (Weidenfeld and Nicolson, London 1968).
2 BELLAH, ROBERT N. 'Reflections on the Protestant Ethic analogy in Asia', *Journal of Social Issues* vol. XIX, no. 1, January 1963, pp. 52–60.
3 BEN-DAVID, JOSEPH 'Religion and capitalism' (book review), *Jewish Journal of Sociology* vol. IV, no. 2, 1962, pp. 299–302.
4 BENDIX, REINHARD 'Max Weber and Jakob Burckhardt', *American Sociological Review* vol. 30, no. 2, April 1965, pp. 176–84.
5 BENDIX, REINHARD *Max Weber: an Intellectual Portrait* (Methuen, London 1966).
6 BENDIX, REINHARD 'The Protestant Ethic—revisited', *Comparative Studies in Society and History* vol. IX, no. 3, 1967, pp. 266–73.
7 BIRNBAUM, NORMAN 'Conflicting interpretations of the rise of capitalism: Marx and Weber', *British Journal of Sociology* vol. IV, no. 2, June 1953, pp. 125–41.
8 DEMERATH III, NICHOLAS J., and HAMMOND, PHILLIP E. *Religion in Social Context: Tradition and Transition* (Random House, New York 1969).
9 DOBB, MAURICE *Studies in the Development of Capitalism* (George Routledge, London 1946).
10 EISENSTADT, SAMUEL N. 'The Protestant Ethic thesis in analytical and comparative context', *Diogenes* no. 59, Fall 1967, pp. 25–46.
11 ELTON, G. R. *Reformation Europe 1517–1559* (Collins–Fontana, London/Glasgow 1963).

12 FISCHOFF, EPHRAIM 'The Protestant Ethic and the Spirit of Capitalism the history of a controversy', in EISENSTADT, SAMUEL N. (ed.) *The Protestant Ethic and Modernization: a Comparative View* (Basic Books, New York 1968).

13 FORCESE, DENNIS P. 'Calvinism, capitalism and confusion: the Weberian thesis revisited', *Sociological Analysis* vol. 29, no. 4, Winter 1968, pp. 193–201.

14 FORSYTH, P. T. 'Calvinism and capitalism', *Contemporary Review* vol. XCVII, June 1910, pp. 728–41, vol. XCVIII, July 1910, pp. 74–87.

15 FREUND, JULIEN *The Sociology of Max Weber* (Allen Lane, The Penguin Press, London 1968).

16 FREUND, JULIEN 'L'éthique économique et les religions mondiales selon Max Weber', *Archives de Sociologie des Religions* no. 26, July–December 1968, pp. 3–25.

17 GELLNER, ERNEST *Thought and Change* (Weidenfeld and Nicolson, London 1964).

18 GEORGE, CHARLES H., and GEORGE, KATHERINE *The Protestant Mind of the English Reformation 1570–1640* (Princeton University Press, Princeton, N.J. 1961).

19 GERTH, H. H., and MILLS, C. WRIGHT *From Max Weber: Essays in Sociology* (Routledge and Kegan Paul, London 1948).

20 GOLLIN, GILLIAN LINDT 'The religious factor in social change: Max Weber and the Moravian paradox', *Archives de Sociologie des Religions* no. 23, January–June 1967, pp. 91–7.

21 GREELEY, ANDREW M. 'The Protestant Ethic: time for a moratorium', *Sociological Analysis* vol. 25, no. 1, Spring 1964, pp. 20–33.

22 GREEN, ROBERT W. *Protestantism and Capitalism: the Weber Thesis and its Critics* (D. C. Heath and Co., Boston 1959).

23 HILL, CHRISTOPHER 'Debate, Puritanism, capitalism and the scientific revolution' (a reply to Kearney, *q.v.*), *Past and Present* no. 29, December 1964, pp. 88–97.

24 HILL, MICHAEL, and TURNER, BRYAN S. 'John Wesley and the origin and decline of ascetic devotion', in HILL, MICHAEL (ed.) *A Sociological Yearbook of Religion in Britain—4* (SCM Press, London 1971).

25 HILTON, R. H. 'Capitalism—What's in a name?', *Past and Present* vol 1, no. 1, February 1952, pp. 32–43.

26 HYMA, ALBERT *Christianity, Capitalism and Communism* (George Wahr, Ann Arbor 1937).

27 ISRAEL, HERMAN 'Some religious factors in the emergence of industrial society in England', *American Sociological Review* vol. 31, no. 5, October 1966, pp. 589–99.

28 JONASSEN, CHRISTEN T. 'The Protestant Ethic and the Spirit of Capitalism in Norway', *American Sociological Review* vol. 12, no. 6, December 1947, pp. 676–86.

29 KEARNEY, H. F. 'Puritanism, capitalism and the scientific revolution', *Past and Present* no. 28, July 1964, pp. 81–101.

30 KENNEDY, ROBERT E. JR. 'The Protestant Ethic and the Parsis', *American Journal of Sociology* vol. LXVIII, no. 1, July 1962, pp. 11–20.

31 KITCH, M. J. (ed.) *Capitalism and the Reformation* (Longmans, London 1967).

32 KNIGHT, FRANK H. 'Historical and theoretical issues in the problem of modern capitalism', *Journal of Economic and Business History* vol. 1, no. 1, November 1928, pp. 119–36.

33 LUETHY, HERBERT 'Once again: Calvinism and capitalism', *Encounter* vol. 22, no. 1, January 1964, pp. 26–38.

34 MCNEILL, JOHN T. *The History and Character of Calvinism* (Oxford University Press, New York 1954).

35 MEANS, RICHARD L. 'Weber's thesis of the Protestant Ethic: the ambiguities of received doctrine', *Journal of Religion* vol. XLV, no. 1, 1965, pp. 1–11.

36 MERTON, ROBERT K. *Social Theory and Social Structure* (The Free Press, New York 1957).

37 MITZMAN, ARTHUR *The Iron Cage: an Historical Interpretation of Max Weber* (Alfred A. Knopf, New York 1970).

38 MOORE, ROBERT 'History, Economics and Religion: a Review of "The Max Weber Thesis" Thesis', in SAHAY, ARUN (ed.) *Max Weber and Modern Sociology* (Routledge and Kegan Paul, London 1971).

39 MUELLER, SAMUEL A. 'Changes in the social status of Lutheranism in ninety Chicago suburbs, 1950–1960', *Sociological Analysis* vol. 27, no. 3, Fall 1966, pp. 138–45.

40 NEUMANN, FRANZ *Behemoth. The Structure and Practice of National Socialism 1933–1944* (Octagon Books, New York 1963).

41 O'BRIEN, GEORGE *An Essay on the Economic Effects of the Reformation* (The Newman Bookshop, Westminster, Md. 1944).

42 PARSONS, TALCOTT ' "Capitalism" in recent German literature: Sombart and Weber', *Journal of Political Economy* vol. 36, no. 6, December 1928, pp. 641–61, vol. 37, no. 1, February 1929, pp. 31–51.

43 PARSONS, TALCOTT *The Structure of Social Action* (The Free Press, New York 1937).

44 ROBERTSON, ROLAND *The Sociological Interpretation of Religion* (Basil Blackwell, Oxford 1970).

45 SALMAN, D. H. 'Psychology and sociology in Weber's theories', *Social Compass* vol. X/6, 1963, pp. 537–9.

46 SAMUELSSON, KURT *Religion and Economic Action*, translated by E. Geoffrey French (William Heinemann, London 1961).

47 SCHELER, MAX 'The Thomist Ethic and the Spirit of Capitalism', *Sociological Analysis* vol. 25, no. 1, Spring 1964, pp. 4–19.

48 SCHNEIDER, LOUIS 'Problems in the sociology of religion', in FARIS, ROBERT E. L., *Handbook of Modern Sociology* (Rand McNally and Co., Chicago 1964).

49 SEE, HENRI *Modern Capitalism* (Noel Douglas, London 1928).

50 SHASKHO, PHILIP 'Nikolai Alexandrovich Mel'gunov on the Reformation and the work ethic', *Comparative Studies in Society and History* vol. IX, no. 3, 1967, pp. 256–65.

51 SHEEHAN, JAMES J. *The Career of Lujo Brentano* (University of Chicago Press, Chicago/London 1966).

52 THE SHORTER CATECHISM OF THE WESTMINSTER ASSEMBLY OF

DIVINES: Facsimile of the first edition with historical account and bibliography by William Carruthers (Publication Office of the Presbyterian Church of England, London 1897).

53 SOUTHEY, ROBERT *Sir Thomas More: or Colloquies on the progress and prospects of society* (London 1829).

54 STARK, WERNER 'The protestant ethic and the spirit of sociology', *Social Compass* vol. XIII/6, 1966, pp. 373–5.

55 TREVOR-ROPER, H. R. *Religion, the Reformation and Social Change* (Macmillan, London 1967).

56 TROELTSCH, ERNST *Protestantism and Progress* (Williams and Norgate, London 1912).

57 TURKSMA, L. 'Protestant ethic and rational capitalism', *Social Compass* vol. IX/5–6, 1962, pp. 445–73.

58 WAGNER, HELMUT 'The Protestant Ethic: a mid-twentieth century view', *Sociological Analysis* vol. 25, no. 1, Spring 1964, pp. 34–40.

59 WALZER, MICHAEL *The Revolution of the Saints* (Weidenfeld and Nicolson, London 1966).

60 WAX, ROSALIE and MURRAY 'The Vikings and the rise of capitalism', *American Journal of Sociology* vol. LXI, no. 1, July 1955, pp. 1–10.

61 WEBER, MAX *General Economic History*, translated by Frank H. Knight (Allen and Unwin, London 1923).

62 WEBER, MAX *The Protestant Ethic and the Spirit of Capitalism* (Unwin University Books, London 1930).

63 WEBER, MAX *The Religion of India. The Sociology of Hinduism and Buddhism*, translated and edited by Hans H. Gerth and Don Martindale (The Free Press, Glencoe 1958).

64 WEBER, MAX *The Religion of China. Confucianism and Taoism* (Macmillan, New York 1964).

65 WEBER, MAX *The Theory of Social and Economic Organization*, translated by A. M. Henderson and Talcott Parsons (Free Press, New York 1964)

6

Protestantism and Capitalism

HAVING SET up the Calvinist theological system in all its
'magnificent consistency' [64:104] Weber then employs one of his
most characteristic methods, that of empathetic understanding.
[34:77–9] In the face of this theological system, what was its
effect on the individual Calvinist? Here there can be little doubt:
there must have been 'a feeling of unprecedented inner loneliness
of the single individual'. [64:104] In the most important area of
his life—the question of his eternal salvation—the Calvinist was on
his own and forced to follow his particular path to a destiny which
had already been determined. No other human being could help
him. Priests were of little help since God could only be known
directly by the chosen. Sacraments provided no means of acquiring grace; and even membership of a church, which was a
strict moral duty, provided no supernatural guarantees since the
external Church included the damned as well as the saved: the
Calvinist belonged to a church for God's glory, not for his
salvation. Thus Calvinism represented the culmination of the
process which had been initiated by the Hebrew prophets and
propelled by Hellenistic scientific thought—*Entzaüberung der
Welt*, the elimination of magic from the world—and Weber
illustrated this by pointing to the Puritan attitude to an event
which was a crucial test of religious meaning (and which for
Spencer and Durkheim had provided a crucial proof of the
socially reinforcing function of religion)—death. 'The genuine
Puritan even rejected all signs of religious ceremony at the grave
and buried his nearest and dearest without song or ritual in order
that no superstition, no trust in the effects of magical and sacramental forces on salvation, should creep in.' [64:105] The English

117

Puritans, it should be noted, were firmly located in the Calvinist tradition. [41:1127]

On the one hand, Calvinism tended to 'tear the individual away from the closed ties with which he is bound to this world', [64:108] and evidence of this is given by the Puritan Baxter, who said of friendship: 'It is an irrational act and not fit for a rational creature to love any one farther than reason will allow us ... It very often taketh up men's minds so as to hinder their love of God.' [64:224] Yet despite the inner isolation of the individual, there was a doctrinal injunction propelling adherents in the direction of social organization. Since the world only exists for the glory of God, the Christian must play his part in this scheme by fulfilling God's commandments to the best of his ability. God requires social achievement of the individual because he desires that social life shall be organized in accordance with his overall purpose. Thus the social activity of Christians in the world must be for the greater glory of God, and the best way of achieving this is to adopt a 'calling' in which the mundane life of the community can be served. In Baxter's phrase: 'God hath commanded you some way or other to labour for your daily bread.' [58:241] In this context Weber emphasized the peculiarly objective and impersonal character of work, which became service in the interest of the rational organization of the social environment. The argument so far had attempted to demonstrate how the tendency to isolate individuals through the doctrine of predestination, coupled with other elements in Calvinist theology, combined to produce a form of compulsive involvement in social life. There remained the *pyschological* problem of how the Calvinist adherents adapted the original idea in the light of their religious interests.

> For us the decisive problem is: How was this doctrine borne in an age to which the after-life was not only more important, but in many ways also more certain, than all the interests of life in this world? The question, Am I one of the elect? must sooner or later have arisen for every believer and have forced all other interests into the background. And how can I be sure of this state of grace? [64:109-10]

To make absolutely sure of his case, Weber takes up the argument that predestination was only a doctrine of theologians and not a popular doctrine. Evidence is cited that in the 1840s the ordinary Calvinists of Holland were similarly imbued with the belief, and that the members of Cromwell's army were acquainted with it. Also in line with his clear distinction between Calvin and Calvinism he points out that, for Calvin himself, predestination presented no problem. He felt himself to be a chosen agent of God and was certain of his own salvation; in fact, the basic answer he gives to the question which the doctrine of predestination provoked was that we should be content with the knowledge that God has chosen, and further than that, we should have implicit trust in Christ, which is the result of true faith. Calvin rejected the idea that it was possible to learn from the conduct of others whether or not they were saved, because this was an unjustifiable attempt to force God's secrets: the elect differ externally in no way from the damned and from God's invisible Church. It was possible for the chosen to *feel* saved, but this kind of subjective experience was possible to some extent for the damned.

Hence as an unintended but equally unavoidable consequence of maintaining a radical doctrine of predestination the question of how to recognize the state of grace became one of 'absolutely dominant importance'. [64:110] This was as true for Beza, Calvin's successor, as it was for the mass of ordinary men—though special importance is given to the latter. The 'idea' of predestination engendered an 'interest' in knowing whether or not the individual belonged among the 'elect' of Calvin's doctrine. 'So, wherever the doctrine of predestination was held, the question could not be suppressed whether there were any infallible criteria by which membership in the *electi* could be known.' [64:110] The need to know where a man stood as far as his state of grace was concerned could not be satisfied by Calvin's personal trust in the expectation of salvation (*certitudo salutis*) resulting from grace—and this was in spite of the fact that formal doctrine continued to uphold this conception. In particular, practical pastoral work which came into close contact with the suffering caused by the official doctrine found Calvin's solution unsatisfactory.

Out of this dilemma arose two mutually connected types of pastoral advice: on the one hand, it was held to be 'an absolute duty to consider oneself chosen, and to combat all doubts as temptations of the devil' [64:111] (lack of self-confidence being

E

the result of insufficient faith and therefore of imperfect grace). The result of this was to breed the self-confident Calvinist saints who were often regarded as a distinct social estate. On the other hand, it was considered most appropriate to engage in intense worldly activity as the means of attaining self-confidence, since it alone removes religious doubts and gives a feeling of certainty of grace. The logic behind this recommended course of action was that, since the only way in which the chosen could approach their distant, transcendent God was by seeing themselves as tools of his divine will (since mysticism and contemplation had been eliminated) the only outlet for this conception was in ascetic activism.

Within this Calvinist scheme the practice of good works, which in Catholicism are a means of attaining salvation, becomes indispensable as a sign of election. Thus, while good works might be useless as a way of attaining salvation, they are a valuable technical means of getting rid of the fear of damnation. 'In this sense they are occasionally referred to as directly necessary for salvation or the *possessio salutis* is made conditional on them.' [64:115] Weber continues, 'In practice this means that God helps those who help themselves. Thus the Calvinist, as it is sometimes put, himself creates his own salvation, or, as would be more correct, the conviction of it.' [64:115]

This particular passage has apparently created certain difficulties, though I see no reason why it should if it is firmly located in the context of Weber's notion of religious ideas and religious interests. Robertson, for instance, thinks that Weber vacillated between saying that the Calvinist logic led in this direction and saying that in practice Calvinists believed that God helps those who help themselves. [46:173] As is so often the case, the original criticism comes from the counter-arguments of Kurt Samuelsson, and we will treat it as Samuelsson puts it forward. [48:43-4] The mistake contained in this criticism is to treat the issue purely in terms of a logical progression. Weber, having logically traced the way in which doctrinal formulations found it necessary to add glosses to the stark theological purity of the doctrine of predestination—glosses that were made necessary by the strong 'interests' generated by the original doctrine—is in no doubt about the official presentation of the importance of activity in a worldly calling. It could only be a *sign* that the diligent person was one of the elect, since no one could know or influence God's judgement. It is certainly not true that Weber merely adds the conditional phrase 'or, as would be more correct, the conviction of it' in order to be safe, as Samuelsson rather naïvely claims. Much more central is the observation that logical considerations are not the only ones that are significant in the theory of ideal 'interests': psychological motives also enter into the discussion, and their relevance to the extension of the doctrine of predestination are vitally important.

The tension produced by the original doctrine of predestination results in the 'interest' of Calvinists in *knowing* whether or not they are among the elect. To a certain extent, this 'interest' *propels* the development of supplementary theological explanations, which, especially in the realm of practical pastoral work, are intended to meet the 'interest'. This is largely achieved by the concept of conscientious worldly activity as a *sign* that the individual belongs among the elect. But this is hardly enough on the personal level because the 'interest', having been produced by such a profoundly important issue as that of eternal salvation, has to be fully met: and this can only be done if the individual can ensure for himself that he is one of the elect. Thus for practical purposes the logical leap is made to the belief that conscientious activity in a calling is a *means* to becoming one of the elect. Weber even provides evidence that St Augustine, an early proponent of the doctrine of predestination, had also made a logical leap in his statement: 'si non es praedestinatus, fac ut praedestineris'—'if you are not predestined, act that you may be predestined'. The most useful analogy to this logical leap is the 'arcing' of an electrical charge: an electrical current will run along a conductor until it meets an impedance—such as, for example, a break in a wire—but if the initial charge is strong enough (and here we are arguing that the 'interest' in eternal salvation was extremely strong) it will jump the gap. In this case, the 'interest' was stronger than the logical interval. (It goes without saying that we are predominantly concerned with 'unofficial' theologies.)

Given the ethical demands of Calvinism and to a lesser extent Lutheranism, both of which put forward a form of salvation by works, there followed an important observation about the way in which moral action was viewed by the adherent. The normal medieval Catholic layman 'lived ethically, so to speak, from hand to mouth' [64:116]: that is to say, his good works did not necessarily form a connected system of life, and certainly not a rationalized one (in the sense of disciplined) but rather remained a succession of individual acts. A cycle of good works, sin and absolution thus typified the ordinary conduct of the layman. The God of Calvinism, on the contrary, 'demanded of his believers not single good works, but a life of good works combined into a unified system. There was no place for the very human Catholic cycle of sin, repentance, atonement, release, followed by renewed sin.' [64:117]

We may at this point briefly refer to a parallel *within* Catholicism, which has sometimes been used as a criticism of Weber's argument but which is dealt with, albeit obliquely, at this stage of his exposition: the parallel in question is the systematically pursued ethical rigorism of the religious orders. As soon as 'planless otherworldliness and irrational self-torture' [64:118] had been to a great extent removed by successive Benedictine reforms, a systematic method of rational conduct was established with the purpose of freeing man from the power of irrational impulses and from dependence on the world.

Weber cites the Cistercians in the course of this parenthesis, and there is excellent corroborative evidence as far as this religious order is concerned. One of the most interesting examples is a paper by François Bucher, which attempts to 'deduce' the character of the Cistercian movement by a study of its architecture. [9:89] He thinks that:

> Even if we knew nothing of the Cistercians except their buildings we would be able to deduce the character of their movement. For an almost absolute unity within a far reaching architectural school presupposes a tightly organized group of men ready to accept with unwavering discipline the laws and the validity of a complete spiritual system which they themselves defined. [9:89]

Above all, the Cistercians worked with a purist ideal of austerity, and this was typified in their architecture, which was based on four principles, almost totally negative: (1) the Augustinian principle of a structure without *affectus*, that is, without emotional expression; (2) the Benedictine principle that the monastic church should be nothing but an *officina*, or workshop for the production of holiness; (3) St Bernard's stipulation that architecture which aimed at evoking an emotional response was unworthy of the independent spirit of the monks; and (4) a general awareness of the extent to which the decline of the Benedictine monastery of Cluny had been associated with the adoption of liturgical and architectural elaborations. An explanation of why this movement did not take on a wider significance for the whole of society is provided by St Bernard's attitude to the lavish decoration of secular churches: this he approved of on the grounds that the masses need more than purely intellectual stimulation. Disclaiming wealth, engaging in manual labour and organizing their lives around a systematic plan, these monks represented the proto-Puritans of the twelfth century. They were also significant in attempting to isolate as far as possible the spiritual activity of the individual monk, to such an extent that their life has been described by one observer as a form of 'solitude in community'. [3:77]

Here are several of the features which have been identified in the Protestant ethic, and Weber gives a number of reasons why their historical significance was different from that of later Calvinism. In the first place, the rational, ascetic life of the monk could only be maintained through the distinction between a systematic, virtuoso life in the cloister and a life of average humanity in the world with its much less evident degree of organization. This was occasionally broken through, such as when the friars took a virtuoso form of Christianity out of the confines of the cloister, but on the whole, the more asceticism the individual practised, the greater was its tendency to drive him away from everyday life in the direction of the life of a monk. The importance of the Reformation, thought Weber, was in reversing this process: 'Sebastian Franck struck the central characteristic ... when he saw the significance of the Reformation in the fact that now every Christian had to be a monk all his life.' [64:121] The spiritual aristocracy of the monks outside and above the world was transformed through the doctrine of predestination into a spiritual aristocracy of the elect saints of God within the world.

To Weber's argument may be added one further parallel and two other sources of contrast between the religious orders and the later Calvinists. The parallel can be seen in the unintended consequences of systematic physical labour when coupled with an ethic of frugality. This has often been epitomized in Wesley's observation that '. . . the Methodists in every place grow diligent and frugal; consequently they increase in goods. Hence they proportionately increase in pride, in anger, in the desire of the flesh, the desire of the eyes, and the pride of life.' [64:175] A very similar process overtook the Cistercians, since they embodied a strong component of physical labour in their practices and observed a degree of asceticism which was explicitly intended to distinguish them from their more 'lax' progenitors, the Benedictines. As their farming activities brought in more and more wealth which could not be consumed they initially found themselves acquiring larger and larger tracts of land, and eventually they too succumbed to the growth of more lax discipline: the Trappist reform occurred in response to such laxity.

But successive monastic reforms also indicate one important source of contrast between monasticism and Calvinism: the influence of monasticism, as well as being restricted to a minority of the Church's adherents, tended to be cyclical rather than a linear progression. Orders would begin as reform movements, run into a process of decay and then give rise to reform movements in their turn. The reason for this seems to be that they would frequently legitimate their 'reformed' observances by reference to an established monastic *tradition*, such as that contained in the Rule of St Benedict: indeed, I have argued elsewhere that it has been the capacity of religious orders in Western Christianity for incorporating traditional rather than charismatic definitions of organization in their foundation documents that has made their accommodation in the Catholic church a process involving minimal conflict. [23:152–70] But as Weber argues, it was the *removal* of traditional attitudes towards social and economic organization which was so characteristic of later Calvinism and so congenial to the development of modern capitalism.

The second feature of those religious orders that went through this cyclical process was their inability to maintain the spiritual isolation of the individual. Most monastic reforms have been in the direction of establishing a characteristically 'eremitical' type of observance—meaning one in which the monk is seen as engaged more in a single-minded pursuit of God than in the service of his community—and it is interesting that the one order that has never needed reform, the Carthusian, has pushed this element to an extreme. However, this goal was difficult to maintain in a permanent face-to-face (or, more appropriately, 'cheek by cowl') community, and a tendency very often set in for goal-displacement, so that the community in itself became more and more the centre of attention. As we have seen, a major feature of Calvin's doctrine of predestination, coupled with his attitude to the things of the flesh, was to *maintain* the goal of isolated individualism.

The outline so far has concentrated on the development within Protestantism, and especially within its Calvinist component, of an ethic which demanded systematic activity in a worldly calling, together with a sustained rejection of the enjoyment of things that belonged to the flesh; the shorthand term for which is 'inner-worldly asceticism'. We have concentrated on the religious aspect of the problem first because it seems to be an area in which there is a considerable amount of confusion, but before we can demonstrate the 'congruence' between the religious ethic and the economic spirit, we must first refer to Weber's account of modern capitalism. In *The Protestant Ethic and the Spirit of Capitalism* this account comes first.

Weber was primarily interested in the *uniqueness* of the modern economic order, and to this extent he was in agreement with Marx. It is important to note, however, that the word 'capitalism' for Weber applied not only to the modern Western world but to a series of different types of profit-making, [52] and this has sometimes not been fully understood by commentators and critics: because of this, some of the early types of capitalism to which critics have pointed to show that capitalism antedates the Protestant Reformation belong properly in a separate category. Similarly, Weber used the word 'rational' in more than one sense, and these have to be distinguished if the precise meaning of his statements is to be judged. To combine these two key terms, we can summarize Weber's main contention by saying that *modern capitalism*, as against other historical types, is characterized by its *formal rationality*. 'Formal' rationality involves an assessment of the extent to which actions are calculated in terms of opportunities, needs and relative costs and are thus directly related to goals that are empirically quantifiable. This contrasts with 'substantive' rationality—a concept that Weber found 'full of difficulties' [66:185]—which refers rather to questions of ultimate ends: 'salvation' would be just such an ultimate end, as would 'the greatest happiness of the greatest number'. Ultimate ends are not capable of being empirically calculated and quantified in the way that 'discrete' ends are, though they may nevertheless influence action. The problem of rationality is one to which we will return in chapter 10.

Accepting for the moment the terms of Weber's enquiry, it can be seen that the whole thrust of his argument rests on the importance for the growth of modern capitalism on the systematic calculation of every aspect of the economic enterprise. A money economy is presupposed, as is the separation of the household from the enterprise itself: also, the importance of a free market means that traditional and substantive ethical restrictions which might limit the monetary evaluation of certain objects must disappear. In other words, formal rationality to Weber involved considerably more than just 'goal-directed behaviour'. It implied the existence of an institutional order in which the possibility of making discrete calculations of the relative profitability of different courses of action was pushed to a maximum, so that the individual actor came across a minimal amount of 'blockage' in the form of entrenched traditional appropriations or ethical restrictions. This, of course, involves a somewhat arbitrary assessment, since like most of the ideal types we are confronted in concrete cases with the problem of calculating the 'mix' between, in this instance, formal and substantive orientations of action. But in terms of the breakdown of tradition and the fact that formal rational calculations were not confined to a particular sector of human activity, it appeared to Weber that Western capitalist societies exhibited formal rationality to a much greater degree than any other society, either past or present.

This is why it seems to me to be a mistake to ignore Weber's comparative studies, as we are told to do by some commentators. Apart from the fact that Weber claimed that even his study of Protestantism was only a part of a study which needed to be pursued much further, there is the additional reason that Weber explicitly went beyond the stage of elaborating two 'relative historical concepts' and converted one of them into the basis for cross-cultural comparisons. The 'Protestant Ethic' is presented as a unique historical constellation, but 'modern capitalism' is defined largely in terms of one pole of the continuum 'formal'/'substantive' rationality, and this aspect at least can be taken out of the context of Western Europe. In *The Protestant Ethic and the Spirit of Capitalism*, only the 'formal' rational element is given a full treatment: the 'substantive' aspect is either implied, or associated by way of contrast with medieval Catholicism.

A crucial historical element, which Weber considered as having contributed significantly to the structure of modern capitalism, was what he termed 'the spirit of capitalism', and he understood by this a specific set of attitudes towards the acquisition of money and related activities. This spirit was distinctive in the important sense of regarding the acquisition of money not as a necessary evil but as an ethically approved end in itself. Furthermore, it gave no limit to the pursuit of gain, and this was an important feature distinguishing it from traditional conceptions of acquisition in which 'enough' was defined as all that is required to enable a man to live as he has always been accustomed to live. Here is one respect in which economic action can be seen as becoming more 'formally' rational by becoming self-legitimating. A further process was the removal of traditional means of conducting economic affairs, so that procedures became systematically reorganized in terms of maximization of gain. Similarly, work itself was not looked at in terms of traditional conceptions, such as that it is a necessary evil, 'the curse of Adam', but as a field in which to realize one's full potential. Although released from traditional constraints, the 'spirit of capitalism' did not entail complete emancipation from discipline and control since it enjoined systematic, continual activity in the pursuit of wealth. It is clear enough in this formulation that Weber intended to high-light the removal of 'substantive' rational restrictions as the basis for the specifically 'formal' rational orientations within Western capitalism.

If we place the religious ethic and the capitalist spirit side by side it becomes immediately apparent that the two are congruent, that there is, in short, significant equivalence between them. Having shown that congruence exists, on the other hand, we have not shown that the religious ethic has played a part in the development of the economic attitudes. The ways in which this link is forged are several.

There is, in the first place, a certain amount of miscellaneous statistical evidence which suggests that there might be a relationship between religious affiliation and social position in the direction which Weber was interested in measuring. However, Weber was not setting out to make a statistical study, and the use of these statistics was quite incidental to his argument. 'He used this material more as a pointer to the significant problems than as a proof.' [42:530] That Weber's first chapter is little more than an extended reflection of the kinds of random observation which had first suggested the existence of a 'problem' can be seen from the way the chapter is constructed, shifting almost randomly from one thought to the next, and from the note on which it ends:

> It will now be our task to formulate what occurs to us confusedly as clearly as it is possible, considering the inexhaustible diversity to be found in all historical material. But in order to do this it is necessary to leave behind the vague and general concepts with which we have dealt up to this point, and attempt to penetrate the peculiar characteristics of and the differences between those great worlds of religious thought which have existed historically in the various branches of Christianity. Before we can proceed to that, however . . .' [64:45–6]

Since the whole of this very short chapter could well be dropped from the book completely without altering the rest of the argument at all, I think that Weber can at worst be accused of 'academic prolixity'—indeed, the end of this chapter is very much on the level of R. K. Merton's 'Foreword to a Preface for an Introduction to a Prolegomenon to a Discourse on a Certain Subject'. [38] It therefore seems in every way ironically appropriate to the rest of his criticism that Samuelsson should regard the statistics on higher education and skilled labourers as 'fundamental to Weber's thesis'. [48:137] Even so, the final judgement which Samuelsson makes on the statistics is that they are merely 'dubious'—a resounding squeak in view of the counterblast with which his book begins.

The second method of proof is one which we will encounter again in chapters 9 and 10, and it rests on the demonstration of a *chronology* apparently working in the opposite direction from that suggested by contradictory materialist interpretations. Thus, if a relationship between two variables, A and B, is normally interpreted by saying that A causes B or that C is simultaneously responsible for both A and B, but a historical sequence can be discovered in which B apparently precedes A, then although this is insufficient to reverse the direction of the relationship, it is at least evidence for the argument that B has on occasion operated as an independent variable.

The materialist view in this case would probably state that incipient capitalism was responsible for the rise of the Calvinistic form of Protestantism; the second view might say that, for example, humanism or secularization caused both. Despite Weber's immense care not to commit the error of making a single overall causal explanation of the 'B causes A' type, his book has continually been saddled with this interpretation. Gordon Walker, for instance, decides that 'The conclusion [of Weber's book] must be that ideas that came to birth in the mind affected economic and material developments and not vice versa'. [63:6] Coupled with this version of 'what Weber said' there is often the implication that capitalism is somehow the *intended* consequence of Puritanism, whereas in fact his view of the operation of ideal factors in history had taken on a much more subtle form by the time he came to conceive the 'Protestant Ethic thesis': '. . . in his work on the *Protestant Ethic*, the role of ideal motives in creating modernity changes in three crucial respects, all of which centre on his discovery, similar to that of Hegel and others, of a complex "cunning of reason" by which people may intend one thing and attain something entirely different'. [39:183] The importance of unintended consequences will later be taken up under the third of Weber's demonstrations of the direction of the relationship between Protestantism and capitalism, but it does mean that whatever chronologies may be revealed are not intended to represent direct and intended causal links.

Weber used a certain amount of chronological evidence on the Puritan colonies on North America, and the following is an example:

. . . without doubt, in the country of Benjamin Franklin's birth (Massachusetts), the spirit of capitalism (in the sense we ~ (18th!

have attached to it) was present before the capitalistic order. There were complaints of a peculiarly calculating form of profit-seeking in New England, as distinguished from other parts of America, as early as 1632. It is further undoubted that capitalism remained far less developed in some of the neighbouring colonies, the later Southern States of the United States of America, in spite of the fact that these latter were founded by large capitalists for business motives, while the New England colonies were founded by preachers and seminary graduates with the help of small bourgeois, craftsmen and yeomen [sic], for religious reasons. In this case the causal relation is certainly the reverse of that suggested by the materialistic standpoint. [64:55–6]

Subsequent criticism of what Weber argued about North America seems to rest on two points: (a) that usury and prices were controlled both in the North and the South, and (b) that Puritanism tended to break down into a modish, socially relaxed existence. [28] As far as (a) is concerned, Weber seems to be aware of the different elements in the North American colonies since he finds their history 'dominated by the sharp contrast of the adventurers, who wanted to set up plantations with the labour of indentured servants, and live as feudal lords, and the specifically middle-class outlook of the Puritans'. [64:174–5] As far as proposition (b) is concerned, this is exactly what Weber himself says: 'To be sure, these Puritanical ideals tended to give way under excessive pressure from the temptations of wealth, as the Puritans themselves knew very well.' [64:174]

Scotland provides another example of supporting chronology. 'At the time of John Knox, the Scotsmen, who later came to dominate the English finance, were semi-tribal rustics renowned for their dissolute ways. Knox and his followers made them into the most perfect examples of worldly asceticism.' [2:11] This, suggests Andreski, reverses the direction of causality which a materialistic interpretation would require. However, the historian Hugh Trevor-Roper thinks that the evidence of Scotland weighs against Weber:

Since Weber himself limited the Protestant ethic to Calvinism, he had no need to explain the economic stagnation of Lutheran

Germany; but what about Scotland? According to Weber's theory, Scotland, with its coal deposits and its strict Calvinist system, should have progressed faster than England, whose Anglican system was regarded by Laveleye as, economically, little better than popery. [60:21]

This is a badly weighted statement. First it attributes to Weber a view which Weber himself explicitly denied when he pointed out that the social and economic environment would necessarily play an important part in whether or not capitalism developed in a particular area, and then it implies that England was monolithically Anglican. One of the reasons why Scotland remained economically retarded may well have been the ease with which emigration to England was possible, as Andreski's note on the domination of English finance by Scotsmen clearly indicates.

Finally, the most important link that Weber draws between the two sets of attitudes is the one to which we have devoted some space in outlining the concept of 'elective affinity'. Weber traces the development in writings by Puritan leaders of an internal adaptation of the Protestant ethic itself. Originally, the ethic had been exclusively concerned with religious ideas, and in Calvin's Geneva the result was a stringently controlled theocracy. After this—no doubt partly as a result of material conditions, though this is the aspect to which Weber intended to return in a further piece of research [64:277]—the direction of change was increasingly towards individualism. Additionally, the ethic gave increasing support to properly disciplined acquisitive behaviour, which came to be seen as a sign of God's blessing.

Weber strongly maintains that this process is *not* merely the permissive 'accommodation' of the ethic to dubious business practices (presumably as a way of placating the religious 'clientele'), and he shows that there was a dynamic process *within the religious system of ideas* through which powerful 'interests' were generated and themselves had to be met by the ethic. This is demonstrated by the fact that devotion to a capitalistic calling was not just 'allowed' but was given *positive* religious significance; also, later Puritan doctrine did not approve every form of acquisition but insisted on maintaining strict discipline and on preserving the ascetic element intact, which no amount of 'accommodation' could have achieved. Eventually, however, capitalistic activity was sanctioned on purely utilitarian motives, though even here—as in the case of Benjamin Franklin—the element of ascetic commitment to intrinsically valued tasks was still kept up. Thus to summarize: there was an 'elective affinity' between the Protestant (and especially Calvinist) ethic and the spirit of capitalism: that it was not purely a case of 'accommodation' to economic conditions on the part of the religious ethic is due to an internal dialectic between religious 'ideas' and religious 'interests', the latter being generated—as has been shown—by the need of Calvinist believers to find their strategies for salvation.

As Weber admitted, this was one-sided and incomplete—not, he hastened to add, because of any *a priori* commitment to an idealist position but because his method of isolating contributory factors in a complex chain of historical interconnections (in which the ideal-type method was centrally important) led to the logical result of taking one thing at a time. However artificial and capable of misinterpretation such a method might be, its pay-off in terms of analytical precision is very high. But Weber did not turn to the other side of this particular coin by studying the effects of economic conditions and attitudes on the Protestant ethic. 'Instead of continuing to ask directly what specific forces account for the appearance of rational bourgeois capitalism in the modern West, he asks inversely, why did anything like it *fail* to appear in any of the other great civilizations of the world?' [42:533]

In both his study of Chinese religion and his study of Indian religion Weber uses the same term—a 'magical garden'—to describe the world-view which interprets the natural order as being pervaded by magical elements. [65:336; 67:227] In both cases, the major statement in his argument is that these Eastern religions did not manage to create the radical tension between this-worldly and other-worldly concerns which in the West, especially under the influence of Calvinistic Protestantism, had brought about the attitudes of rational calculation and manipulation within social and economic life that were so necessary in the growth of capitalism. In contrast to the tremendous tension towards the 'world' which Puritanism created as a result of its rational, ethical imperative—and which, like a stretched spring, propelled its adherents into a systematic, ascetic confrontation with worldly affairs—Confucianism created very little tension

> between nature and deity, between ethical demand and human shortcoming, consciousness of sin and need for salvation, conduct on earth and compensation in the beyond, religious duty and socio-political reality. Hence, there was no leverage for influencing conduct through inner forces freed of tradition and convention. [67:235–6]

It is above all the dead weight of tradition and the function of different religious beliefs in breaking through this obstacle to economic development that interests Weber, and to this extent Confucianism provided no basis for the type of radical impingement on the world that occurred in the West.

To take an example that Weber clearly regarded as crucial: one of the great achievements (in terms of economic development) of Protestantism had been 'to shatter the fetters of the sib' [67:237]: by viewing man as a mere creature of a hidden, transcendent God and as owing strict duty overwhelmingly to him, the Puritans had been led to appraise all human relations, including the relations of a man to his family, in terms of ethical criteria that were unbounded by primary relationships. The significance of this for an economic system which demands impersonality in business transactions and a separation of the business enterprise from the household need hardly be pointed out. Confucianism, on the other hand, placed a strong valuation on primary group-relations and tended to tie the individual strongly to his sib members.

Although the importance of the religious factor was a key interest in Weber's study of China, he went far beyond this to an analysis of Chinese social structure. While this indicated many unfavourable conditions for the development of capitalism there were also factors that might have given rise to its growth: among these were the absence of legal restraints on usury or trade. Hence, 'From a purely economic point of view, genuine bourgeois capitalism might have developed . . .' [67:100] The factor which was significantly absent was the 'particular mentality' which in the West had been provided by ascetic Protestantism. Confucianism, he concluded, enjoined adjustment to, rather than mastery of, the world. An interesting alternative interpretation is given by Yang, who observes that there *was* a possibility of world-tension, which might have provided sufficient leverage for the kind of development that occurred in the West. Confucianism and Taoism, he argues, kept harking back to the ideal qualities of the *tao* (the governing principle of the cosmic and social order), and they put forward a view of the 'golden past' when the *tao* was thought to be in perfect operation.

> This meant that the given world was at ethical variance with the *tao* and the 'golden past'. . . . Thus, in Confucianism and in the general Chinese moral tradition, there was pressure for transforming the given world in conformity to ideals which were often disguised under the label of the *tao* or the 'golden past'. [72:xxxvii–xxxviii]

But he then goes on to concede that in historical reality, it was traditionalism, not the innovating potentiality from the ideal of the *tao* and the 'golden past', which became the dominant orientation for Confucianism and Chinese society. It was precisely this process of 'traditional leverage' as a source of change that was earlier used to characterize monastic reforms. The implications of tradition, it was argued, are cyclical rather than linear, and this would apply also to the dynastic cycles of traditional China.

Weber also emphasized the lack of a radical tension between this-worldly and other-worldly concerns in the Indian religions. The aim of the latter, he thought, was to achieve 'a state of ecstatic Godly possession through orgiastic means, in contrast to everyday life, in which God was not felt as a living power. Also, it involved an accentuation of the power of irrationality, which the rationalization of inner-worldly life conduct precisely restricted.' [65:337] Escape from, rather than systematic engagement in the world became the true sphere of interest of the educated Hindu or Buddhist. Since the *gnosis* (or special knowledge of the other-worldly) which is the goal of Indian religion is not a source of rational domination over man and nature but the means of mystical and magical domination over the self and others, its implications are charismatic rather than rational.

As a brief conclusion to this account of the Protestant ethic, a comment is required on its implications for contemporary Western societies. This seems to be a programme which Weber suggested in his open-ended speculation on future developments towards the end of *The Protestant Ethic and the Spirit of Capitalism*. [64:182] Looking at the context of Weber's remarks, however, it is immediately apparent that he viewed the spirit of religious asceticism which was such an important component of Puritanism as being irrelevant to the maintenance of mature capitalism. He clearly thought that a 'materialistic' explanation, which he found inadequate to account fully for the genesis of Western capitalism, might well give an adequate explanation of highly developed capitalism. Even here, however, he left open the possibility of 'new prophets' or 'old ideas' breaking in on the process of rationalization. One might well question the relevance of contemporary research that makes the 'historical leap' from Weber's account to the study of contemporary educational success, political preference or social mobility, and which often uses somewhat broad categories of religious affiliation and practice. In so far as it relates to this brand of vulgarization, there are excellent reasons for accepting Greeley's call for a moratorium on 'the Protestant Ethic' and his contention that 'it is one thing to say that Calvinism furnished spiritual justification to the middle class of the 17th Century and quite another to say that Protestantism makes for differential upward mobility patterns in the 20th. Such a conclusion may be correct . . . but it hardly follows logically from anything in Weber.' [21:30]

REFERENCES

1 ANDERSON, DONALD N. 'Ascetic Protestantism and political preference', *Review of Religious Research* vol. 7, no. 3, Spring 1966, pp. 167–71.

2 ANDRESKI, STANISLAV 'Method and substantive theory in Max Weber', *British Journal of Sociology* vol. XV, no. 1, March 1964, pp. 1–18.

3 ANSON, PETER FREDERICK *The Religious Orders and Congregations of Great Britain and Ireland* (Stanbrook Abbey Press, Worcester 1949).

4 BALL, DONALD W. 'Catholics, Calvinists, and rational control: further explorations in the Weberian thesis', *Sociological Analysis* vol. 26, no. 4, Winter 1965, pp. 181–8.

5 BARNES, HARRY ELMER *An Introduction to the History of Sociology* (University of Chicago Press, Chicago/London 1948).

6 BENJAMIN, A. CORNELIUS 'Mysticism and scientific discovery', *Journal of Religion* vol. XXXVI, no. 3, July 1956, pp. 169–76.

7 BOUWSMA, WILLIAM J. 'Swanson's Reformation', *Comparative Studies in Society and History* vol. X, no. 4, 1968, pp. 486–91.

8 BRESSLER, MARVIN, and WESTOFF, CHARLES F. 'Catholic education, economic values, and achievement', *American Journal of Sociology* vol. LXIX, no. 3, November 1963, pp. 225–33.

9 BUCHER, FRANÇOIS 'Cistercian architectural purism', *Comparative Studies in Society and History* vol. III, no. 1, 1960, pp. 89–105.

10 BULLOUGH, BONNIE, and BULLOUGH, VERN 'Intellectual achievers: a study of eighteenth-century Scotland', *American Journal of Sociology* vol. 76, no. 6, May 1971, pp. 1048–63.

11 CARSCH, HENRY 'The protestant ethic and the popular idol in America', *Social Compass* vol. XV/1, 1968, pp. 45–69.

12 CLARK, S. D. 'Religion and economic backward areas', *American Economic Review* XLI, no. 2, May 1951, pp. 258–65.

13 DATTA, LOIS-ELLIN 'Family religious background and early scientific creativity', *American Sociological Review* vol. 32, no. 4, August 1967, pp. 626–35.

14 DEMANT, V. A. *Religion and the Decline of Capitalism* (Faber and Faber, London 1952).

15 EISENSTADT, SAMUEL N. (ed.) *The Protestant Ethic and Modernization: a Comparative View* (Basic Books, New York 1968).

16 FISCHOFF, EPHRAIM 'The Protestant Ethic and the Spirit of Capitalism: the history of a controversy', in EISENSTADT, SAMUEL N. (ed.), *The Protestant Ethic and Modernization: a Comparative View* (Basic Books, New York 1968).

17 FLINT, JOHN T. 'A handbook for historical sociologists', *Comparative Studies in Society and History* vol. X, no. 4, 1968, pp. 492–509.

18 GOLDSTEIN, BERNICE, and EICHHORN, ROBERT L. 'The changing Protestant Ethic: rural patterns in health, work, and leisure', *American Sociological Review* vol. 26, no. 4, August 1961, pp. 557–65.

19 GREELEY, ANDREW M. 'Influence of the "religious factor" on career plans and occupational values of college graduates', *American Journal of Sociology* vol. LXVIII, no. 6, May 1963, pp. 658–71.

20 GREELEY, ANDREW M. 'Continuities in research on the "religious factor"', *American Journal of Sociology* vol. 75, no. 3, November 1969, pp. 355–9.

21 GREELEY, ANDREW M. 'The Protestant Ethic: time for a moratorium', *Sociological Analysis* vol. 25, no. 1, Spring 1964, pp. 20–33.

22 HAGEN, EVERETT E. 'How economic growth begins: a theory of social change', *Journal of Social Issues* vol. XIX, no. 1, January 1963, pp. 20–34.

23 HILL, MICHAEL *The Religious Order in a Sociological Context: A Study of Virtuoso Religion and its Legitimation in the Nineteenth Century Church of England*, Ph.D. thesis (University of London 1971).

24 HUGHES, H. STUART *Consciousness and Society* (Vintage Books, New York 1958).

25 JOHNSON, BENTON 'Ascetic protestantism and political preference', *Public Opinion Quarterly* vol. XXVI, no. 1, Spring 1962, pp. 35–46.

26 JOHNSON, BENTON 'Theology and party preference among Protestant clergymen', *American Sociological Review* vol. 31, no. 2, April 1966, pp. 200–8.

27 KNOX, RONALD A. *Enthusiasm* (Clarendon Press, Oxford 1950).

28 KOLKO, GABRIEL 'Max Weber on America: theory and evidence', in NADEL, GEORGE H. (ed.), *Studies in the Philosophy of History* (Harper Torchbooks, New York 1965).

29 LAPIERE, RICHARD *The Freudian Ethic* (George Allen and Unwin, London 1960).

30 LENSKI, GERHARD Review of Andrew M. Greeley, *Religion and Career*, *American Journal of Sociology* vol. LXXI, no. 2, September 1965, pp. 200–1.

31 MCCORMACK, THELMA 'The Protestant Ethic and the spirit of socialism', *British Journal of Sociology* vol. XX, no. 3, September 1969, pp. 266–76.

32 MACINTYRE, ALASDAIR 'A mistake about causality in social science', in LASLETT, PETER, and RUNCIMAN, W. G., *Philosophy, Politics and Society*, second series (Basil Blackwell, Oxford 1964).

33 MACK, RAYMOND W.; MURPHY, RAYMOND J.; and YELLIN, SEYMOUR 'The Protestant Ethic, level of aspiration, and social mobility: an empirical test', *American Sociological Review* vol. 21, no. 3, June 1956, pp. 295–300.

34 MARTIN, DAVID A. (ed.) *50 Key Words in Sociology* (Lutterworth, London 1970).

35 MAYER, ALBERT J., and SHARP, HARRY 'Religious preference and worldly success', *American Sociological Review* vol. 27, no. 2, April 1962, pp. 218–27.

36 MEANS, RICHARD L. 'Weber's thesis of the Protestant Ethic: the ambiguities of received doctrine', *Journal of Religion* vol. XLV, no. 1, 1965, pp. 1–11.

37 MEANS, RICHARD L. 'Protestantism and economic institutions: auxiliary theories to Weber's Protestant Ethic', *Social Forces* vol. 44, no. 3, March 1966, pp. 372–81.

38 MERTON, ROBERT K. 'Foreword to a preface for an introduction to a prolegomenon to a discourse on a certain subject', *The American Sociologist* vol. 4, no. 2, May 1969, p. 99.

39 MITZMAN, ARTHUR *The Iron Cage: an Historical Interpretation of Max Weber* (Alfred A. Knopf, New York 1970).

40 NEEDHAM, JOSEPH 'Buddhism and Chinese science', in SCHNEIDER, LOUIS (ed.), *Religion, Culture and Society*, op. cit., pp. 353–8.

41 THE OXFORD DICTIONARY OF THE CHRISTIAN CHURCH, edited by F. L. Cross (Oxford University Press, London 1963).

42 PARSONS, TALCOTT *The Structure of Social Action* (The Free Press, New York 1937).

43 PARSONS, TALCOTT 'Max Weber's sociological analysis of capitalism and modern institutions' in BARNES, HARRY ELMER, *An Introduction to the History of Sociology*, op. cit.

44 PHOTIADIS, JOHN D. 'The American business creed and denominational identification', *Social Forces* vol. 44, no. 1, September 1965, pp. 92–100.

45 RIEFF, PHILIP *The Triumph of the Therapeutic* (Chatto and Windus, London 1966).

46 ROBERTSON, ROLAND *The Sociological Interpretation of Religion* (Basil Blackwell, Oxford 1970).

47 ROSENBERG, HANS *Bureaucracy, Aristocracy and Autocracy* (Harvard University Press, Cambridge, Mass. 1958).

48 SAMUELSSON, KURT *Religion and Economic Action*, translated by E. Geoffrey French (William Heinemann, London 1961).

49 SCHARF, BETTY R. *The Sociological Study of Religion* (Hutchinson, London 1970).

50 SCHNEIDER, LOUIS 'Problems in the sociology of religion', in FARIS, ROBERT E. L. (ed.), *Handbook of Modern Sociology* (Rand McNally and Co., Chicago 1964).

51 SCHNEIDER, LOUIS (ed.) *Religion, Culture, and Society* (John Wiley and Sons, New York 1964).

52 SHILS, EDWARD A. 'Some remarks on "The Theory of Social and Economic Organisation"', *Economica* vol. XV, no. 57, February 1948, pp. 36–50.

53 SMOUT, T. C. *A History of the Scottish People 1560–1830* (Collins, London 1969).

54 SPRENKEL, OTTO B. VAN DER 'Max Weber on China', in NADEL, GEORGE H. (ed.), *Studies in the Philosophy of History* (Harper Torchbooks, New York 1965).

55 SUMMERS, GENE F.; HOUGH, RICHARD L.; JOHNSON, DOYLE P.; and VEATCH, KATHRYN A. 'Ascetic protestantism and political preference: a re-examination', *Review of Religious Research* vol. 12, no. 1, Fall 1970, pp. 17–25.

56 SUTTON, F. X. 'The social and economic philosophy of Werner Sombart: the sociology of capitalism', in BARNES, HARRY ELMER, *An Introduction to the History of Sociology*, op. cit.

57 SWANSON, GUY E. *Religion and Regime* (University of Michigan Press, Ann Arbor 1967).

58 TAWNEY, R. H. *Religion and the Rise of Capitalism* (Penguin Books, Harmondsworth, Middlesex 1961).

59 TRENT, JAMES W., and GOLDS, JENETTE *Catholics in College* (University of Chicago Press, Chicago/London 1967).

60 TREVOR-ROPER, H. R. 'Religion, the Reformation, and social change', *Historical Studies* no. 4, 1963, pp. 18–44.

61 VAUGHAN, TED R.; SMITH, DOUGLAS H.; and SJOBERG, GIDEON 'The religious orientations of American natural scientists', *Social Forces* vol. 44, no. 4, June 1966, pp. 519–26.

62 VEROFF, JOSEPH; FELD, SHEILA; and GURIN, GERALD 'Achievement motivation and religious background', *American Sociological Review* vol. 27, no. 2, April 1962, pp. 205–17.

63 WALKER, P. C. GORDON 'Capitalism and the Reformation', *Economic History Review* vol. VIII, no. 1, November 1937, pp. 1–19.

64 WEBER, MAX *The Protestant Ethic and the Spirit of Capitalism* (Unwin University Books, London 1930).

65 WEBER, MAX *The Religion of India. The Sociology of Hinduism and Buddhism*, translated and edited by Hans H. Gerth and Don Martindale (The Free Press, Glencoe 1958).

66 WEBER, MAX *The Theory of Social and Economic Organization* (The Free Press, New York 1964).

67 WEBER, MAX *The Religion of China. Confucianism and Taoism* (Macmillan, New York 1964).

68 WEISSKOPF, WALTER A. 'The American business creed and economic theory', *Journal of Religion* vol. XXXIX, no. 1, 1939, pp. 32–8.
69 WHYTE, WILLIAM H. *The Organization Man* (Penguin Books, Harmondsworth, Middlesex 1961).
70 WILEY, NORBERT 'Religious and political liberalism among Catholics', *Sociological Analysis* vol. 28, no. 3, Fall 1967, pp. 142–8.
71 WILSON, BRYAN R. 'Essay review: religion and career', *The School Review* vol. 73, no. 2, 1965, pp. 156–72.
72 YANG, C. K. Introduction to WEBER, MAX, *The Religion of China*, op. cit.

I am not sure that Weber's Lutheran opponent are taken seriously enough here – striking omissions from the bibliography include H M Robertson's Rise of Economic Individualism and in talking of Calvin Weber seems to talk more reverence over Calvin Linsey! Sociologists must be Marxist admit that Weber could be wrong!

7

The Theoretical Basis of Charismatic Legitimacy

WE ENDED our chapter on the study of Protestantism and capitalism by questioning some of the recent vulgarized versions of 'the Weber thesis'. We begin this chapter by noting that a recent thoroughgoing criticism of the Weberian concept of charismatic authority took as its point of departure the concept's 'current fashionable use', and suggested that it had 'become by now one of the most popular pieces of coinage in the academic exchange market'. [39:ix–x] In order to examine the concept of charisma we must reverse the sequence: thus the account of charisma will first of all be set against the more general background of authority in religious and political groups. Because the legitimation of authority is a process common to a wide range of institutions, it will be necessary to go outside the scope of Weber's 'sociology of religion' as narrowly defined, a procedure which several recent critics of the concept of charisma have adopted. Furthermore, I think it is necessary to locate the concept in the framework of Weber's sociology of ideas, in the same way that the analysis of the Protestant ethic was discussed in terms of this aspect of his thinking. There are, indeed, many continuities between these two important parts of Weber's analysis of religion.

One of the most frequent sources of criticism of the concept of charismatic authority centres on whether or not it is a *relational* term—usually expressed as the need to emphasize the 'recognition' of a charismatic claim and hence its 'dependence' on the surrounding social structure. This, it should be pointed out, is a question that properly belongs to the more general notion of 'legitimate authority', and this is the point at which we take up the discussion. Weber initially argues that 'power' is the most comprehensive term we can use to depict the probability that one actor in a social situation will be able to exert his will over others (who may or may not resist)—which means that every situation in which the probability of successful self-assertion is distributed unequally among a number of social actors is a power situation. However, it is possible on the basis of induction from experience to argue that when there occur recurrent commands from a superior to a group of persons, there will exist some minimum level of voluntary submission, and it is possible to argue further that the parties involved in any such recurrent system of super- and sub-ordination will attempt to establish and propagate the belief in its 'legitimacy', which may be based on various criteria. Legitimation is thus 'the representation by rulers and acceptance by ruled of the credentials on which this differential distribution of power is based'. [20:42] Weber was quick to point out the extent to which such 'acceptance' might be 'feigned'. [36:326-7]

There are a number of ways of portraying the important differences between power and authority. One is to trace the etymology of the Latin term '*Auctoritas*', from which the word 'authority' derives. This term comes from a root meaning 'to augment', and thus authority *adds* to a mere act of will by providing the criteria on which obedience ought to be based. Implied in this formulation is the idea that authority is that property which gives a command its persuasive force, since 'authority is not something working by itself, but rather an implementation of something else'. [5:21] This 'something else' may be the grounds on which compliance is claimed by the person(s) issuing commands, or it may be the grounds on which subordinates perceive those commands to be based; or, if a system of authority is to be relatively enduring, it may be a composite of both of these images. In this latter case we may refer to the authority as legitimate since it is based on consensus between ruler and subordinate over the criteria on which compliance is based. When these criteria become an integral part of the calculations made by members of a society or of a more specific social group with regard to the issuing of and compliance with orders, we can interpret legitimation as 'the primary link between values as an internalized component of the personality of the individual, and the institutionalized patterns which define the structure of social relations'. [25:201]

Friedrich has noted an important concomitant of this interpretation, which will emerge in the later discussion of charisma. Authority, he says, is very often seen in the perspective of its 'psychological penumbra'. [9:45] The fact that persons in positions of authority are often endowed with esteem, respect and admiration results in these attributes being identified with authority. However, in any situation of authority it is important that the actors involved should in the last analysis recognize the *criteria* on which it is based. Here we can trace yet another example of the way in which Weber gave autonomy to ideal elements in social action by claiming that a normative definition of the legitimacy of any form of authority would exert an influence on political action, since *'Weber argues in effect that the political experience of a society flows to a significant degree from its ideas of legitimacy'.* [33:133, original italics] It will be immediately apparent that in emphasizing the element of shared values in the definitions of the situation of those with power and those without power, Weber has directed attention principally at the *relational* aspect of authority.

Although this preliminary account of legitimate authority, by emphasizing the element of shared values, has presented a broadly static, consensual image, there are important implications in it for the analysis of conflict. In the first place, we have used as our 'population' of actors those who *perceive* themselves as part of the same community. It may well be that certain social groups do not identify their 'reference group' with their 'membership group' and consequently do not share the prevailing definition of legitimacy in a particular society or institution. Thus authority need not be monolithic. While for considerable periods of time a majority of the members of a particular society, or of specific parts of a given society, may be identified to some extent with the values and norms of the system, other groups may show very little commitment to these values and may accept them as binding only to a very limited extent. Another possibility is for groups to accept the normative system but to claim that they (as against those who are actually placed in positions of authority) are the true repositories of basic values. The 'perceived images' of authority are not homogenous among the members of a particular society, and change is most likely to come from leverage exerted by those groups which find most tension between their 'perceived image' of authority and the reality of the existing system of authority. [4:89] Contained in this is the important notion of the way in which legitimacy provides relatively enduring images of the system under which authority is exercised, and the influence these may have when the political realities are seen to have changed. It may therefore be argued that 'any institutional system is never fully "homogenous" in the sense of being fully accepted or accepted to the same degree by all those participating in it. These different orientations to the central symbolic spheres may all become foci of conflict and of potential institutional change.' [6:xliv]

Even more important in the study of religious institutions is the fact that, whatever the attitudes of a particular group to the basic values on which the system is based, these may change after the initial onset of institutionalization. Institutionalization entails an effort to maintain the legitimacy of the system's values, symbols and norms, but change in the direction of institutionalization may well result in shifts in the balance of power among different groups in the system and consequent changes in their orientation to the system as a whole. There is a particularly interesting example of this process in the early development of the Christian church. Institutionalization in this particular case involved the gradual concentration of power in a distinct priestly hierarchy and an increasing accommodation to the norms of the previously hostile surrounding society. The impact of these institutional changes has often been interpreted as an important factor in the fourth-century development of monasticism as a distinct social and geographical movement. Workman, for instance, sees monasticism in its origin as 'the protest of the lay spirit against any conception of religion which excluded the laity from the highest obligations or the supremest attainment'. [38:13] And Timothy Ware uses the conversion of Constantine as a symbol of fundamental changes in the institutional character of Christianity: 'It is no coincidence that monasticism should have developed immediately after Constantine's conversion at the very time when the persecutions ceased and Christianity became fashionable. The monks with their austerities were martyrs in an age when martyrdom of blood no longer existed; they formed the counterbalance to an established Christendom.' [34:45]

Eisenstadt refers to the possibility of 'anti-systems' developing within any institutional system, and argues that although these anti-systems may often remain latent for long periods of time they may also constitute 'important foci of change under propitious conditions'. [6:xlv] It may well be that the existence of contradictions and conflicts over the basic issue of legitimacy in a particular system can still be accommodated within the overall system or partially insulated as a sub-system—in the example we have used, for example, monastic groups were eventually incorporated within the church's system of authority, albeit with a considerable degree of internal autonomy—but the possibility of conflict and change is always present. Evidently, schism and its management should be seen more as an endemic property of religious institutions than as an occasionally intervening element. [37]

Starting from the concept of legitimacy as the normative nexus in reference to which social relationships are conducted in any society, or indeed in any group having differentiated authority roles, Weber then went on to consider the grounds on which such legitimacy might be claimed and accepted. This he did in terms of the three familiar ideal-types of legitimate authority, which can best be seen as the major 'styles' in which the claim to and acceptance of legitimacy on the part of the holder of authority on the one hand and his subordinates on the other might be phrased. This will be our point of departure for a consideration of the concept of charisma: in the meantime, we might usefully simplify the discussion so far in the set of diagrams on pages 145–6.

Weber states that the validity of claims to legitimacy may rest on one or a combination of more than one of three 'pure types' of authority:

1. Rational grounds—resting on a belief in the 'legality' of patterns of normative rules and the right of those elevated to authority under such rules to issue commands (legal authority).
2. Traditional grounds—resting on an established belief in the

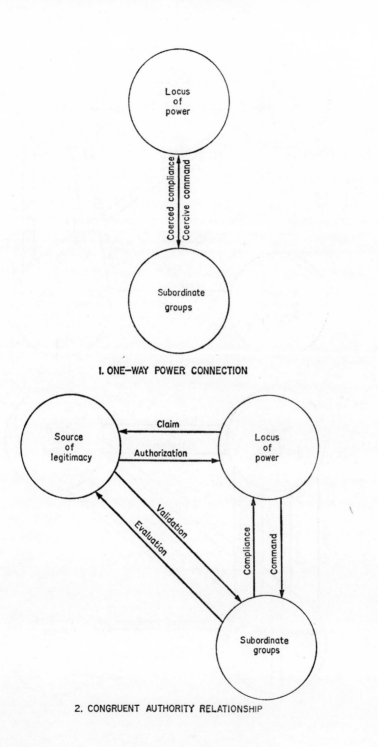

1. ONE—WAY POWER CONNECTION

2. CONGRUENT AUTHORITY RELATIONSHIP

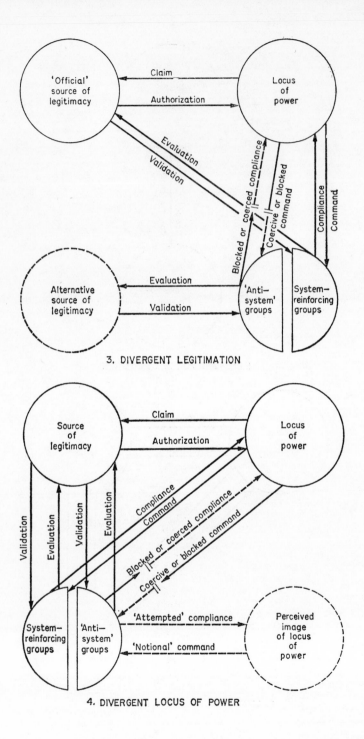

3. DIVERGENT LEGITIMATION

4. DIVERGENT LOCUS OF POWER

sanctity of immemorial traditions and the legitimacy of the
status of those exercising authority under them (traditional
authority); or finally,

3. Charismatic grounds—resting on devotion to the specific
and exceptional sanctity, heroism or exemplary character of
an individual person, and of the normative patterns or order
revealed or ordained by him (charismatic authority).
[36:328]

A distinction is then drawn between legal authority, where
obedience is owed to the legally established impersonal order,
and is extended to persons occupying offices of authority under
it only as long as they issue commands compatible with the legal
limits of their competence, and traditional authority, where
obedience is owed to the *person* of the chief who occupies a
traditionally sanctioned position of authority and behaves in
accordance with traditional prescriptions. In charismatic authority the charismatic leader as such is obeyed as a result of personal
trust in him, and the only restriction on the leader is the extent to
which his revelation, heroism or exemplary qualities 'fall within
the scope of the individual's belief in his charisma'. [36:328]
There follow in Weber's account two points of clarification. The
first is that the concept of 'charisma'—'the gift of grace'—has
been taken from the vocabulary of early Christianity, and had
been used by Rudolf Sohm in his *Kirchenrecht* (1892) in a way that
clarified its usage as far as early Christian organization was concerned. 'It is thus nothing new', Weber adds. [36:328]

There are two main passages referring to charismatic endowment in the New Testament, and they have interesting implications for the sociological use of the concept. In the Epistle to the
Romans, Paul juxtaposes the 'enthusiastic' exercise of charisma
with its institutional varieties, and the *New English Bible* clearly
brings this out in its translation: 'The gifts we possess differ as
they are allotted to us by God's grace, and must be exercised
accordingly: the gift of inspired utterance, for example, in proportion to a man's faith; or the gift of administration, in administration.' The other gifts mentioned are teaching, exhortation,
charity, leadership and mercy. 1 Corinthians 12 contains a long
passage about the 'gifts of the spirit' and lists the following

varieties of 'gifts': wisdom, knowledge, faith, healing, miracles, prophecy, distinguishing true and false spirits, ecstatic utterances and interpretation of ecstatic utterances. Here there is exclusive concern with the 'enthusiastic' varieties of charisma. The passage in Romans, on the other hand, specifically includes administration, and it shows how 'charisma' in this fundamental usage could be made the basis of ecclesiastical organization and offices.

This we will subsequently consider in greater detail, but it is important to note that the source from which Weber derived his concept of charisma was primarily concerned with the way in which Christian organization was attached to this quality of spiritual endowment rather than to any other principle of administration. As Sohm noted in his *Kirchenrecht*:

> The doctrine of the constitution of the ecclesia which was derived from the divine word, but in truth was apostolic is that the organization of Christianity is *not legal but charismatic*. Christianity is organized by the distribution of *gifts of grace* (Charismata) which at the same time enables and calls the individual Christians to different activities in Christianity. The charisma is from God. . . . And thus the service (*diakonia*) to which the Charisma calls, is a service imposed by God, and an office in the service of the church (ecclesia) and not of any local community. [10:14]

The implication of the concept in its original usage is undoubtedly to distinguish the organizational base of the Christian church from that of the surrounding social institutions, and this we will find has been a recurrent theme in charismatic restatements within ecclesiastical organizations, but it also has the effect of setting limits on the institutional contexts in which charisma may be located. Much of the debate about the concept is concerned with the extent to which it can be lifted out of its restricted religious setting and generalized to include other types of specific 'callings', especially within the political sphere. Weber clearly intended it to be a generalized concept, since his typology of legitimate authority is one of his most generalized uses of ideal-typical models.

Weber's second point of clarification is to emphasize that the concept of 'pure' charisma stands at one end of a continuum

which is concerned with its transformation: 'Later on the transformation of pure charisma by the process of routinization will
be discussed and thereby the relevance of the concept to the
understanding of empirical systems of authority considerably
increased.' [36:329] This was expressed more categorically in the
statement that '. . . in its pure form charismatic authority may be
said to exist only in the process of originating'. [36:364] Quite
clearly, Weber intended that charismatic authority should be seen
as part of a historical process rather than as an isolated and remote
type of authority.

The use of ideal types and the criticisms levelled at them have
already been briefly reviewed in the section on the Protestant
ethic. Many of their difficulties can be dealt with in the context of
Weber's three pure types of legitimate authority. Above all, the
types are intended to be abstractions from aspects of concrete
reality rather than a comprehensive empirical account of that
reality: 'the idea that the whole of concrete historical reality can
be exhausted in the conceptual scheme about to be developed is
as far from the author's thoughts as anything could be'. [36:329]
Nor can we expect any empirical historical example of authority
to fall unambiguously into any single category in the three-part
typology—to be, in Weber's phrase, 'as an open book'. An
analogy may show more clearly how ideal types are used to
analyse an empirical 'mix'.

The analogy which comes nearest to elucidating the use of
ideal types is that of colour printing. The three basic 'primary
pigments' are blue, yellow and red, and different combinations of
these three pigments can produce an almost complete range of
'secondary' colours. This is the principle used in colour printing.
Suppose, for example, that we wished to make a print copy of
an original painting with an immense complexity of colours. The
procedure—much simplified—would be to photograph the
picture three times using each time a different colour filter which
permits only certain colour rays to penetrate, and to make a
separate printing-block for each primary colour. To get the
yellow block the blue–green filter is used, for the red block a
yellow–green filter and for the blue block a red–orange filter.
Having gone through this process of 'filtering out' the 'irrelevant'
primary colours for each block we are then in a position to assess

the relative contribution and density of each one separately and—if we are making a copy—we can combine all three blocks to reproduce the complexity of the original.

This is a process exactly parallel to the one Weber used in the device of the ideal type. We have already seen how he attempted to 'filter out' the 'extraneous' factors in the rise of modern Western capitalism in order to assess more precisely the specific contribution of the Calvinist ethic: here he was interested in isolating only one of the variables present, and his study is thus 'incomplete'. The three-part typology of authority is an even better use of the device because it represents an attempt to provide a more general set of categories through which we can analyse one aspect of the differential distribution of power, namely the distinct bases of legitimate authority. The three types of legitimate authority have in common with the three blocks of the colour printer the fact that they are crude accentuations of elements contributing to a complex whole, but just as the printer uses these devices in order to extricate and later to reconstruct an intricate work of art, so the only justification for the use of ideal types is that they enable the sociologist to disentangle, and thus to explain as far as possible the 'infinite richness' of reality. [35:105] While we would not expect to find much obvious use of primary colours as such in the work of a painter, we could nevertheless 'extract' them from a finished picture, and this is how we use ideal types in an empirical historical setting.

This analogy may serve to throw light on one of the points that figures prominently in sociological treatments of the concept of charisma, namely the argument that charismatic authority is somehow 'on its own'. This would appear to be the view of Edward Shils, who thinks that 'Max Weber's classification of types of legitimate authority suffers from its tendency to isolate charismatic authority from the traditional and rational–legal types'. [30:3] He then goes on to argue that charisma is 'dispersed' in all types of legitimate authority. This seems to me to represent a misdirected criticism: all three components of Weber's typology of legitimate authority might be said to 'suffer from the tendency to be isolated', the reason being that by working with the pure models offered in the typology—the 'primary colours' in this kind of analysis—we are better able to assess their 'mix' in concrete historical circumstances. Thus it makes sense to propose that we do not try to develop a model of charismatic authority which is less 'isolated' than the pure type. The argument for such a reformulation, as demonstrated by Shils, is that since charisma is 'dispersed' in other forms of authority relationship we should incorporate it more firmly in these other categories rather than making it analytically distinct. This is not an altogether fair account of Shils' argument since he does give other reasons for his interpretation of Weber—and these we will shortly consider—but on a methodological level the counter-argument can be advanced that it is more fruitful to maintain the distinctions between our abstract models, since this makes possible an analysis of the relative contribution of each component in an empirical 'mix'.

Moreover, there is sometimes a degree of uncertainty about whether those who adopt Shils' line of argument mean by it merely that in empirical examples of (apparently) charismatic authority, traditional and rational–legal elements will be found in combination—a position which is very much the one put forward in Weber's own work—or whether they wish to import 'charismatic' elements into the *types* of traditional and rational–legal authority—a much more questionable procedure. I can find no other sense than this in, for example, Oomen's statement that: 'It is sufficient for the present purpose to keep in mind that "charisma" is analytically separable although present in other types of authority.' [24:87] The consequence of such an attempt to weaken the boundaries between different 'pure' types emerges in the same writer's later discussion of empirical examples of charismatic authority—in brief, it becomes impossible to 'filter out' other types of authority.

Oomen in fact takes an approach to the study of charismatic leadership which is extremely useful, and which has been applied with great insight by Berger to the study of the Israelite prophets: that is, to consider the importance of individuals with an established traditional or rational–legal position of authority as charismatic figures. He suggests, for instance, that the control over the press and propaganda which can be exercised by individuals in established rational-legal authority positions may make the presentation of their charismatic claims much easier. Presumably, as sociologists we wish to disentangle the relative contribution of the different types of legitimation, but this becomes extremely difficult when we allow our abstract constructs to interpenetrate. Oomen finally admits that in his case it is impossible: '. . . we are not in a position to establish the proportion of authority derived from their charismatic and rational-legal authority respectively'. [24:96]

So far in this chapter we have looked at the general features of the concept of legitimate authority and have tried to anchor the subsequent discussion in terms of the three-part typology set out by Weber. We have commented on the methodological status of these pure types of authority and, again on a methodological level, we have argued that there are good reasons for their conceptual isolation: these reasons apply as much to the types of traditional and rational-legal authority as they do to the pure type of charisma and its inseparable process of routinization. Nevertheless, the ideal type of charismatic authority is undoubtedly the source of a profound disagreement which goes beyond these primary methodological concerns (though it cannot be denied that they often intervene in the debate), and the most frequently encountered criticism of the concept is the one that regards it as a *residual category*. Apter refers to it as 'a normative residual category sandwiched between two stable types of authority, the traditional and the rational-legal'. [2:763] Friedland similarly regards the concept as a residual category to explain situations which cannot otherwise be illuminated by recourse to traditional or legal–rational models and regards it as Weber's way of accounting for large-scale change which could not be accommodated within the 'stable systems' of traditional and rational–legal authority. [7:19] If we are to 'reserve' the use of charisma, perhaps we might ask just how stable are the other two types of authority.

If we formulate the problem in these terms, some interesting features emerge. Bendix prefaces his account of the struggle for power under legal domination with the comment: 'The system of legal domination is as subject to transformation as are the systems of charismatic and traditional authority, and Weber utilized his analysis of legal rationality and of bureaucracy to identify the "problematics" of legal domination. Any system of domination undergoes change when the beliefs in its legitimacy and the practices of its administrative organization are modified. Such changes of belief occur in and through the struggle for power, which in the modern state may lead to changes of control over the bureaucratic apparatus but not to its destruction.' [3:431] Despite the strong attribution of stability which characterizes rational-legal authority, Weber saw it as containing inherent strains and even a basic incompatibility. Nowhere does this emerge with greater clarity than in his studies of law.

The concept of natural law, Weber argued, had become 'deeply discredited' as the result of social and ideological conflicts which had arisen as groups in revolt against the existing order *appealed* to natural law to legitimate their activities—the American revolution was a case in point. At the same time, the established authorities appealed to natural law to legitimate the *status quo*. We will see in chapter 12 how the plausibility of the foundation documents of Christianity was subjected to much the same fragmentation by competing social groups. As a result 'Weber's thesis apparently was that the modern legal order is sustained by both a formal and substantive theory of natural law and hence by a more or less incompatible set of beliefs concerning its legitimacy'. [3:432] The implications of this incipient source of conflict between the claims for substantive justice by legal ideologists on the one hand and the legal formalism of the system of judicial decisions on the other, together with his more familiar distinction between the logic of bureaucracy and the values of democracy, are that rational-legal authority is typified by deeply embedded strains and is therefore to be regarded as potentially and sometimes chronically in a process of change.

The dynamic potential of traditional legitimacy appears on the surface to be a contradiction in terms, but this is a source of change which has considerably more significance than has often been attributed to it. In the previous two chapters it was shown that in the case of China and of monastic orders in the West, a strongly valued tradition provided a source of leverage around which support for changes in the structure of authority could be mobilized. Some of the implications of this will now be expanded. It is important to note that traditional authority *shares* with charismatic authority the feature of a personal capacity on the part of the leader to define for himself the limits of the obligations owed to him by his followers—the difference between tradition and charisma being that in the former the leader's scope in this respect is limited while in the latter, theoretically at least, it is not. The limit on the leader's personal initiative in traditional authority is provided by the sanction of immemorial tradition. The customary way of conducting affairs sets the boundaries of a traditional leader's legitimacy, and the less clearly defined these boundaries are, the more personal initiative he will possess. However, it is immediately apparent that traditional authority does provide a mechanism of change, for if it can plausibly be argued by those over whom the traditional leader exercises power that the limits of entrenched usage have been overstepped, this provides a possible basis for a challenge to the leader's legitimacy and some-times a motive for his replacement. This is precisely the process that Yang envisaged when he noted that both Confucianism and Taoism kept harking back to a 'golden past' when the *tao* was thought to be in perfect operation, and thus there was a source of world-tension or leverage in the comparison that could be made between the decadence of the present and the sacred traditions of the past.

The reason for arguing that this is a useful approach to the study of change within religious and especially Christian insti-tutions is that they often appear to embody very strongly the notion of a period in their history which has been characterized by a particularly high level of authenticity, both in belief and practice, and is therefore to be valued above all as a model for emulation. This golden age of pristine purity may be identified differently by competing groups within the institution, as is amply shown in the differential content given to the notion of 'the Primitive Church' by different Christian groups, but the use made of such appeals has generally been to contrast unfavourably the contemporary structure of authority with that of the pristine model. It might be argued that rather than use the concept of tradition, we might find it more valuable to interpret this process as the search for the charismatic origins of contemporary insti-tutional roles—and it will later be shown that this too has been a powerful source of innovation in established Christian organiza-tions—but the traditional component has also played an unmistakable part in religious change. A brief example from the history of religious orders in Western Christianity will demonstrate this.

In the Benedictine Order, the Rule of St Benedict has always provided the central focus for successive reforms, which have tended to refer back to the injunctions contained within it for their legitimation. Since the Rule was for a long period the most important source of whatever uniformity existed between the autonomous Benedictine abbeys, it acquired a very strong valuation. However, to look at the Rule with its eminently practical and meticulous regulations of daily conduct, all of which are oriented to the substantively rational goal of a quasi-familial type of existence, one is struck above all *not* by its charismatic appeal to new obligations and its negative evaluation of institutional structures, but by its attempt to reproduce within a permanent community the traditional microcosm of the surrounding society, and to orient it towards a unified system of religious progress in its members. Hence, when the subsequent reforms of the Benedictine Order—such as those of Cluny and Cîteaux—took place, they were typically attempts to return to the pristine purity of the Rule, and as a result they made highly detailed restatements of injunctions contained within it. While the exponents of a strongly valued tradition might be expected to make capital over an issue like the wearing of skins, furs and warm underpants—as the Cistercian rebels certainly did in their criticisms of Cluny—this does not seem to fit at all well into the Weberian concept of charisma, with its total transformation of obligations and its shattering of traditional stereotypes.

Other evidence of the importance of traditional reinstatements for legitimating change in religious institutions can be found in the competing versions of tradition in Anglican schools of 'churchmanship', [15] but the major point is that historical traditions—and 'unofficial' versions of historical traditions—may serve to provide the leverage for legitimate institutional change, which can be generated by the tension between a highly valued past and a devalued present. The historical account need not be historically accurate for this process to operate, and it may well be that a mythical version of history carries more effect. In chapter 11 we will find that similar mythical versions of a 'golden past' form an important component of some theories of secularization.

Taking the argument one step further, it can be seen that some of the supporting data that sociologists have used to define leaders as charismatic can be transferred very readily to the category of traditional authority. This is precisely the criticism which can be levelled at David Apter's charismatic portrait of Nkrumah, who is placed in the role of a leader who has 'replaced the chief's authority by meeting the same functional requirements through new social structures'. [1:8] This functional similarity is then used by Apter to minimize the problem of Nkrumah's acceptibility to the masses; but a rather different interpretation is possible: 'Does the fact that Nkrumah performs the same functions as the chief make him as acceptable as the chief to the ordinary Ghanaian still in the grip of traditional institutions?' [1:8] Shils is another writer who adopts as his criterion of 'charismatic' a source of legitimacy which can readily be accommodated within traditional conceptions. Political leaders in underdeveloped countries, he argues, believe themselves to possess 'the spirit of the nation, that spirit which slumbered long and which is now awake in them'. [30:3] The spirit of the nation seems more a traditional than a charismatic image.

There are indeed respects in which charismatic and traditional authority become closely identified, and many of the problems surrounding the convergence that may occur between charisma and tradition emerge most clearly in the process of routinization. Many of the difficulties are identified in the following quotation from Runciman, who argues that:

the borderline between charismatic and traditional authority is harder to delimit than Weber's almost pedantic definitions would suggest. Once obedience to charismatic authority has become a habit, what does it mean to say that it is charismatic? If it means (as in the case of a church) that it retains some sort of of 'magical' attributes, this is equally true of many rulers who are by Weber's definition traditional. If on the other hand, it means that it remains in some sense personal, then so, once again, can traditional authority; and to say that stability is the distinguishing criterion is to turn Weber's basic insight on this topic into a circular definition. Of course, as has already been remarked, Weber emphasized that his ideal types are likely to exist in combination; but he gives no account of a procedure which would enable us to analyse a combination into its components. [28:160]

On the contrary, Weber *did* provide a procedure which would make easier the unravelling of components in combination, and he showed how it could be applied in his historical and comparative research: the procedure was to elaborate precisely those 'pedantic definitions' about which Runciman apparently has reservations, and then to use them in such a way that the other factors in a historical situation were 'filtered out'. If this is understood, then the concept of charisma becomes much less precarious and provides a very important insight on a whole range of phenomena within religious and political movements alike. In the following chapter we will argue strongly that there is a place for the concept of charisma in our sociological tool-kit, and that the sociology of religion is an extremely fertile area for its use. Furthermore, it can be shown that by starting from a 'pedantic definition' a crucial set of continuities can be drawn between the concept of charisma and its routinization, and the previous outline of the Protestant ethic. Both properly belong in Weber's sociology of ideas.

REFERENCES

1 AKE, CLAUDE 'Charismatic legitimation and political integration', *Comparative Studies in Society and History* vol. IX, no. 1, 1966, pp. 1–13.

2 APTER, DAVID E. 'Nkrumah, charisma, and the coup', *Daedalus* vol. 97, no. 3, Summer 1968, pp. 757–92.

3 BENDIX, REINHARD *Max Weber: an Intellectual Portrait* (Methuen, London 1966).

4 EASTON, DAVID 'The perception of authority and political change', in FRIEDRICH, CARL JOACHIM, *Authority*, op. cit.

5 EHRHARDT, ARNOLD A. T. 'Christianity and authority', *Diogenes* no. 41, Spring 1963, pp. 117–35.

6 EISENSTADT, SAMUEL N. *Max Weber on Charisma and Institution Building* (University of Chicago Press, Chicago 1968).

7 FRIEDLAND, WILLIAM H. 'For a sociological concept of charisma', *Social Forces* vol. 43, no. 1, October 1964, pp. 18–26.

8 FRIEDRICH, CARL JOACHIM (ed.) *Authority* [American Society of

Political and Legal Philosophy. Nomos 1] (Harvard University Press, Cambridge, Mass. 1958).

9 FRIEDRICH, CARL JOACHIM 'Authority, reason, and discretion', in FRIEDRICH, CARL JOACHIM, *Authority*, op. cit.

10 FRIEDRICH, CARL JOACHIM 'Political leadership and the problem of the charismatic power', *Journal of Politics* vol. 23, no. 1, February 1961, pp. 3–24.

11 HENDEL, CHARLES W. 'An exploration of the nature of authority', in FRIEDRICH, CARL JOACHIM, *Authority*, op. cit.

12 HILL, CHRISTOPHER *Puritanism and Revolution* (Panther Books, London 1968).

13 HILL, MICHAEL (ed.) *A Sociological Yearbook of Religion in Britain—4* (SCM Press, London 1971).

14 HILL, MICHAEL *The Religious Order in a Sociological Context: A Study of Virtuoso Religion and its Legitimation in the Nineteenth Century Church of England*, Ph.D. thesis (University of London 1971).

15 HILL, MICHAEL, and TURNER, BRYAN S. 'John Wesley and the origin and decline of ascetic devotion', in HILL, MICHAEL (ed.), *A Sociological Yearbook of Religion in Britain—4*, op. cit.

16 JOUVENEL, BERTRAND DE 'Authority: the efficient imperative', in FRIEDRICH, CARL JOACHIM, *Authority*, op. cit.

17 KEEN, MAURICE *The Outlaws of Medieval Legend* (Routledge and Kegan Paul, London 1961).

18 LEACH, EDMUND 'The legitimacy of Solomon. Some structural aspects of Old Testament history', *Archives Européennes de Sociologie* vol. VII, no. 1, 1966, pp. 58–101.

19 MARCUS, JOHN T. 'Transcendence and charisma', *The Western Political Quarterly* vol. XIV, no. 1, Part 1, March 1961, pp. 236–41.

20 MARTIN, DAVID A. (ed.) *50 Key Words in Sociology* (Lutterworth, London 1970).

21 MICHELS, ROBERT *First Lectures in Political Sociology*, translated by Alfred de Grazia (Harper Torchbooks, New York 1965).

22 NEUMANN, FRANZ *Behemoth. The Structure and Practice of National Socialism 1933–1944* (Octagon Books, New York 1963).

23 NYOMARKAY, JOSEPH *Charisma and Factionalism in the Nazi Party* (University of Minnesota Press, Minneapolis 1967).

24 OOMEN, T. K. 'Charisma, social structure and social change', *Comparative Studies in Society and History* vol. X, no. 1, 1967, pp. 85–99.

25 PARSONS, TALCOTT 'Authority, legitimation, and political action', in FRIEDRICH, CARL JOACHIM, *Authority*, op. cit.

26 RATNAM, K. J. 'Charisma and political leadership', *Political Studies* vol. XII, no. 3, October 1964, pp. 341–54.

27 ROBERTSON, ROLAND *The Sociological Interpretation of Religion* (Basil Blackwell, Oxford 1970).

28 RUNCIMAN, W. G. *Sociology in its Place* (Cambridge University Press, Cambridge 1970).

29 SHILS, EDWARD 'Tradition and liberty: antinomy and interdependence', *Ethics* vol. LXVIII, no. 3, April 1958, pp. 153–65.

30 SHILS, EDWARD 'The concentration and dispersion of charisma. Their

bearing on economic policy in underdeveloped countries.' *World Politics* vol. 11, no. 1, 1958, pp. 1–19.

31 SHILS, EDWARD 'Charisma, order, and status', *American Sociological Review* vol. 30, no. 2, April 1965, pp. 199–213.

32 SHILS, EDWARD 'Charisma', in *International Encyclopaedia of the Social Sciences*.

33 SPENCER, MARTIN E. 'Weber on legitimate norms and authority', *British Journal of Sociology* vol. XXI, no. 2, June 1970, pp. 123–34.

34 WARE, TIMOTHY *The Orthodox Church* (Penguin Books, Harmondsworth, Middlesex 1964).

35 WEBER, MAX ' "Objectivity" in Social Science and Social Policy', in *The Methodology of the Social Sciences*, translated and edited by Edward A. Shils and Henry A. Finch (Free Press, New York 1949).

36 WEBER, MAX *The Theory of Social and Economic Organization*, translated by A. M. Henderson and Talcott Parsons (Free Press, New York 1964).

37 WILSON, JOHN 'The sociology of schism' in HILL, MICHAEL (ed.) *A Sociological Yearbook of Religion in Britain—4*, op. cit.

38 WORKMAN, HERBERT BROOK *The Evolution of the Monastic Ideal* (Charles H. Kelly, London 1913).

39 WORSLEY, PETER *The Trumpet Shall Sound* (MacGibbon and Kee, London 1968).

8

Charisma: Routinization or Evaporation?

IN CHAPTER 7 it was argued that the concept of charismatic authority becomes much less problematic and precarious when it is located in the theoretical framework of types of legitimate authority. The fact that charisma has been questioned as an isolated and in many ways eccentric concept largely stems from this failure to put it in its full context. Charismatic legitimacy is not merely a residual category for explaining social change, since both rational-legal and traditional authority contain dynamic elements. Traditional authority in particular contains an important source of potential leverage, which has been little exploited by sociologists in their studies of social or religious systems that incorporate the myth of a period of pristine authenticity in their history. Above all, the types of legitimate authority are constructed as accentuations and exaggerations of features that would rarely, if ever, be found in such abstract purity in empirical reality, and charismatic authority is no different from the other two types in this respect. However, Weber seems to have anticipated that the interpretation of charismatic authority might cause problems, because in his remarks on the methodological basis on the ideal types of legitimate authority he explicitly dealt with it. He did this by expanding the concept of 'pure' charisma into a continuum which depicted the routinization of charisma. A central issue in the development or decay of any charismatic movement was the death of the original leader and the substitution in place of the leader's personal authority of a more permanent, institutionalized structure of authority. This Weber saw as only one aspect of the process of routinization, which involved both structural and ideological changes. To this we will shortly turn; but some important roots of the process must first be analysed in the *career* of charismatic leaders.

If charismatic legitimacy depends on the recognition by followers of signs and proofs, which demonstrate that the individual claiming authority has personal access to exceptional inspiration, then we will find a valuable line of investigation in tracing the whole *career* of individuals in authority in order to identify exactly when they appear to be manipulating symbols that can validly be termed charismatic, and when they fit more closely into the alternative categories of authority. A recent study has noted that 'built into the repertoire of tactics and strategies of charismatics is the knowledge (intuitive or otherwise) that in a traditional setting the value of the message is judged by the personal qualities of the bearer. Thus it is through image-making and accentuation of personal qualities that the charismatic obtains a lever on the public and facilitates his recognition.' [36:5] On this basis we can criticize the tendency to look for evidence of charisma only among leaders already *in power*, since this ignores the fact that once in power a leader can, through propaganda and other means which are by then at his disposal, significantly manipulate his image so as to project an aura of charisma. I do not think we should place too much emphasis on the *conscious* manipulation of symbols, because this leads only too easily to the kind of reified notion of charisma which is illustrated in Apter's statement that Nkrumah 'understood neither charisma nor his normative obligations. He did not realize that charisma in a voluntaristic environment is based on populism, and that when it declined, that same populism was likely to turn the leader and his government into enemies of the people.' [4:788] However, if we rid the discussion of this unwarranted assumption we can usefully analyse the career of at least one religious leader in terms of his appeal to different sources of legitimacy.

Norman Cohn's account in *The Pursuit of the Millennium* of the career of Jan Bockelson, the messianic leader of the Anabaptists of Münster, contains some fascinating insights on the charismatic career of a religious revolutionary. [8] The establishment of Anabaptism in Münster as a New Jerusalem was originally accomplished by disciples of the Dutch Anabaptist leader, Jan Matthys, and it was in the role of disciple that Bockelson first arrived in the town. The arrival of Matthys himself consolidated the Anabaptist position, and he and Bockelson began systematically to eliminate the Lutheran and Roman Catholic elements in the population, which precipitated a siege by the Roman Catholic Bishop. By March 1534 Matthys had established an absolute dictatorship with himself as head, but the same Easter he received a divine command to lead a handful of men against the Bishop's forces, and was consequently cut to pieces, thus creating a vacuum in the structure of authority.

In this situation, Bockelson's acquisition of authority was highly significant, and Cohn sees it as a mixture of political ambition and belief in his own divine purpose:

> He had much shrewdness; he knew how to arouse enthusiasm in the masses and how to use it for his purposes when it was aroused. On the other hand it seems certain that he was himself easily moved to quasi-mystical enthusiasm . . . Bockelson's first important act was—characteristically—at once a religious and a political one. Early in May he ran naked through the town in a frenzy and then fell into a silent ecstasy which lasted three days. When speech returned to him he called the population together and announced that God had revealed to him that the old constitution of the town, being the work of men, must be replaced by a new one which would be the work of God. [8:268]

There are a number of useful observations to be made at this point. First of all, there existed a crisis situation with the death of Jan Matthys: Matthys, the dictator by terror methods of the Anabaptist theocracy, had been removed and the population was in the grip of a siege by the Bishop. The importance of crisis in precipitating what we might term a 'charismatic context' has been noted by several writers. Davies sees three types of crisis as being possible determinants of a charismatic upsurge: (1) feelings of insecurity or anxiety about basic needs; (2) frustration of expected demands due to rising expectations, and (3) persistence of unresolved conflicts between internal or external forces. [9] Eisenstadt has similarly pointed to the importance of charismatic symbols on those occasions or in those situations in which 'routine is to some extent broken or disturbed'. [10:xxvii] Weber made the crucial point himself—though 'without giving it adequate emphasis and elaboration' [34:742]—when he noted that in times of 'psychic, physical, economic, ethical, religious, political distress' the natural leaders 'have been holders of specific gifts of the body and spirit; and these gifts have been believed to be supernatural, not accessible to everybody'. [15:245] Of the followers' devotion to the charismatic leader he says: 'It is a devotion born of distress and enthusiasm.' [15:249]

Another feature of Bockelson's claim to charismatic legitimacy is his demonstration of possession by supernatural forces. In his discussion of the different varieties of charismatic endowment, Weber specifically mentions the importance of trances and seizures as evidence of supernatural possession, and he even notes that for a long time 'it has been maintained that the seizure of the berserk is artificially produced through acute poisoning', and that 'Shamanic ecstasy is linked to constitutional epilepsy, the possession and the testing of which represents a charismatic qualification.' [15:245-6] To this extent, he continues, they are

> just as little edifying to us as is the kind of 'revelation', for instance, of the Sacred Book of the Mormons, which at least from an evaluative standpoint, perhaps would have to be called a 'hoax'. *But sociology is not concerned with such questions.* In the faith of their followers, the chief of the Mormons has proved himself to be charismatically qualified, as have 'heroes' and 'sorcerers'. [15:246, my italics]

In other words, no leader can be labelled charismatic unless he is accredited with the possession of such a quality by his followers: his claim must be evaluated by the 'population' which constitutes his potential followers in the light of those characteristics that may be regarded as having a source in revelation or inspiration, and if this claim is validated, then obedience to the leader—since he is seen as having access to the most highly valued repository of intuitions about the natural world—is a matter of obligation. Recognition is the relational aspect of charismatic authority, because what one 'population' may recognize as a charismatic qualification (epilepsy, for instance) another may recognize as an illness that requires treatment. It is the definition that actors in a situation give to it that is of primary importance, rather than a purely external evaluation of it.

Related to the importance for charisma of this kind of possession and to the more general recognition of charismatic qualifications is the observation—which is very rarely made—that in his most rigorous formulation of the concept of charisma Weber made an even more explicit step away from the 'individualistic' conception when he referred to it as the 'quality of a personality' (*Qualität einer Persönlichkeit*), indicating an abstract category rather than a 'person', a concrete individual. He also qualifies his definition by stating that charisma is a quality 'believed to be extraordinary' (*als ansseralltäglich geltend*). [12:157] The emphasis in these phrases is clearly towards a sociological construction rather than to some vague, quasi-mystical conception of 'Great Men' in history. Nevertheless, we do not have to abdicate the innovatory potential of the concept *entirely* to such determinist notions as that of a 'culture base', [18:119] which dictates the full range of ideas available for articulation, as I hope to show.

There are two further lines of enquiry to be drawn out of the account of the Münster Anabaptists, the first of which can best be traced by following the narrative. Bockelson's tactic of establishing a charismatic claim included denuding himself—the pun is not entirely inappropriate—of all other symbols of authority. The anti-institutional character of charismatic leadership is well demonstrated in this case by the initial break with traditional channels of authority. After establishing his charismatic status, Bockelson seems to have met with only minority opposition, and Cohn notes that the leader's prestige reached its height at the end of August 1534, after the Bishop's forces had been effectively beaten off. At this point Bockelson began to adopt alternative symbols of authority, for he had himself proclaimed King—the Messiah of the Last Days—and gradually accumulated many of the trappings and emblems of secular monarchy. As a response to the increasing luxury of the King and his court and the concomitant poverty of the mass of the people, millennial prophecies promising better things to come were stepped up by means of 'spectacular stunts', including divine trumpets, banquets and public executions. However, the discontent caused by both the siege and the affluence of Bockelson's monarchy brought back into operation the tech-

niques of terror and repression, and thus the situation gravitated
from one in which both charismatic and traditional types of
legitimation were employed to one involving more and more an
overt display of coercion. In this case, charismatic domination
seems to have become embedded in a more traditional type of
authority, and subsequently power relationship.

The other line of enquiry is even more interesting, for it shows
just how important is the role of ideas in understanding charisma.
We note from Cohn's account that: (a) Bockelson already had a
position of considerable power when Matthys was killed; and
(b) the first activity that Bockelson engaged in after his original
demonstration of charismatic possession was the promulgation
of *new obligations* in the form of a new political structure with
himself as head. It is no exaggeration to say that the lack of
evidence of new obligations in the programme of many figures
who have uncritically been labelled 'charismatic' has been a major
cause of the dilution of the concept. Similarly, the notion that
charismatic leaders only arise outside an existing institutional
structure has diverted attention from individuals within institutions who have made charismatic claims. Tucker, whose treatment of charisma is one of the most perceptive in recent sociological literature, has integrated the concept of leader and message
in a succinct way:

> I do not mean to suggest that a charismatic leader acquires
> charisma exclusively because of his inspirational sense of
> mission and belief in the movement, or even that his personality
> *per se*, independently of the content of his message, is sufficient
> explanation for his impact upon his followers. We cannot
> properly say of charismatic leaders that 'the medium is the
> message', although it is a large part of it. They offer to followers
> and potential followers not simply and solely their extraordinary
> selves as instruments of leadership, but also a formula or set
> of formulas for salvation. [34:750-1]

The importance of the charismatic message is given a most
impressive treatment in Berger's reappraisal of the social location
of Israelite prophecy. [5] It was in the study of the prophetic
movement of ancient Israel that Weber discovered the archetype
of the charismatic leader, and to this extent his formulation can be

said to stand or fall on the evidence which has since been accumulated about these historical figures. The effect of Berger's research is to give less emphasis to the non-institutional location of the pre-exilic prophets, but at the same time to provide a much better understanding of the place of charisma in the autonomous generation of religious ideas. Weber had recognized that the prophetic books of the old Testament were based on an earlier form of prophecy called Nabiism, which was an ecstatic religious practice common to other religious traditions as well as to ancient Israel.

In the old Testament Nabiism first emerges in the form of war prophecy, where the Israelite prophets appear as bands of military dervishes who proclaim the holy wars of Yahweh against the Canaanites. Their social location at this time was in the loosely organized, semi-nomadic armies of the Israelite tribal confederacy, but with the establishment and consolidation of the monarchy, especially under Solomon, and the accompanying demilitarization of the peasantry and growth of a permanent military organization under the King, this type of prophecy became obsolete. However, in the ninth century B.C. and subsequently a new kind of prophecy emerged, characterized not by ecstasy as a source of inspiration but by the development of a group of political and military ideologists who formed 'a stratum of genteel intellectuals'. [40:279] Furthermore, their message was no longer one of good fortune but rather one of judgement and doom, and these 'emissary prophets' were seen as standing in opposition to the official institutional structure of the monarchy and priesthood. Their interest was not in acting as spokesman for protest movements but in 'gratuitous oracles' based on ethical considerations. Moreover, Weber was quite explicit that it was not so much the message they brought that resulted in their independent social location as the reverse: 'The complete inner independence of the prophets was not so much a result as a most important cause of their practice'. [40:278-9] Because they were socially detached their message was gratuitous: 'One does not pay for evil omens nor expose oneself to them.' [40:279] Thus Weber was quite categorical in fixing the social location of prophecy *outside* the institutional setting.

However, Berger finds the problem more complex as a result

of recent historical scholarship, which suggests a much closer relationship between the prophets and the official religious institutions. In the first place, he agrees that there did quite unmistakably occur a new orientation in Israelite prophecy in the eighth century B.C., but the sociological problem is to determine how this new orientation related to the institutional structure of Israelite religion. Here he notes the enormous influence of Protestant historical scholarship on our image of Old Testament history, and in particular: 'One of the stereotypes connected with this image is the notion of the prophets as opponents of the priests, brave individualists defying the religious authorities of their time . . . In this way, the prophets are made to appear as proto-Protestants of an earlier dispensation.' [5:942–3] Berger indicates how the Protestant historians deduced this priest/prophet dichotomy by quoting a more recent account of the canonical prophets by Jepsen in which the following argument appears: 'Everything professional, everything which would make of God a certain possession and would want to dispose of Him, is alien to them [the canonical prophets]. . . . They cannot dispose of God, but He disposes of them. Their preaching can therefore never become a profession.' [5:943] The word 'therefore' in the final sentence clearly expresses the sociological reasoning, for it shows that the social location of the prophets is deduced from the content of their religious message. This is the procedure that Berger finds most questionable, and his main argument is that Weber, whose studies of ancient Judaism first appeared in 1917–19, though basing his research on the best historical scholarship then available, was limited in his analysis by the tendency of the historical accounts to adopt this established Protestant perspective.

More recent scholarship has regarded the earlier prophetic form of Nabiism as having been incorporated *within* the official religious institutions, with the result that the official religion contained two elements: one was the 'sacramental' element, consisting in actions on behalf of the community directed towards the divinity; and the other was the 'sacrificial' element, consisting in actions on behalf of the divinity addressed to the community. The sacramental functions were those that could be labelled priestly, and the sacrificial ones correspond with the prophetic function. Such functions were not always differentiated, but in

some cases special cultic officials would be assigned to the prophetic function. In sociological terms, the incorporation of
originally personal, ecstatic charismatic elements into an official
religious institution represents a routinization of charisma, and
although Berger rejects the term 'charisma of office' in favour of
'charismatic office' he nevertheless shows how various degrees of
'domestication' occurred in the prophetic element: 'At first, only
the time of prophetic utterance was liturgically fixed. Later, the
content of such utterances was fixed too, so that it contained
nothing but the prophetic style.' [5:944] Given the evidence that
the routinized charismatic role of prophet existed within the
official religious institution, one writer has even reversed the
logic of deduction from social location by arguing: 'If the *nabi* is
attached to the sanctuary, it is clear than one must not put too
much emphasis on the pronouncements in the prophetical
"books" which seem to be directed against the cult [= official
institutions].' [5:946] Once again, by a logical skid the medium
has become the message.

Berger's solution to these conflicting interpretations, based on
an emerging consensus between Biblical scholars, is vital for our
later discussion of routinized charisma. He suggests that the
'canonical prophets began their careers as Nabis, socially located
within the cultic institutions, but their message drove them beyond
the cultic definitions of their function'. [5:948] The process by
which this was achieved can be seen as the *radicalization* of the
message, and this radicalization involved 'the staggering idea that
Yahweh might abandon Israel as such'. [5:948] This process
eventually pushed the prophets beyond the functions of their
office in the official religious institutions. The canonical prophets
stand out because of the astounding novelty of their message—
and this is precisely the aspect of 'new obligations' which Weber
saw as typical of charismatic movements. I do not think we need
to distinguish the charismatic office of the cultic prophets from
Weber's notion of office charisma, as Berger does, if we understand by Weber's concept of routinization (Berger's 'domestication') *not* that this represents an 'evaporation' of originally
personal charismatic features but their embodiment in a latent
form in an institutional setting, such that they are always available
as a source from which new obligations may be articulated. This we

will shortly consider, but for the moment let us concentrate on the aspect of 'new obligations'.

The dominant theme in Weber's work was that ideas—and especially religious ideas—must be seen *to some extent* as having a historical efficacy of their own, and therefore they cannot entirely be understood as 'reflections' of underlying social and economic relationships. A charismatic 'breakthrough' represents 'the sudden eruption into history of quite new forces, often linked to quite new ideas'. [5:949] To put it another way, we cannot always postulate a situation in which the 'interests' of a particular group of people in a society are somehow articulated and consciously 'to hand'. Some Marxist writers have indeed used the notion of 'interests' being available against the concept of charisma, for example by suggesting that 'followers with possibly utopian or at least diffuse and unrealized aspirations cleave to an appropriate leader because he articulates and consolidates their aspirations'. [44:xiv] The implication of this statement—especially the phrase *'appropriate* leader'—is that individuals with the requisite predispositions which may perhaps be identified with features of 'the authoritarian personality', [9] shop around for a leader on whom they can project *their* aspirations. Against this we can place the observation that charismatic leaders 'characteristically strive to *accentuate* the sense of being in a desperate predicament. . . . And they propound certain ideas, ranging from the most nebulous to the most definite and concrete, as a way out of the predicament.' [34:751]

The process of 'crisis-production' is well illustrated by the Israelite prophets who, as Berger shows, radicalized their prophecy in just such a direction by proclaiming the frightening idea that Yahweh might abandon his people. Hence the charismatic message is not simply dictated by existing interests, but is significant in initiating a radical definition of the situation of its own. Berger rightly claims that the more recent evidence on the social location of Israelite prophecy strengthens rather than weakens the notion of the innovating characteristic of charisma. Although charismatic claims may be made by individuals who are socially marginal—perhaps coming into a society as strangers and legitimating their authority partly on this criterion—they may also emanate from individuals located in the institutional fabric of society, and may thus take the form of a process of 'radicalization' from within rather than challenge from without. In other words, the message does not necessarily imply the medium. Using Weber's railway analogy which was described above (page 107), we can say that the ideas contained in the charismatic message are the important factors that influence the change in direction of a historical process—these are the switchmen that operate the points—but, pushing the analogy further, the question of whether or not the process gets under way and the speed at which it takes place depends on the driver of the engine. Even so-called 'Great Men' in history have to stay on the rails if they are to become part of history! Once positioned on the new stretch of track, to press the analogy, we are once again involved in the process of 'elective affinity', which was fully treated in chapter 5: in the case of charisma this is one aspect of the process of routinization.

Charismatic authority originates as something 'out of the everyday' (*Ausseralltäglich*) and is therefore precarious, since it is not possible to live 'out of the everyday' for any length of time; as a result, there is a return of the charismatically initiated process to a more everyday existence (*Veralltäglichung des Charisma*): this is 'routinization'. Above all, if the ideas of a charismatic leader are to exert any historical influence they must form the basis for a charismatic group—typically containing the leader and his disciples—and on this basis must develop into a charismatic movement. However, as soon as a sizable following is attracted the original ideas will undergo a process of transformation as the needs and desires of the followers select out of an elect into the charismatic message those features that manifestly coincide with those needs. Thus the ideas achieve their historical importance at the expense of their initial purity. A similar process occurs at the level of organization, and centres on the critical issue of how a successor to the original charismatic leader is designated. Weber lists six methods: (1) an organized search for another bearer of charisma, such as the Dalai Lama of Tibet; (2) the use of oracles, revelation of divine judgement; (3) choice of a successor by the charismatic leader himself and his acceptance by the community of the faithful, for example the selection of Peter by Jesus; (4) choice of a successor by the staff of the charismatic leader and his recognition by the community; (5) an assumption that charisma is inseparable from a blood line and is thus hereditary; (6) transmission by magical or religious means, as for instance in a coronation ceremony.

The observation that charisma can be transmitted to a wide range of institutional roles, many of which will also contain traditional components (as in the case of sacred kingship) and rational-legal components—by election of successors, for example —does seem to create problems, because it might appear that all institutions contain charismatic elements, and such a possibility is sufficient justification in Worsley's view for dropping the term charisma and referring to a 'mythological charter' where the term 'charisma of office' had previously been used. [44:xlix–1] Parsons, Shils and Eisenstadt, on the other hand, regard the pervasiveness of institutional charisma as implying something very close to Durkheim's notion of the sacred. Indeed, Parsons, dates his own conversion to the latter opinion as recently as 1963: '. . . this individualistic emphasis in Weber's treatment of the concept of charisma has tended to obscure the fact that he treated it not *only* as a quality of an individual person, but also of a normative *order*. The latter reference, for example, is a necessary basis for making use of the important concepts of lineage-charisma (*Gentilcharisma*) and charisma of office (*Amtscharisma*). In this latter context Weber's concept of charisma is identical with Durkheim's concept of the sacred'—and in a footnote he adds '. . . it was only in connection with the present book [the Fischoff edition of *The Sociology of Religion*], and then only on a careful second reading, that I was able to see the resemblance of Weber's charisma in its normative social aspect of Durkheim's concept of the collective sacred. . . .' [42:xxxiv]

So apparently we have two alternatives. Either we take Weber's statement that 'in its pure form charismatic authority may be said to exist only in the process of originating' [41:364] at its face value, and deny that routinization is in any way connected with charisma since it represents its 'evaporation' or transformation into some other type of authority relationship. We may also add to this the criticism view of Worsley that the original attribution of charisma is largely determined by the 'interests' of the followers: in this case we are left with a concept of charismatic innovation that is so restricted as to be virtually trivial. Or alternatively we may apparently view charisma as being so dispersed and pervasive throughout a whole range of institutional areas that its innovatory potential becomes almost nebulous and the term becomes synonymous with 'the central features of man's existence': this option blurs much of the precision which the concept of charisma as a type of legitimate authorty and 'a source of *new obligations* contains.

Without trying to understate these conflicting views, I think we can synthesize some of the more disparate elements by means of the concept of 'latency'. Although the process of routinization is concerned with the development of more formalized roles and ideological definitions, and thus depicts a movement towards traditional or rational-legal types of legitimation, we still hold open the possibility that any institution that claims a charismatic pedigree will retain in its structure of roles a latent form of charisma which is always available as a source of legitimacy for office-holders who are involved in 'the process of innovation. It is also important to note that the claim to be an incumbent in an institution which has such a charismatic pedigree may provide an important measure of leverage when conflicts occur with other institutions which, it can be claimed, have no pedigree of this type.

Perhaps the most important aspect of the 'latency' process is the one that Berger identifies as *radicalization*. The possession of office charisma does not necessarily imply the personal charismatic propagation of new obligations, but it does provide a valid basis on which this may be accomplished. Eisenstadt regards the test of any charismatic leader as:

> his ability to leave a continuous impact on an institutional structure—to transform any given institutional setting by infusing into it some of his charismatic vision, by investing the regular, orderly offices, or aspects of social organization, with some of his charismatic qualities and aura. Thus here the dichotomy between the charismatic and the orderly regular routine of social organization seems to be obliterated—to be revived again only in situations of extreme and intensive social disorganization and change. [10:xxi]

By maintaining the view which sees routinized charismatic institutions as retaining the 'imprint' of their founder we are in a much better position to analyse some of the most crucial 'break-throughs' in the history of Christianity, and on this we will conclude our chapter.

The New Testament account of the events surrounding Christ's death and resurrection is in many ways a classic example of the transfer of power from a charismatic leader to his followers. The statement which is always used to indicate the transfer of leadership from Jesus to Peter is given in Matthew 16:13–20, when Jesus asks his disciples: 'Who do you say I am?' Peter replies, 'You are the Messiah, the son of the living God', and he is then given an apparent position of leadership over the disciples: 'You are Peter, the Rock; and on this rock I will build my church, and the powers of death shall never conquer it. I will give you the keys of the Kingdom of Heaven; what you forbid on earth shall be forbidden in heaven.' There then follows an account of the Transfiguration and the events leading up to the death of Jesus.

In all the Gospel accounts of the resurrection the significant observation is made that an apostolic commission is being given to the disciples to continue their work of spreading the charismatic message. The disciples are described as being gloomy and despondent, and the appearance of Jesus has the important function of revitalizing their mission. Matthew adds an interesting point of detail—which clearly indicates that the authorities were concerned to break the continuity of this charismatic movement—when he writes that after the tomb had been found empty

some of the guards went into the city and reported to the chief priests everything that had happened. After meeting with the elders and conferring together, the chief priests offered the soldiers a substantial bribe and told them to say, 'His disciples came by night and stole the body while we were asleep.' They added, 'If this should reach the Governor's ears, we will put matters right with him and see that you do not suffer.' So they took the money and did as they were told.

The New Testament account also appears to solve one of the problems that Tucker has seen to be crucial for the continuance of a movement which originates in the personal charismatic qualities of a leader. He regards the cult of the leader's death as militating against the transmission of charisma to his successors, and thus charisma does not become 'depersonalized'. [34:754] The different accounts of the resurrection not only serve to reinforce the authority of Peter (Mark 16:7; Luke 24:12; John 21:2–22), but in the case of Luke provide the basis for the charismatic endowment of the apostles which was to occur at Pentecost (Luke 24:49).

In the early history of Christianity we note two of the features of the core group consisting of master and disciples that Wach thought so important for the origin and spread of charismatic movements. On the one hand 'The circle is the supporting and nourishing ground out of which everyone who belongs gains his strength; it is the concrete revelation of the "power" of the master. Attracted by this power, moved by it, and defined through it, the disciples assemble in a circle around the master; followers and helpers assemble in ever wider circles.' [35:21] However, it is characteristic of those movements which have become historically significant that 'the master points not only to himself; he also directs the disciple away from himself'. [35:18–19] Hence the Christian apostolate grew out of the notion of a group of delegates who were sent out by a divine commission, and there is an important conception in the earliest documentary sources that the apostolate was taken to be a charismatic gift *before* it came to be seen as an institution. A church historian has identified one of the key features of charismatic routinization: 'As far as Paul is concerned the connection between the activity and power of the apostle and his personality is accidental, the apostle being nothing more than the servant and administrator of goods belonging to God, and from whom nothing more is demanded than faithfulness.' [16:106] In other words, the transmission of charisma from an originally personal leader involves a process of *depersonalization* and objectifying of the charismatic endowment. [22:240] We have already noted that the cult of a dead leader may be one mechanism through which the transmission of charisma may become blocked. To this we must add the further qualification that when the transfer of charismatic power is seen as being restricted to the original group of disciples, there may also occur a process of blocking, which prevents routinization. This did not happen in early Christianity, though the two views were for a time in competition.

An example of the successful blocking of charismatic routinization is provided by the more recent history of the Catholic Apostolic Church. [19] This group originated in the climate of prophetic millennialism and pentecostal revelations of the 1820s and '30s. Two features resulted in the church's rapid institutionalization and less rapid but seemingly inevitable disappearance. It had, in the first place, a middle- and upper-class membership which found the liturgical and architectural accompaniments of the Catholic revival more congenial than the more spontaneous, emotional style characteristic of less well-heeled sectarianism. Hence a hierarchy of Apostles, Angels, elders, prophets, deacons and underdeacons was soon established, with twelve 'second-called' Apostles at its head. The second feature that blocked any transmission of charismatic roles was the Church's self-conception of being 'an emergency group, having come into being in view of the imminence of the second Advent'. [29:234] When conflict arose over the question of new apostles being called to fill the gaps caused by the death of many of the original ones, the Chief Apostle, Cardale, firmly resisted the proposal. In adopting this strategy, however, the group's eventual demise was virtually assured, and as a recent study shows, the original movement now lingers on with very few members. On the other hand, the schismatic offshoot known as the New Apostolic Church, which originated after the conflict over reappointment of Apostles, still claims some 700,000 members in different parts of the world.

In early Christianity the development of the doctrine of the apostolate played a most important part in providing a guaranteed pedigree from which to exert 'leverage' on heretical protest groups, since

> the Church's organization had to be such that at any time assurances could be given that it was connected by a direct, organic and guaranteed link to the events which were creative of the faith and the means of salvation. . . . For doctrine and organization to be a real bulwark against heresy, they had to have a transcendent origin, an exclusive character, and the value of a norm. [16:112]

However, the depersonalization of charismatic qualifications which was implicit in their attachment to a formal office in the church's hierarchy was itself a source of schismatic upheaval, and this radical element reappeared continually in heretical movements. The Montanist heresy in the latter half of the second century has been seen as an attempt to revert to the primitive fervour of the earliest period of Christian history in the face of growing institutionalization. The Donatist heresy of the fourth century was in principle concerned with the lack of personal qualifications on the part of the consecrator of a local bishop. The growth of an individual, personally charismatic form of monasticism in fourth-century Egypt, which has since been taken as the prototype of the various developments in Christian monasticism, also represents a form of anti-institutional protest.

Examples of extra-institutional charismatic resurgence could be multiplied almost endlessly. On the other hand, the argument that a charismatic origin which becomes institutionally routinized has important implications for innovation *within* the institution, quite apart from that which can be explained by traditional and rational-legal legitimations, is the one that we wish to maintain, in opposition to the view that routinization is synonymous with evaporation.

> The truly decisive question, then, is, whether the growth of a priestly bureaucracy in Christianity has de-Christianized Christianity; in more technical terms, whether the charismatic spirit has fully departed from it, leaving behind nothing but empty forms, fossils, as it were, whether they are words or gestures or dogmas or rituals or any other evidences of a one-time living and burning religious life. [31:206]

Some sociologists have thought that Weber did mean fossilization when he spoke of routinization, but it is possible to demonstrate the impact of latent charisma even in the case of that superficially most uncharismatic of institutions, the Church of England. The changes that this institution experienced in the nineteenth century must be attributed to a number of influences—among them rational-legal conceptions and traditional reinstatements—but at least one component was a 'charismatic resurgence'.

The Thirty-Nine Articles in the Book of Common Prayer have

been given a variety of interpretations, and the most charitable view of them is perhaps contained in the *Oxford Dictionary of the Christian Church*, which states: 'Though not ostensibly vague, they avoid unduly narrow definitions.' [24:1349] Nevertheless, Article 26—'Of the Unworthiness of the Ministers, which hinders not the effect of the Sacrament'—takes a clear position on the Donatist controversy. It is worth quoting at length:

> Although in the visible Church the evil be ever mingled with the good, and sometimes the evil have chief authority in the Ministration of the Word and Sacraments, yet forasmuch as they do not the same in their own name, but in Christ's, and do minister by his commission and authority, we may use their Ministry, both in hearing the Word of God, and in the receiving of the Sacraments. Neither is the effect of Christ's ordinance taken away by their wickedness, nor the grace of God's gifts diminished by such as by faith and rightly do receive the Sacraments ministered unto them; which be effectual, because of Christ's institution and promise, although they be ministered by evil men.

The Article then goes on to make provision, in the interests of ecclesiastical discipline, for the removal of ministers who are found to be guilty of malpractice. But the effect of this statement is undoubtedly the emphasis it places on the *depersonalized* possession of qualifications which are then *objectively* dispensed by appealing to the authority of the founder: in other words, it is concerned with charisma of office. Given the possibility of such a claim to a source of legitimacy which was in one important respect quite distinct from that of the surrounding institutions, the holders of routinized charismatic offices in the Church of England had a point of 'leverage' against these other institutions.

It was precisely this point that the leaders of the nineteenth-century Oxford Movement adopted as an important ideological weapon, and if we look at the immediate background to their 'innovations' (which in a limited historical context they definitely were) we can understand why. The Church of England had always had a very close relationship with the State apparatus—in the eighteenth century it became virtually the ecclesiastical wing of the secular establishment—and on the whole it had not rejected the privileges it gained from this alliance. But the arrival of a Whig government under the premiership of Earl Grey gave the situation a completely different meaning. The Whigs were committed to reform of the Church of England—Grey had even given the bishops something on which to ponder in the form of an incomplete biblical exhortation to 'set their house in order' (see 2 Kings 20:1)—and the Government proceeded to suppress ten Irish bishoprics. The notion of crisis which could be stimulated by the rallying call 'The church in danger' was amplified by the possibility that the churchmen on whose behalf the Tractarian leaders spoke 'had no considered theory of the Church' [11:319] and thus had no solid basis for resisting incursions by the State.

Again we see two of the common features of a charismatic reorientation—the perception, even the accentuation, of crisis and the absence of other institutional means towards articulating a solution. The Tractarians in response to this perceived threat put forward a doctrine of the Church of England as a '*perfecta societas* set over against the State', [21:112] and Newman in particular appealed to the charismatic pedigree of the Church. In the first of the *Tracts for the Times* which were the Oxford Movement's manifesto and from which they derived their name, Newman began by reminding his clerical readership of the exceptional features of their office: 'It is plain then that he [the bishop] but *transmits*; and that the Christian Ministry is a *succession*. And if we trace back the power of ordination from hand to hand, of course we shall come to the Apostles at last . . . all we, who have been ordained Clergy, in the very form of our ordination acknowledged the doctrine of the Apostolical Succession.' [7:65] But this argument is then turned into an exhortation: 'Therefore, my dear Brethren, act up to your professions. Let it not be said that you have neglected a gift; for if you have the Spirit of the Apostles on you, surely this *is* a great gift. "Stir up the gift of God which is in you."' [7:66]

The whole of the church history of the nineteenth century is indeed a very instructive comment on the immense importance for ecclesiastical institutions of claims to legitimacy involving office charisma. The claims and counter-claims of the Church of England and the Roman Catholic Church over the validity of Anglican Orders culminating in Leo XIII's encyclical *Apostolicae Curae* are one example. The curious ecumenical experiment known as the Order of Corporate Reunion, which, rather like an ecclesiastical chain-letter, proposed a scheme whereby clergy in a number of different churches would be ordained by bishops from other bodies, presumably with the intention of eventually establishing a unified church with a single valid apostolic succession, is another example. [6; 39, chap. 5] One should perhaps also mention the even more curious brand of ecclesiastical entrepreneurs known as *Episcopi Vagantes*, whose obscure claims to valid episcopal consecration resulted in what can only be called 'free-floating office charisma'. [1] The basic point, however, is a serious one. The routinization of charisma is not a process involving the 'evaporation' or 'fossillization' or originally personal charisma. The latter retains a degree of latency which may emerge as extra-institutional challenge or intra-institutional leverage: in either case, it is a source of innovation.

In the last two chapters it has been argued that Weber's category of charismatic authority, if rescued from the ravages of 'current fashionable usage', provides an indispensable tool for the analysis of social change, and that it is of special importance in the study of religious movements. By locating it firmly against the background of the concept of legitimacy and in the context of the two alternative types of traditional and rational-legal authority— bearing in mind that these are the filters through which we approach the mixture of concrete empirical reality—it may perhaps emerge as less of a precarious residual category than it has some-times been presented. Above all, charisma is a source of new ideas and obligations, and in the perspective of Weber's sociology of ideas it can be seen as one way in which shifts occur in the histori-cal process, only to be drawn again into the mainstream of histori-cal development, though not without leaving an imprint which may provide a subsequent source of innovation. Since religious ideas in their origin are *par excellence* ideas with a large measure of 'interest-free' autonomy, we may expect to find charismatics important in the religious sphere: furthermore, the claim to divine inspiration and revelation involves an explicitly religious orien-tation, and it is just such a claim that is often made by a charismatic.

Similarly, in traditional societies, where personal incumbency is a significant defining characteristic of institutional authority roles, the personal claim of the charismatic leader is more likely to meet with a resonant response on the part of his audience.

REFERENCES

1 ANSON, P. F. *Bishops at Large* (Faber and Faber, London 1964).

2 APTER, DAVID E. *The Gold Coast in Transition* (Princeton University Press, Princeton 1955).

3 APTER, DAVID E. *Ghana in Transition* (Atheneum, New York 1966).

4 APTER, DAVID E. 'Nkrumah, charisma, and the coup', *Daedalus* vol. 97, no. 3, Summer 1968, pp. 757–92.

5 BERGER, PETER L. 'Charisma and religious innovation: the social location of Israelite prophecy', *American Sociological Review* vol. 28, no. 6, December 1963, pp. 940–50.

6 BRANDRETH, H. R. T. *Dr Lee of Lambeth* (SPCK, London 1951).

7 COCKSHUT, A. O. J. *Religious Controversies of the Nineteenth Century: Selected Documents* (Methuen, London 1966).

8 COHN, NORMAN *The Pursuit of the Millennium* (Paladin, London 1970).

9 DAVIES, JAMES C. 'Charisma in the 1952 campaign', *American Political Science Review* vol. XLVIII, no. 4, December 1954, pp. 1083–1102.

10 EISENSTADT, SAMUEL N. *Max Weber on Charisma and Institution Building* (University of Chicago Press, Chicago 1968).

11 FABER, GEOFFREY *Oxford Apostles* (Penguin Books, Harmondsworth, Middlesex 1954).

12 FABIAN, JOHANNES 'Charisma and cultural change: the case of the Jamaa movement in Katanga (Congo Republic)', *Comparative Studies in Society and History* vol. 11, no. 2, 1969, pp. 155–73.

13 FAGEN, RICHARD R. 'Charismatic authority and the leadership of Fidel Castro', *Western Political Quarterly* vol. XVIII, no. 2, Part 1, June 1965, pp. 275–84.

14 GELLNER, ERNEST 'Pouvoir politique et fonction religieuse dans l'Islam marocain', *Annales* no. 3, May–June 1970, pp. 699–713.

15 GERTH, H. H., and MILLS, C. WRIGHT *From Max Weber: Essays in Sociology* (Routledge and Kegan Paul, London 1948).

16 GOGUEL, MAURICE *The Primitive Church*, translated by H. C. Snape from the French original of 1947 (George Allen and Unwin, London 1964).

17 HARRISON, PAUL M. *Authority and Power in the Free Church Tradition* (Princeton University Press, Princeton 1959).

18 HOULT, THOMAS FORD *The Sociology of Religion* (Holt, Rinehart and Winston, New York 1958).

19 JONES, R. K. 'The Catholic Apostolic Church—a study in diffused commitment', in HILL, MICHAEL (ed.) *A Sociological Yearbook of Religion in Britain—5* (SCM Press, London 1972).

20 KNOX, RONALD A. *Enthusiasm* (Clarendon Press, Oxford 1950).

21 LASKI, HAROLD J. *Studies in the Problem of Sovereignty* (Yale University Press, New Haven 1917).

22 MARCUS, JOHN T. 'Transcendence and charisma', *The Western Political Quarterly* vol. XIV, no. 1, Part 1, March 1961, pp. 236–41.

23 NEUMANN, FRANZ *Behemoth. The Structure and Practice of National Socialism 1933–1944* (Octagon Books, New York 1963).

24 THE OXFORD DICTIONARY OF THE CHRISTIAN CHURCH, edited by F. L. Cross (Oxford University Press, London 1963).

25 RUDGE, PETER F. *Ministry and Management* (Tavistock Publications, London 1968).

26 RUNCIMAN, W. G. *Sociology in its Place* (Cambridge University Press, Cambridge 1970).

27 SALISBURY, W. SEWARD 'Faith, ritualism, charismatic leadership and religious behaviour', *Social Forces* vol. 34, no. 3, March 1956, pp. 241–5.

28 SCHLESINGER, ARTHUR, JR. 'On heroic leadership and the dilemma of strong men and weak peoples', *Encounter* vol. XV, no. 6, December 1960, pp. 3–11.

29 SHAW, P. E. *The Catholic Apostolic Church* (King's Crown Press, New York 1946).

30 SOBEL, B. Z. 'The tools of legitimation—Zionism and the Hebrew Christian movement', *Jewish Journal of Sociology* vol. X, no. 2, 1968, pp. 241–50.

31 STARK, WERNER 'The routinization of charisma: a consideration of Catholicism', *Sociological Analysis* vol. 26, no. 4, Winter 1965, pp. 203–11.

32 STARK, WERNER *The Sociology of Religion. A Study of Christendom: Volume IV. Types of Religious Man* (Routledge and Kegan Paul, London 1969).

33 THOMPSON, KENNETH A. *Bureaucracy and Church Reform* (Clarendon Press, Oxford 1970).

34 TUCKER, ROBERT C. 'The theory of charismatic leadership', *Daedalus* vol. 97, no. 3, Summer 1968, pp. 731–56.

35 WACH, JOACHIM 'Master and disciple: two religio-sociological studies', *Journal of Religion* vol. XLII, no. 1, 1962, pp. 1–21.

36 WADDELL, R. G. 'Charisma and reason: paradoxes and tactics of originality' in HILL, MICHAEL (ed.) *A Sociological Yearbook of Religion in Britain—5* (SCM Press, London 1972).

37 WALLERSTEIN, IMMANUEL *Africa. The Politics of Independence* (Vintage Books, New York 1961).

38 WALLIS, WILSON DALLAM *Messiahs: their Role in Civilization* (American Council on Public Affairs, Washington 1943).

39 WALSH, WALTER *The Secret History of the Oxford Movement*, 3rd edn. (Church Association, London 1898).

40 WEBER, MAX *Ancient Judaism*, translated and edited by Hans H. Gerth and Don Martindale (The Free Press, New York 1952).

41 WEBER, MAX *The Theory of Social and Economic Organization* (The Free Press, New York 1964).

42 WEBER, MAX *The Sociology of Religion*, translated by Ephraim Fischoff, introduced by Talcott Parsons (Methuen, London 1965).

43 WILSON, BRYAN R. *Religious Sects* (Weidenfeld and Nicolson, London 1970).

44 WORSLEY, PETER *The Trumpet Shall Sound* (MacGibbon and Kee, London 1968).

9

The Halévy Thesis

CLOSELY RELATED to Weber's thesis of a link between Calvinism and the growth of capitalism is the interpretation given by
Elie Halévy to the importance of religious ideology in preventing
a political revolution in the late eighteenth and early nineteenth
centuries in Britain. 'The Halévy thesis' is in many respects the
political corollary, applied in a more restricted historical and
geographical context, of the broader thesis put forward by Weber,
and there are some interesting parallels between the two. They
were both developed at about the same time (Halévy's first
account was published in 1906), and the major premiss of both is
that religious ideas may exert an important autonomous influence
within a process of social change. A recent assessment of the
current status of the Halévy thesis might almost have been taken
from one of the more sympathetic accounts of Weber's important
study: 'The present status of the Halévy thesis is most curious.
Again and again, in current historical literature, one encounters
the casual but firm assumption that the thesis has been discredited
or at least significantly modified.' [5:292] But the statement that
follows indicates the real difference between the two, for of the
Halévy thesis it is noted: 'Yet in fact there has been no serious or
sustained analysis of it. And the few brief critiques contradict each
other more than they do the thesis itself'. [5:292] While Weber's
work has generated an almost unparalleled amount of sociological
and historical research, the important insight of Halévy has been
almost totally ignored.

In this chapter, Halévy's original interpretation will be developed as being potentially a very valuable device for understanding
the role of religious ideas in social change. Just as it was earlier
suggested that one of the proofs of the Weber thesis lies in the use

of *chronology* as a technique for gauging the relative autonomy of religious factors, so it will be found that the historical sequence that can be traced between religious and political movements has become an important issue in the arguments of sociologists and historians over the extent to which religion ever operates as an independent variable. In the following chapter, the wealth of material on millennial movements—and especially the studies of cargo cults—will be set in the framework of alternating religious and political solutions to the problems experienced when societies undergo a process of rapid social change.

Halévy was primarily interested in the history of nineteenth-century England, but he drew his background material from as far back as the early eighteenth century. His main preoccupation was with explaining 'the extraordinary stability which English society was destined to enjoy throughout a period of revolutions and crises; what we may truly term the miracle of modern England, anarchist but orderly, practical and business like, but religious, and even pietist'. [3:339] And he clearly saw that no simple answer could be given using the evidence of English religious institutions, for he regarded them as intricate and complex and a source of disorder, even anarchy, in the seventeenth century. However, the key to the problem in his view lay with the eighteenth-century Methodist and Evangelical revival: it is crucial to an understanding of his explanation that he was interested not simply in Methodism, nor solely in the influence of this religious movement on the emergent industrial working class, but in the broader permeation of the Methodist revival through the Evangelical movement. Thus he summarized his position: 'We shall witness Methodism bring under its influence, first the dissenting sects, then the establishment, finally secular opinion.' [3:339] It is perhaps ironic that the aspect of Halévy's thesis that might have provided the basis for a thoroughgoing Marxist analysis of religious legitimation among members of a ruling class, and for which evidence will later be given, has been so little pursued, as a result of the preoccupation with Methodism and its supposed influence on the working class.

The period in which the Methodist revival began (Halévy dates its origin as 1739, the year in which Wesley began his field-preaching among the Kingswood miners) is seen as one of general

disturbance characterized by economic and political crisis and by
strikes and riots. 'Similar conditions a half-century later must have
given rise to a general movement of political and social revolution,'
notes Halévy in an historicist parallel which is intended to convey
the significant effect of the religious revival. [3:341] But in 1739
the revolt assumed a different form as the discontented workers
came under the influence of Wesley and his followers and substituted
a new religious fervour in place of their mood of incipient revolt.

In pointing to the fact that John and Charles Wesley and their
colleague George Whitfield were all Anglican clergymen with a
deep commitment to the defence and regeneration of the established church, Halévy indicates the impeccable social location
of the original leaders of the movement. On the other hand,
partly owing to the 'radicalization' of the message being preached
—which Halévy describes as an 'eccentric style of preaching' and
'doctrinal extravagance'—the Methodists found themselves barred
from many Anglican churches and thus became increasingly a
marginal group on the frontier of the Church of England, and it
was here that the vast organization of Methodism was founded.
Halévy obviously regarded as central to his thesis the 'double
environment' of Methodism, which it derived from its Anglican
origins and its increasingly close identification with nonconformist dissent. Viewed thus, Methodism takes on the role of a
movement which filled both a social *and* an ideological vacuum,
and in doing so opened up the channels of social and ideological
mobility (for this is what Halévy goes on to argue), which worked
against the polarization of English society into rigid social
classes, each with a distinct ideology that could be given religious
expression.

The importance of Methodism is thus to be seen in terms of its
distinctiveness, both from nonconformist dissent, which Halévy
regarded as taking on many of the characteristics of a relaxed and
to a large extent inert religious observance in the eighteenth
century, and Anglicanism, which became closely identified with
the privileges and abuses of the secular establishment. 'An
Established Church apathetic, sceptical, lifeless; sects weakened by
rationalism, unorganized, their missionary spirit extinct. This was
English Protestantism in the 18th century.' [3:359] In this environment the influence of Methodism was more quickly felt among the

nonconformist groups than by the Church of England, Halévy argued—though there is evidence to suggest that its impact on the Church of England was being felt by the end of the eighteenth century. In one sense, the effect on nonconformity was an unintended consequence of the Methodist revival, at least as far as John Wesley was concerned, since the original goal had been to revitalize the Church of England, but Halévy thinks it became impossible for the Methodist societies to remain faithful to a church which repudiated them: a separate organization also brought with it certain compensations in the form of enhanced ministerial status and freedom of action. As a result, Methodism 'exported' Anglicanism and adopted an interstitial role in terms of its organization between the Church of England and nonconformity:

> In short, the Methodist connexion adopted a position intermediate between the Establishment and the older Nonconformist bodies. It thus constituted a transition between the former and the latter, which became the more insensible when new sects arose in turn from Wesleyanism and occupied the space between the Connexion and the original sects. [3:363]

Halévy's model of social mobility through religious mobility is equally interesting, although in the absence of detailed historical research it remains hypothetical. In order to become a member of the establishment, he argues, it was necessary for a wealthy dissenter to join the Church of England: 'If a successful man of business wished to enter the governing class, to entertain at his country seat the clergy or the gentry of the neighbourhood, to obtain a title or a position in the Civil Service, he must not be a Dissenter'. [3:370] Here there seems to be an implied equation between dissent and business success, and Halévy elsewhere depicts the social composition of nonconformity as being primarily lower middle class. The argument continues:

> Puritan nonconformity thus tended to become a transitional creed, a stage in the history of an English family. The unskilled labourer becomes in turn a skilled workman, an artisan, the head of a small business, a business man possessed of a modest capital, and as he rises out of the barbarism in which the working class was plunged, he becomes a Nonconformist. If he himself rises still higher on the social ladder, or if his children rise

after his death, he or they go over to the Church of England. [3:371]

The significance of Wesleyan Methodism in this process was that it stood in an intermediate position between dissent and established religion and was thus able to ease the transition from one to another:

> The constitution of the Wesleyan body rendered the transition imperceptible. And what is most characteristic of the new spirit in Dissent is its acceptance of this subordinate position. The middle-class Nonconformist was content to be despised by the members of a Church which his own family might some day enter. He compensated himself by indulging an even deeper contempt for the common people of the fields or factories from whom his family had emerged. [3:371]

Halévy's notion of social and religious progress moving in parallel presents an interesting reworking of the idea, which was discussed in the section on Comte in chapter 2, of religion as a source of 'supernatural blinkers'. The nonconformist bourgeois is seen as possessing much the same pair of blinkers as Comte's Protestant or Gibbon's recluse fanatic, only in this case their purpose is the one which is more normally associated with blinkers, which is to keep the wearer on a forward track. The interpretation of the role of religion in social change which Halévy develops relates also to more recent findings in the sociology of education. Educational movement, like religious movement, may be regarded symbolically as an indicator of social position, and various pieces of research, including an interesting study by Himmelweit on the social background and attitudes of school-teachers, suggests that over-conformity to the prevailing norms of the most prestigious educational institutions may be more typical of individuals who have been upwardly socially mobile than of others. [8] At all events, there is an explicit hypothesis in Halévy's account which it might be possible to test.

The logic of the next part of his argument is the common stock of many discussions of 'the religious factor', and takes the form of a successive elimination of other factors which might be held responsible for the features observed, leaving religion as the only other variable present which might explain them. The problem for

Halévy is: 'why was it that of all the countries of Europe England has been the most free from revolutions, violent crises and sudden changes? We have sought in vain to find the explanation by an analysis of her political institutions and economic organiza- tion'. [3:371] England's political institutions were such that society might have lapsed into anarchy had there existed in England—and here the emphasis given by Halévy is important to note—a *bourgeoisie* which was animated by the spirit of revolution. Similarly, the system of economic production was sufficiently disorganized to make revolution possible had there only existed middle-class leaders who could have provided the working class with articulate and effective leadership. 'But the élite of the working class, the hard-working and capable bourgeois, had been imbued by the Evangelical movement with a spirit from which the es- tablished order had nothing to fear.' [3:371]

Halévy's view of the *bourgeoisie* as potential providers of rev- olutionary leadership for the new industrial proletariat might appear almost bizarre unless we bear in mind that Halévy was working with an implied contrast between English and French history at the end of the eighteenth and beginning of the nine- teenth centuries. In both societies there existed a powerful *traditional* ruling class against which the aspirations of both the proletariat and the new middle class might be directed. In France the aspirations of the bourgeoisie had been blocked, with radical consequences, but in England there existed sufficiently fluid channels of social mobility, together with an inbuilt mechanism of anticipatory socialization through the 'transitional' creed of Evan- gelicalism, to allow a more stable accommodation of the newer social groups into the established order. In brief, the Halévy thesis, rather than concerning itself primarily with the question of an 'opiate for the masses', is an early version of the *embourgeoise- ment* thesis.

The next stage of Halévy's argument is concerned with the origins of the trade-union leadership after 1815. He remarks that Continental observers have always pointed to the distinctive charac- teristics of the leaders of the English labour movement, who are

sometimes blamed for their middle-class morality and want of imagination, at others praised for their solid virtue and capacity for organization. Perhaps these qualities and defects are inseparable; in any case they derive from a common origin. The majority of the leaders of the great trade-union movement that would arise in England within a few years of 1815 will belong to the Nonconformist sects. They will often be local preachers, that is practically speaking ministers. Their spiritual ancestors were the founders of Methodism. In the vast work of social organization which is one of the dominant characteristics of nineteenth-century England, it would be difficult to overestimate the part played by the Wesleyan revival. [3:372]

And it is clear that Halévy regarded the conservative, Tory strain in Wesleyan Methodism—which was strongly embodied in John Wesley's own leadership and ably perpetuated in the nineteenth-century leadership of Jabez Bunting—as one of its most characteristic features. He quotes from the 1792 statutes of the Wesleyan body, which state: 'None of us shall either in writing or in conversation speak lightly or irreverently of the Government. We are to observe that the oracles of God command us to be subject to the higher powers; and that honour to the King is there connected with the fear of God.' [3:373]

Finally, having traced the links upwards from dissent through Methodism to the Church of England, Halévy forges an important link down from the Church of England to Methodism: he attributes a decisive influence to the Evangelical movement in the Church of England.

To be sure John Wesley had been driven from the church of which he was an ordained priest. But he had left a rear-guard behind him which persisted in the attempt to realize his original dream, not the creation of a new sect, but the regeneration of the Church herself . . . If the Wesleyan sect, with its hierarchic constitution, and frank political conservatism, constituted the High Church of Nonconformity, the new Low Church or evangelical party was a species of Anglican Methodism. [3:379]

Thus a mutual accommodation took place: Wesley exported Anglicanism to the new social strata, which might have been expected to provide radical leadership for the industrial working class; while in turn, the Evangelical movement in the Church of England imported much of the fervour and a few of the techniques, including in some cases itinerant preaching, [1] of the Wesleyan revival.

There is little doubt that the evangelizing success of Wesleyanism stimulated a parallel movement in the Church of England, and it is principally through the efforts of this movement that Halévy sees influence being brought to bear on the governing élite, especially in the early years of the nineteenth century. The 'Clapham Sect', one of the most characteristic embodiments of the Evangelical movement in the Church (it was not a 'sect' in any sociological meaning of the term but an informal grouping of like-minded individual members of the Church of England), consisted of wealthy Anglicans who were 'at bottom conservative in their attitude to the social order', [12:294] but their role in Halévy's view was very much one of upward linkage: 'This was a group of laymen who linked the Evangelical clergy with the world of politics and business to which they belonged.' [3:380] Nor were the members of the Evangelical movement narrowly committed to the Church of England, for 'they systematically refused to interest themselves in the theological differences which held Protestants apart'. [3:382] This was to prove of immense value in the programme which the Evangelicals did so much to propagate and which was subsequently such a marked feature of the Victorian ethos—the programme of individual moral (as against collective social) reform.

This is a fairly comprehensive, though necessarily brief, summary of the Halévy thesis. Its major concern is with the importance of social and religious linkage and mobility, and little space has been devoted in the initial outline to the important secondary theme of religion as an 'opiate', which channelled off secular revolutionary fervour. In part, this is more appropriately considered in the context of criticisms and elaborations of Halévy's interpretation, but it can also be treated in terms of the attention which was given by the governing élite of the late eighteenth and early nineteenth centuries to the issue of the moral regeneration of English society. Wesley may well have exported from within the Church of England a conservative ethic to potentially disaffected social groups, but the Evangelicals in the Church of England reimported much of Methodism's fervour and moral preoccupations, and the final stage of this process can perhaps best be

? dating.

seen as the redirection of religious concern—at a time of serious social and political crisis in England—into the growth of foreign missions. We will shortly return to this topic.

Much as Fischoff has viewed the proponents and opponents of Weber's thesis regarding the rise of capitalism in the West in terms of their attitudes to capitalism, Himmelfarb sees the reactions of historians of Wesleyanism in a similar polemical perspective: either they accept Halévy's thesis for good and bad—'that is, they accept the fact that a conservative and counter-revolutionary force might have had liberalizing and humanitarian effects' [5:293]—or they reject it for good and bad by denying that Wesleyanism had the significant influence that has been attributed to it [10], or, finally, they accept the large measure of influence that Methodism had, but emphasize its 'progressive' role in the radical Methodist offshoots, the trade union movement and the Labour Party—this is the point that Halévy himself makes in later volumes of his *History*.

Radical historians are seen as mostly following the line of interpretation set out by the Hammonds, and as viewing evangelicalism as an instrument of suppression and reaction in the service of the ruling class: 'Repressive, inhibiting, intolerant, obsessed with spiritual salvation and tormented with the fear of eternal damnation, it distracted men from their economic and social grievances and effectively destroyed any impulse to rebellion'. [5:293] However, the Hammonds also acknowledged that some of the 'unintended' consequences of Methodism might have benefited the working class, for they argue: 'The teaching of Methodism was unfavourable to working-class movements; its leaders were hostile and its ideals perhaps increasingly hostile; but by the life and energy and awakening that it brought to this oppressed society it must, in spite of itself, have made many men better citizens, and some even better rebels.' [5:294] One brief comment on the intended or unintended effects of Evangelicalism in stifling revolutionary fervour: it is not sufficient to *imply*, from the observation that the Methodist and Evangelical movements appear to have mobilized working-class support in an anti-revolutionary direction, that this was the result of conscious manipulation by the ruling class. To put forward such an argument one would need evidence of the way in which Evangelicalism was legitimated *by* the ruling class, and this is why it is so important to consider groups like the Clapham Sect.

E. P. Thompson is a notable proponent of the Halévy thesis, though not of the underlying tone of approval found in Halévy. If anything, he pushes the thesis even further and 'portrays a Methodism that was even more influential than Halévy's and more insidious than Hammonds''. [5:294] Thompson's contribution to the debate is highly significant in the present context because his argument is based throughout on the establishment of a *chronology* in which political activism turns into religious withdrawal. This is certainly one perspective in which to analyse the link between religion and social change: whether it can be seen as the *only* perspective, even using the same historical data as Thompson, is dubious.

The basis of Thompson's argument is the same as Halévy's—that Methodism was closely linked with Toryism and had an ambivalent attitude towards the Church of England, and thus the Wesleyans 'fell ambiguously between Dissent and the Establishment, and did their utmost to make the worst of both world, serving as apologists for an authority in whose eyes they were an object of ridicule or condescension, but never of trust'. [15:385] One of the results of the Establishment's disparagement of Methodism was, according to Thompson, to make it easier for the movement to engage in 'moral espionage'. During the Napoleonic Wars, the gains of Methodism were—according to this account—greatest among the new industrial working class; and the ministerial bureaucracy which was developing at the same time made it easier for the ministers to impose discipline on their followers. In this they served the establishment well, since the Church of England was too 'distanced' from the poor (another echo of Halévy) to have much effect on them. However, Thompson diverges from Halévy on the question of Methodism's social composition. Halévy, being primarily interested in Wesleyan Methodism, sees it more as a religion of the striving bourgeoisie: Thompson locates its class base lower than this when he argues that 'the Methodists—or many of them—*were* the poor'. [15:386] At the same time, he draws on the Weber thesis to suggest that Methodism was a simple extension of the Puritan ethic in a changed environment and was thus exceptionally well adapted 'both to self-made mill-owners and manufacturers and to foremen, overlookers, and sub-managerial groups'. [15:390-1] Therefore, the problem in Thompson's view is one of explaining how, at the beginning of the nineteenth century, Methodism was able to serve simultaneously as the religion of the industrial bourgeoisie and of wide sections of the proletariat.

As far as the bourgeoisie are concerned, Thompson largely accepts the interpretation of Weber and Tawney of the utility of the Puritan work-ethic. He also notes Weber's observation that the capitalist requirement of a disciplined work-force has always encountered 'the immensely stubborn resistance of . . . pre-capitalist labour', [15:392] and that this was especially important in the transition to a system in which labour was exclusively measured in money earnings. The systematization of factory production required that the labour force should be imbued with a disciplined and methodical ethic—a goal that was expressed in the words of a contemporary, 'It is, therefore, excessively the interest of every mill-owner to organize his moral machinery on equally sound principles with his mechanical . . .' [15:397]—and it is in providing such an ethic for the industrial proletariat that Thompson finds an important catalyst im Methodist theology.

If we avoid Thompson's dubious connotation of Methodist theology with 'promiscuous opportunism', [15:348] there are some valid elements of 'elective affinity' between it and the ethic of work-discipline. The Arminian component of Wesleyan Methodism, which emphasized that grace was freely available to all who believed, became conditional on three means of maintaining grace: the first was through service to the church; the second was through religious exercises, especially the reliving of the conversion experience; and the third was through methodical discipline in every aspect of life. Above all, the channelling of spontaneity into 'enthusiastic' religious practices meant that Wesleyan emotionalism was *intermittent* and allowed for the methodical, disciplined and repressed character of everyday life, so that the 'Sabbath orgasms of feeling made more possible the single-minded weekday direction of these energies to the consummation of productive labour'. [15:406]

Having thus established the utility of Methodism as a work-discipline, the next step of the argument is to explain 'why so many working people were willing to submit to this form of psychic exploitation'. [15:411] During the period 1790–1830 three reasons are given: (1) direct indoctrination; (2) the sense of community that Methodism invoked; and (3) the compensation it provided when revolutionary impulses were stifled. Indoctrination was achieved primarily through the evangelical Sunday schools, with their insistence on morality and discipline—'religious terrorism' is the epithet that Thompson takes from Lecky. [15:415] The notion of Methodist fellowship, represented in class and group meetings, provided a new basis of community to replace those that had been disrupted by the urbanization of the Industrial Revolution: this is a process that has often been noted in the growth of sectarian and other face-to-face religious groups during periods of rapid social change. [14]

The third reason given is one that requires close analysis, for Thompson presents a view of Methodism as 'the chiliasm of despair', a form of hysterical reaction to the defeat brought about by counter-revolutionary repression. Himmelfarb notes 'the difficulty presented by Thompson's proposition, which is that England was on the brink of revolution from 1790 to 1832. If Methodism prevailed so widely among the masses and penetrated so deeply into their individual and collective psyche, where did the impulse and perennial threat of revolution come from?' [5:294–5] In one sense, this criticism is justified. In attributing such immense importance to Methodism as a source of the work-discipline that was demanded by the capitalist system, Thompson gives it greater prominence than Halévy as a stabilizing influence. And yet, when it comes to a question of dating the growth of Methodism he is considerably more careful and precise. He notes that the phenomenon of Methodist conversion appears to run in waves between 1790 and 1832, and states specifically that the most substantial growth in Methodist numbers occurred after the eve of the French Revolution, when counter-revolutionary feeling was strongest. Furthermore, he qualifies his account by referring to his explanation as hypothetical: 'This is not the customary reading of the period; and it is offered as an hypothesis, demanding closer investigation'. [15:427]

His interpretation is that the working class was imbued with strong radical hopes before the 1790s, and that they turned only temporarily to religion when these hopes were crushed: 'whenever hope revived, religious revivalism was set aside, only to reappear with renewed fervour upon the ruins of the political messianism which had been overthrown'. [15:427] The advance in numbers lends some weight to Thompson's argument. On the eve of the French Revolution, Methodism claimed about 60,000 adherents in Great Britain, which 'indicated little more than footholds in all but a few of the industrial districts'. [15:427] In 1800 there were 90,619; in 1810: 137,997; in 1820: 191,217; in 1830: 248,529. Furthermore, years that showed most revivalist activity are seen as being periods of maximum political awareness and activity. At this point in the discussion the idea of chronology is brought in.

Thompson rejects the argument that religious revivalism and political activism ran in parallel. Instead, he finds it possible (and *tentatively* suggests) that 'religious revivalism took over just at the point where "political" or temporal aspirations met with defeat'. [15:428] The only precise general example given of this is the wave of revivalism that began in 1813 in the aftermath of Luddism (1811–12) and then gave way to a political revival in the winter of 1816–17. The particular example given is that of the Pentridge 'rising' of June 1817, *after* which a Primitive Methodist revival is claimed to have taken place in the area. More recent evidence suggests that the chronology in this particular case should be reversed: Primitive Methodist activity preceded the 'rising'. [13:42 and 43n.] On empirical grounds, it cannot be claimed that Thompson succeeds in demonstrating the interesting hypothesis that there occurred 'something like an oscillation, with religious revivalism at the negative, and radical politics (tinged with revolutionary millenarianism) at the positive pole'. [15:429]

Eric Hobsbawm's counter-argument to the Halévy thesis asserts basically that Methodism was never as pervasive nor as potent as had been suggested, and that there was no revolution because the ruling class knew when to make concessions and thus never lost control. Behind his argument, however, is a notion of chronology which differs from that of Thompson and which Thompson explicitly attacks. While maintaining a similar position over the prevalence of revolutionary feeling in large parts of the country between 1790 and the late 1840s, he adopts Lenin's view that a deterioration in the conditions of the masses, together with an increase in their political activity, are not sufficient conditions for the emergence of revolution: also necessary is a crisis in the affairs of the ruling order and a body of revolutionaries who are capable of directing and leading the movement—these, he argues, were absent. While this argument detracts somewhat from the emphasis given by Thompson to the 'chiliasm of despair' that was available in Methodism, it does not fundamentally undermine Halévy's original thesis, which was explicitly concerned with the way in which potential working-class leadership was diverted. Hobsbawm's subsequent statement that 'Methodism was not responsible for the moderation and flexibility of the Parliamentary politicians or the Utilitarian radicals' [6:116] appears to be a much more serious challenge to Halévy—whose insistence on the upward permeation of the Wesleyan revival involves us in a consideration of Evangelicalism among the governing élite—until Hobsbawm makes it clear that he will not give any attention to this aspect of the problem: 'In order to demonstrate [that Methodism had no such responsibility] . . . it is necessary to discover—in so far as this is possible—what effect it had on the politics of the British *working classes* in our period . . .' [6:116, my italics] Thus the discussion gravitates from Wesleyan Methodism, which is generally accepted as a group with conservative leadership and a strong lower middle-class element, to the more radical Methodist seceding groups, the Kilhamites or New Connexion (1797), the Primitive Methodists (1811)—'the most purely "proletarian" of the major sects' [6:118]—and the Bible Christians (1815).

Using information drawn from the Religious Census of 1851, Hobsbawm concludes that in the new industrial cities and in some mining areas organized religion *as a whole* was weak, and that the different branches of Methodism could be expected to have a major political influence on popular agitations only in the North, Midlands, East Anglia and the extreme South-west (still a sizable area, although Bristol, Birmingham and London—where a great deal of revolutionary unrest was centred—are specifically excluded). Wesleyan Methodism is seen to have only one stronghold, in the West Riding of Yorkshire. Projecting back from 1851, Hobsbawm argues that at the beginning of the nineteenth century Methodism was numerically much weaker: 'It does not seem likely that a body of, say, 150,000 out of 10 million English and

Welsh in 1811 could have exercised decisive importance.' [6:120] Nor does there appear to be much evidence of the 'moderating influence' of Wesleyans in their early nineteenth-century strongholds, for Luddism and other radical activities were well evidenced in those areas of the West Riding where Wesleyanism was strongest. In fact, 'The truth is that Methodism developed in this area and so did Radicalism.' [6:121] In Cornwall, on the other hand, Wesleyanism was strongest among the miners, who were also weak in radical political activity; but the correlation does not point to the influence of Methodism, since the structure of Cornish industry was responsible for the lack of working-class consciousness. In view of these and similar pieces of evidence, Hobsbawm suggests that although the official leadership of Methodism wished to retain its conservative position, the movement was not strong enough numerically to have much influence, nor were its leaders able to prevent the rank-and-file from forming radical offshoots and from engaging in radical agitation.

The question of chronology is brought up to explain why the effectiveness of official Wesleyan conservatism has often been exaggerated. Hobsbawm challenges the assumption that workers in early industrial Britain turned towards various sects *as an alternative* to revolutionary or radical politics. To some extent they did—though the only examples cited are drawn from continental mystical and quietist sectarianism—but 'there is another kind of religion which might seize the miserable mass of the people at such times. Preachers, prophets and sectarians might issue what the labourers would regard as calls to action rather than to resignation.' [6:123–4] Instead of adopting Thompson's unitary continuum of activism-quietism, in which religious movements are closely identified with the quietist pole and political ones with the activist, Hobsbawm broadens the scope of his analysis to include both quietist and activist religious movements. In this way, the chronological links between religious and political radicalism run in parallel. Methodism is seen as advancing when radicalism advanced, and religious revivals 'normally did *not* occur when economic conditions were coming to their worst, for instance, at the bottom of trade depressions. The periods when Wesleyanism [a more specific application of the perspective] recruited most rapidly . . . were also, with the one exception of the boom-years

1820–4, periods of mounting popular agitation . . .' [6:124]
Reversing the Halévy thesis completely, Hobsbawm argues that
workers became Methodists and radicals for the same reasons,
the logic of this argument is somewhat vague.

Thompson and Hobsbawm maintain quite different interpretations, both of the significance of Methodism and of the chronological links between religious revival and political radicalism, and
yet there has never been a direct confrontation between the two
views. Thus in two of the most important recent treatments of
certain aspects of the Halévy thesis the issues remain unresolved.
However, it can be maintained that too much attention has been
concentrated on the direct influence of Methodism on its (sup-
posedly) working-class membership, and that the major emphasis
of Halévy's construction lies elsewhere. To take up the point made
by Hobsbawm, could part of the explanation for the flexibility of
the ruling class at the beginning of the nineteenth century be
given in terms of the influence of Methodism and Evangelicalism?

An article by Kiernan suggests that it could. [11] Although not
directly intended as an empirical test of the Halévy thesis (Halévy's
name appears only twice in footnotes, and then only in connection
with points of detail), it comes much closer to an understanding
of his argument, because firstly, it concentrates on a wider social
and religious context than that of working-class Methodism; and
secondly, it draws a contrast between the socio-political situation
in England and contemporary developments in France. Kiernan
sets out to document the influence of the French Revolution on the
Evangelical revival in England, and especially on elements within
the upper class, in the late eighteenth and early nineteenth centuries. Some of the implications of his research provide even
better grounds for a Marxian analysis than the accounts of Hobsbawm and Thompson.

The Methodist revival, which began in 1739, is seen as being
greatly influenced in its first 100 years by the complex socio-
economic changes that accompanied its development. But around
the year 1800:

> there was a sudden acceleration, a broadening of a sectarian
> cult into something like a national faith. It may be permissible
> to say that in general, as in this case, religious impulses begin at

the lower social levels, in response to changes to which the mass
of people are more sensitive, because more directly exposed,
than those above them; and that the latter move from hostility
to acceptance only when an external shock comes to emphasize
the dangers of internal discontent. Jacobinism, which abolished
the Christian calendar in France, helped to establish the Victorian Sabbath in England. [11:44]

This identification of all 'religious influences' with lower social
origins is untenable as a generalized hypothesis—certain *types* of
religious expression may originate in this way, but these, as well as
their precise social location, are a subject of immense complexity.
[18] Nevertheless, in so far as the urban lower-middle class and
artisans may be argued to have 'a definite tendency towards
congregational religion, towards religion of salvation, and finally
towards rational ethical religion', [18:96] this may validly be
applied to the inception of Methodism: its 'acceptance' by more
privileged social groups is a matter for detailed historical enquiry
rather than *a priori* assumption. But it is in establishing this upward permeation that Kiernan's study is most important.

Around 1800, it is suggested, the religious enthusiasm of the
Evangelical revival 'was recognized as a possible support of order
and stability'. [11:44] The eighteenth-century upper class had
begun by deriding or denouncing much of the enthusiasm of the
Wesleyan revival, and this in itself was a positive factor when
revivalism came to be enlisted in defence of the established order:
'In religion as in politics, an idea which is to disarm discontents
must at some time, in some sense, have seemed both to friend and
foe an idea of rebellion'. [11:45] Since Jacobinism was so closely
associated with atheism, Christianity became synonymous with
loyalty to the existing social order. However, the Church of
England was not as it stood at the time of the French Revolution
in a strong position to meet the new needs. Its hierarchy, especially
at the top, was closely identified with the governing élite, and its
parochial clergy were either pauperized or had plural livings. Its
theology too had been much influenced by the idea of 'the reason-
ableness of Christianity', but 'a public creed only looks "reasonable" . . . so long as the prevailing relations between man and man
are accepted as reasonable. And when an upper class appeals to

common sense, others follow its example. Reason was now divided against itself. Burke, with tremendous passion, appealed to men's good sense; but so did Thomas Paine'. [11:46] (In just the same way, Weber argued that natural law had become 'deeply discredited' as a result of its use as an ideological weapon, as was shown above—page 153.) There thus appeared side by side two different conceptions of religion: on the one hand, the 'civic religion' of a stable, established society; in contrast to this stood the salvation religion of individual conversion provided by Methodism and the broader Evangelical movement.

In order to regain social stability, some form of common ground was needed between the upper and lower classes, but Kiernan gives evidence of initially substantial opposition from conservatives within the ruling class to the notion of evangelicalism as such a source of common ground: 'To bring the respectable round to this point required both hard experience and able advocacy. The distance they had to travel may be seen by comparison of Burke's *Reflections* (1709) with Wilberforce's *Practical View* (1797)—both addressed to the upper classes, and both immediately applauded by them.' [11:47] While Burke provided an orthodox conservative defence of the Church of England, the Evangelical William Wilberforce (a member of the 'Clapham Sect') advocated the need for a new religious solution to the perils threatening property and political stability. Thus he stated his political case quite openly: his intention was 'to suggest inferior motives to readers, who might be less disposed to listen to considerations of a higher order'. [11:48] In other words Wilberforce was concerned to legitimate, in terms that would gain the support of members of the ruling class, the *political* advantages of a set of *religious* beliefs which he quite genuinely held: 'what was emotionally necessary to him, he could recommend to others as politically necessary. He had no novel ideas; his mind fused together Wesley's conviction that man's soul was in danger, and Burke's that society was in danger. His book came out, appropriately, at the crisis of the great naval mutinies.' [11:48] By combining these two convictions, Wilberforce presented the characteristic Evangelical diagnosis that what lay behind the social crisis of his time was a moral, rather than a political problem: thus it involved all social classes, and Christianity was the only thing that could save the social fabric from falling apart—'Moderating the insolence of power, [Christianity] ... renders the inequalities of the social state less galling to the lower orders, whom also she instructs, in their turn, to be diligent, humble, patient.' [11:48]

Not that Wilberforce argued in favour of some form of simulated religion with which to control the masses. Religion could not merely be set up to serve the State (just as Durkheim later argued that it was no simple practical solution to the incidence of suicide) [2:374-6], and thus Burke's prescription was dismissed: 'Whereas Burke had put the religious horse squarely before the political cart, Wilberforce concealed the horse behind the cart. Or, more properly, he transformed the characters of both.' [11:49] The appeal that Wilberforce made to Evangelical Christianity was in its own way a radical one, since at the time it was a derided, even a suspect creed. But its theological fluidity, its egalitarian distribution of sin and eternal damnation (without disturbing the existing social structure), and the way in which it channelled the sense of social crisis into a conception of individual guilt, left unchallenged the basic structure of English society. As Kiernan notes of the sweeping denunciations of national vice and calls for contrition on the part of the Evangelicals: 'Implicit in such sweeping judgements was a denial of any peculiar blame attaching to griping landlord or brutal mill-owner.' [11:50] But if the rich could not be condemned for grinding the faces of the poor, they were certainly accused, along with the poor, of Sabbath-breaking, since Sabbatarianism was an important plank in the Evangelicals' programme of moral reform. Circulation of the Bible (the British and Foreign Bible Society, which was largely an Evangelical enterprise, was founded in 1804) was another form taken by the national reformation of morals, and it is not without significance that the period 1790-1810 saw a very rapid growth in the number of societies devoted to foreign missionary work: in this way, evangelical fervour was 'exported' in a quite literal sense.

It would be too crude to portray the political consequences of the Methodist revival and the Evangelical revival which it stimulated in the Church of England as intended consequences. Kiernan sometimes comes near to this—as, for instance, when it is claimed that there was in the revival after 1800 'a strong admixture of pretence' [11:54]—although the documentation gives considerable support to most of the arguments. On the other hand, Wilberforce can be credited with having made *manifest*, at an important stage in the history of the Evangelical revival in the Church of England, some of its more politically advantageous *latent* features. Furthermore, Wilberforce was an influential member of the ruling class, and if we are to understand the complex of influences which, in Hobsbawm's view, lay behind the maintenance of sufficient control and flexibility on the part of the ruling class to prevent the development of a revolutionary situation, we must look at the views of legitimators and apologists like Wilberforce *as well as* at detailed statistics of Methodist growth and influence.

The Halévy thesis, we have argued, is not primarily a statement about working-class religiosity (a concept largely disclaimed by Halévy) but about the social and religious linkage and mobility that Methodism made possible, and the resulting influence that Methodism was able to exert, first of all on dissent, '*then the establishment*, finally secular opinion'. [3:339, my italics] By concentrating so much attention on the influence (or lack of it) that the different branches of Methodism were able to exert on their (supposed) working-class membership, the effects of the permeation of Methodism *via* Evangelicalism into the establishment itself, and its propagation by some apologists as a political expedient, have tended to be overlooked. Paradoxically, this same area might provide a valuable empirical test of at least one Marxian hypothesis: that is to say, if religion's function as an opiate for the masses depends in part on its adoption and assiduous inculcation by the ruling class, it is important to find evidence of the latter's perception of this link. Kiernan's variation on Halévy's original thesis provides some valuable evidence for the conclusion that Evangelicals such as Wilberforce managed, from within the ruling class itself, to legitimate the growing but often suspect Evangelical revival in the Church of England on the grounds of its contribution to the maintenance of the *status quo* as well as on purely religious grounds.

The Halévy thesis contains several interesting insights, both on a particular historical level and on a broader theoretical level, into the relationship between religious beliefs and organization and the process of rapid social change. Because it has been so widely ignored, attention has in the main been devoted to a detailed restatement of the original thesis and an examination of more recent elaborations and criticisms of it. Of particular importance in the study of religion and social change is the means by which religion as an independent variable is isolated from other variables: thus Halévy selects three institutional areas—economic, political and religious—and, by a process of eliminating the economic and political variables successively, puts forward an explanation in which religion is the key variable. One line of criticism has been to reassert the significance of the other variables. Hobsbawm, for instance, argues that greater weight should be given to the political structure—though even here, it has been suggested, there are still important components of the Halévy thesis that remain untouched. Another line of criticism—and of elaboration—has adopted a procedure that has produced valuable results in recent discussions of the place of religion in social change. This procedure is what has already been referred to as the tactic of *chronology* and it is to a more detailed consideration of its varied uses that we turn in the following chapter.

REFERENCES

1 BALLEINE, G. R. *A History of the Evangelical Party in the Church of England* (Church Book Room Press, London 1951).

2 DURKHEIM, EMILE *Suicide* (Routledge and Kegan Paul, London 1970).

3 HALÉVY, ELIE *A History of the English People in 1815*, translated by E. I. Watkin and D. A. Barker (T. Fisher Unwin, London 1924).

4 HALÉVY, ELIE *A History of the English People 1830–1841* (T. Fisher Unwin, London 1927).

5 HIMMELFARB, GERTRUDE *Victorian Minds* (Weidenfeld and Nicolson, London 1968).

6 HOBSBAWM, ERIC J. 'Methodism and the threat of revolution in Britain', *History Today* vol. VII, 1957, pp. 115–24.

7 HOBSBAWM, ERIC J. *Primitive Rebels* (Manchester University Press, Manchester 1959).

8 HOLLANDER, EDWIN PAUL, and HUNT, RAYMOND GEORGE (eds.) *Current Perspectives in Social Psychology* (O.U.P., New York 1967) (2nd edition).

9 INGLIS, K. S. *Churches and the Working Classes in Victorian England* (Routledge and Kegan Paul, London 1963).

10 KENT, JOHN *The Age of Disunity* (Epworth Press, London 1966).

11 KIERNAN, V. 'Evangelicalism and the French Revolution', *Past and Present* vol. I, no. 1, February 1952, pp. 44–56.

12 THE OXFORD DICTIONARY OF THE CHRISTIAN CHURCH, edited by F. L. Cross (Oxford University Press, London 1963).

13 PEEL, J. D. Y. *Herbert Spencer: the Evolution of a Sociologist* (Heinemann, London 1971).

14 ROBERTS, BRYAN R. 'Protestant groups and coping with urban life in Guatemala City', *American Journal of Sociology* vol. 73, no. 6, May 1968, pp. 753–67.

15 THOMPSON, E. P. *The Making of the English Working Class* (Penguin Books, Harmondsworth, Middlesex 1968).

16 WARNER, WELLMAN J. *The Wesleyan Movement in the Industrial Revolution* (Longmans, Green and Co., London 1930).

17 WEBER, MAX *The Protestant Ethic and the Spirit of Capitalism* (Unwin University Books, London 1930).

18 WEBER, MAX *The Sociology of Religion*, translated by Ephraim Fischoff; introduced by Talcott Parsons (Methuen, London 1965).

19 WICKHAM, E. R. *Church and People in an Industrial City* (Lutterworth, London 1957).

[Handwritten notes:]

Hill ignores here the real origins of Evangelicalism (Walsh must be taken seriously here) and also takes no account of Harold Perkin who sees Methodism as the analgesic at the birth of a viable class society. (cf Hist Rev Dec 1972). Pollard also needs noting in his studies of the disciplines imposed on the working class.

Perkin. H. — origins of Modern English Society 1780 – 1880.
Turner Jm. — Methodism & Chartism Egyts Rile Evan 1965.
Turner Jm. — Methodism, Revolution and Social change (Hist 1973)
Wait 1974.
Morland.

IO

Religion and Social Change: Millenarism and the Problem of Rationality

IN TERMS of chronology, the extent to which religion can be seen as initiating or operating as an independent variable in a process of social change will depend to a large extent on the point at which religious beliefs and organization are seen to impinge on that process. Three examples of this have already been indicated. In the account of the Weber thesis it was clear that a great deal of significance was attached on both sides of the debate to the question of when Calvinism 'happened' in relation to capitalism, and Weber himself gave a number of examples to support his causal analysis. E. P. Thompson's tentative hypothesis that working-class millennialism was a response to the frustration of political aspirations, and thus represented a channelling-off of revolutionary fervour in terms of a continuum of activist (political) and quietist (religious) poles, depended for its proof on the establishment of detailed chronologies. The contrasting interpretation of Eric Hobsbawm that both political and religious activism may be seen as moving in parallel, and therefore requiring two continua of religious *and* political activism–quietism, was also expressed in this chronological way.

To some extent, of course, all chronologies are arbitrary because they demand cut-off points within which segments of a historical process may be analysed, and a quite different interpretation might well emerge if a different segment of history were abstracted. This seems to have especially dogged the use of the alternative concepts of charismatic and traditional legitimacy: in a narrow historical context an individual may appear to be an innovator when in a broader context—obtained by pushing back the initial cut-off point—he may appear to be drawing on a traditional, albeit widely neglected, source of ideas. Religious ideas which in one context appear as initiators of a process of social change may in another appear as transitional or even as dependent upon an earlier process. Here again, the 'Protestant Ethic' thesis immediately suggests itself as an example.

However, there are at least two ways of limiting—not, it should at once be added, of eliminating—the 'extraneous' factors in such cases. The first, for which a strong argument has been made in previous chapters, is by the use of precise concepts. While these may often refer to, or be subsumed under, general theoretical statements, they will always require a more detailed empirical content at the level of operation. That is not to say that they can be derived purely from their context, but it does imply that concepts need to be tested and reformulated continually in the light of available empirical data.

A second way of identifying more exactly some of the relation-ships between religion and social change is to take 'episodes' in which the religious symbolism associated with a process of rapid social change adopts a position of extreme rejection towards the surrounding society. In episodes of this sort it is likely that religious symbols will throw into clear relief the tensions gener-ated within different social groups by the changes that they experience, and there may often be a strong relationship between the religious goals and broader social and political aspirations. The study of millennial movements in particular shows how intimate is the connection between religious and political aspira-tions. A number of interpretations have been advanced deriving from different theoretical perspectives: it will be useful to review these in terms of the chronological links they find between religious and political movements.

There is now a vast literature on millenarian movements of different kinds, but two of the more influential contributions, which both appeared first in 1957, are Norman Cohn's *The Pursuit of the Millennium*—a study of European millenarian move-ments in the Middle Ages—and Peter Worsley's *The Trumpet Shall Sound*—a study of recent 'cargo cults' in Melanesia. [16;68] Since these present quite different interpretations of millenarian movements, they will form the basis of the discussion.

Cohn begins by defining the term 'millenarian' as including any religious movement that pictures salvation as: (a) collective, in the sense that it will be enjoyed by all the faithful as a group; (b) terrestrial, in the sense that it will be realized on this earth rather than in some other worldly heaven; (c) imminent, since it will come soon and suddenly; (d) total, because it will completely transform life on earth and bring complete perfection rather than some lesser improvement; (e) miraculous, in the sense that it will be accomplished by, or with the help of, supernatural agencies. These five characteristics are worth noting, because they have since been adopted in general theoretical statements with very little elaboration.

Even within the limits of this model, Cohn notes a wide variety in the way the millennium and the route leading to it have been imagined. Violent aggression and mild pacifism, ethereal spirituality and earthbound materialism are only two of the contrasts found in different millennial movements. However, the main theme of Cohn's study is 'the millenarianism that flourished amongst the rootless poor of western Europe between the eleventh and the sixteenth centuries; and . . . the circumstances that favoured it'. [16:14] Furthermore, although the sources of millennial beliefs were diverse—Jewish and early Christian beliefs provided some of the background, the twelfth-century Cistercian abbot Joachim of Fiore provided a new impulse, and the various heretical sects that went under the name of the Brethren of the Free Spirit yet another—Cohn is interested in how these beliefs were modified in the course of being transmitted to the poor.

The social–psychological explanation of these movements and the chronology that Cohn traces between political revolt and revolutionary millenarianism are in important respects similar to the interpretation of Methodism that E. P. Thompson puts forward, although Cohn is careful to state that he does not regard the movements with which he is concerned as having been involved in an early form of class struggle, nor as being entirely concentrated in lower social strata. One of his most significant observations is that the millennial movements of the Middle Ages 'occurred in a world where peasant revolts and urban insurrections were very common and moreover were often successful'. [16:281] The general pattern, which is seen in all the examples cited, is for a millennial movement with fantastic and 'unrealistic' expectations to arise *after* an organized insurrection with specific and limited objectives had got under way. A key influence in such changes of orientation is seen to be a prophet who was able to mobilize social groups which had no institutionalized means of defending or furthering their interests. Cohn does not actually use the word 'charismatic', though the stress he lays on the articulation of new obligations by such prophets together with their accentuation of a sense of catastrophe strongly supports this view: one of his examples, the Anabaptist Bockelson, has already been shown to have possessed a clearly charismatic element. Thus Cohn argues that in every instance

'. . . the mass insurrection itself was directed towards limited and realistic aims—yet in each instance the climate of mass insurrection fostered a special kind of millenarian group. As social tensions mounted and the revolt became nation-wide, there would appear, somewhere on the radical fringe, a *propheta* with his following of paupers, intent on turning this one particular upheaval into the apocalyptic battle, the final purification of the world. [16 : 284]

In a subsequent article, Cohn has provided an even clearer statement of this fundamental perspective. He argues that millennial movements had very little in common with the mass uprisings 'which they tried to exploit' [15:38] (a phrase which suggests rather more *Real-politik* on the part of millennial movements than is perhaps justified). The contrasts he draws between the 'realistic' aims of political movements and the 'unrealistic' fantasies of the religious revolutionaries are, however, of considerable importance in the understanding of prophetic 'radicalization'. Four main examples are given, the first of which is the millennial fringe of the English peasants' revolt. The political objectives of this revolt of 1381 are set against the background of a labour shortage after the Black Death, as a result of which the peasants saw an opportunity for demanding that manorial dues be commuted for cash rents and villeinage be replaced by wage labour. However, to the rebel gathering at Blackheath, John Ball preached a much more radical set of demands. Basing his sermon on the text, 'When Adam delved and Eve span, Who was then a gentleman?' Ball argued in favour of an ideal of equality based on the notion of a Golden Age at the beginning of creation when all men had been created free and equal. On the analogy of the wise husbandman in the Bible who gathered the wheat into his barn and burnt the tares, Ball argued that the tares—in the form of the great lords, the judges and the lawyers—should now be destroyed. When these evil nobles had been destroyed, he prophesied, the millennium in which all men would live in an egalitarian State of Nature would be ushered in. Cohn finds this millennial element behind some of the by-products of the peasants' revolt, such as 'the burning of the palace of the Savoy and the destruction of all its treasures by Londoners who would take nothing whatsoever for themselves . . .' [16:204] Despite the formal distinction between realistic and unrealistic goals, Cohn does suggest that though 'the majority of the insurgents were simply moved by specific grievances to demand specific reforms, it seems certain that millenarian hopes and aspirations were not altogether lacking'. [16:203]

The second example is the early stage of the Hussite revolution in Bohemia between 1419 and 1421. The Hussite movement was broadly concerned with the establishment of a national church in Bohemia and with improving the status of the laity against the clergy, but the eventual resistance of the authorities to this move-ment provoked a radical offshoot in the form of utopian com-munities, the most important of which renamed the hill on which it had settled 'Mount Tabor' (according to a tradition which said that this was where Christ would make his Second Coming). Here the Taborites denounced the Church of Rome and awaited the millennium. As persecution of these groups increased, so did prophecies of an imminent millennium, and as a result many of the poor sold their belongings and gave their money to the Taborite preachers. One of the latter then announced that it was the duty of the Elect to kill sinners in order to hasten the final event, and the movement swung from pacifism to aggression. Once again, as with the extreme wing of the peasants' revolt, an important component of Taborite radicalism was the belief in the return of a Golden Age of equality in which taxes, rents and private property would be abolished; and the extermination of lords, nobles and wealthy merchants was to precede the return to a State of Nature. By 1430, Taborite armies had penetrated as far as Leipzig, Bamberg and Nuremberg in Germany, but in 1434 they suffered a crushing defeat at the battle of Lipany and thereafter declined rapidly.

The German peasants' revolt of 1525 is given as a third example of a realistic political movement that gave rise to a millennial offshoot. 'The German peasants, a prosperous and rising class, were concerned to increase the autonomy of their communities and to defend their traditional rights against encroachments by the new territorial states.' [15:38] Moreover, Cohn sees the struggles of peasant communities against their lay and clerical lords as having been well disciplined, and relatively successful in gaining a degree of autonomy. In the region of Thuringia, the peasants' revolt came late and was more anarchic, encouraged by the millennial preachings of Thomas Müntzer, whose use of eschatological symbols from the Old Testament—though based on a similar rejection of private property and class distinctions as those of the other two examples—was a little more original. Nimrod, who was supposed to have built the Tower of Babel (identified with Babylon) was popularly regarded as the originator of private property and first builder of cities: by appealing to the peasants to cast down Nimrod and his Tower, Müntzer was making an explicit call to insurrection. Müntzer and his followers suffered a military defeat in May 1525.

A final example is the millenarianism of the Radical Anabaptists who, in the midst of a number of revolts in the capitals of ecclesiastical states in north-west Germany, established their 'New Jerusalem' at Münster in 1534–5. Space has already been given to the messianic reign of Jan Bockelson, and it will be sufficient to note that the 'realistic' background to this movement is seen as the attempt by the powerful and wealthy guilds in these ecclesiastical cities to restrict the economic privileges and immunities of the local clergy, who were almost entirely exempt from taxation.

Looking at the political goals of all those movements which formed the background to medieval millennialism, Cohn concludes that they were 'limited and realistic aims. On the other hand the aims of the millenarian group in each case corresponded not to the objective social situation and the possibilities it offered but to the salvationist fantasies of a handful of free-lance preachers; and they were accordingly boundless.' [15:38] Leaving aside for a moment any discussion of the terms 'realistic', 'objective social situation' and 'salvationist fantasies', which raise issues of central importance for the study of religion and social change, there is here a clear rebuttal, on the basis of the medieval data, of the view that millennial movements are pre-political phenomena: 'It has sometimes been argued that a revolutionary millennarian group fulfils the function of preparing the way for more realistic social movements. This was not the case with the movements which have just been described, for each of these appeared only when an organized insurrection of a decidedly realistic kind was under way.' [15:39]

The interpretation that Cohn opposes—that millennial movements are an embryonic form of political protest and eventually emerge as such—has a long pedigree in a number of sociological and anthropological studies relating to nativistic movements and cargo cults, a common theme of which is the way millenarianism gives religious sanction to political and economic aspirations among native groups in a colonial or culturally deprived situation. Among these studies Worsley's book *The Trumpet Shall Sound* gives the most coherent Marxist account of the pre-political elements in cargo cults.

In the first place, Worsley identifies the social location of activist millenarian movements substantially, but not entirely, among lower social groups. At the same time he leaves the option open for the appearance of millenarism among the members of quite diverse social strata, and there is an element of ambivalence in his argument. On the one hand, he interprets Cohn's data on medieval millennial movements as supporting his contention that 'it was amongst the lowest strata, particularly amongst the uprooted and disorientated peasants who had been turned into unskilled urban workers or into beggars and unemployed, that millenarian fantasies took strongest root'. [68:224] Cohn, however has argued that millenarian groups cannot be so precisely located since there are important examples in which upper-class membership was predominant. [15:35-8] Worsley's response is to claim that the class interests of workers and peasants result in a more direct form of conflict, which gives their millennial movements a mass appeal and an intransigent position, and thus Cohn's upper-class groups are *coteries*, not movements. [68:xl]

This somewhat *ad hoc* distinction is further weakened by Worsley's adoption of an 'action frame of reference' when he deals with the lower-class element in these movements, for instead of using an objective criterion to assess their membership he argues that '. . . it is amongst people who *feel* themselves to be oppressed and who are longing for deliverance that they have been particularly welcomed . . .' [68:225, my italics] (presumably on the assumption, which was pointed out in connection with Worsley's criticism of the concept of charisma, that collective perceptions and objective interests somehow coincide). The fact that Worsley also adopts the concept of 'relative deprivation' because it 'helps us to include *all* kinds of wants within our theoretical framework . . .' [68:lv] concedes even more ground to Cohn's position.

However, Worsley sees the aspirations of millenarian movements, where they have been closely associated with lower social groups, as potentially revolutionary, in that they reject the dominant values and ideology of the ruling class. This potential for violent conflict has resulted in their being proscribed and persecuted by Church and State, and the example of early Christianity can be used to show that the more orthodox conception of the millennium, identifiable even before the time of Constantine's conversion and the establishment of Christianity as the official religion of the Roman Empire, viewed it as a remote event without radical political consequences. Against this official dogma, millenarian movements assumed an anti-authoritarian, heretical form. He argues that, over and above this conflict basis, millennial movements also serve a significant political function in that they integrate previously small, isolated social groups—typically those found in 'stateless' decentralized societies—and mobilize them in the face of an external threat which can be presented as a common enemy. In colonial societies, with their segmented tribal structure, the external threat comes in the shape of the European, and it is against European dominance that cargo cults can be seen as mobilizing concerted action.

At this point the notion of chronology is introduced. Out of the utopian goals of such millenarian movements there arise 'more advanced movements' with more limited secular political objectives, and the impact of these—the reverse of that suggested by Norman Cohn and E. P. Thompson—is to 'drain off' the activism of the religious movements. The corollary of this is that millennialism in societies where political organization *does* exist is of a pacifist type:

Where millenarism survives in countries with popular secular political organizations, it is generally escapist and quietist. It rarely looks forward to the millennium as an immediate possibility. Even the Jehovah's Witnesses movement, which still looks to an imminent millennium, is a pacifist body. [68:232]

It should perhaps be added that even passive resistance implies a radical stance towards the established authorities (and perhaps a more 'realistic' appraisal of the political odds), and that the undercurrent of 'subversion' which resulted in the Witnesses' suppression in Australia and New Zealand in the Second World War and their persecution in the Soviet Union is not altogether consistent with the label 'passive resignation': the Witnesses also manage to maintain a highly aggressive form of symbolism in their descriptions of Armageddon. Worsley argues for the division of movements into active and passive alternatives rather than millenarian and non-millenarian types, and he claims that all activist movements result either in the emergence of secular political organization or turn into cults of passive resignation, found only in backward areas with low levels of political consciousness.

For Worsley the functions of prophetic leadership in the Melanesian cargo cults, rather than diverting the existing 'realistic' goals of radical political movements, is to appeal above the narrower divisions of clan and tribe to a source of legitimacy which is supernatural and therefore transcends the existing social foundations.

By this projection on to the supernatural plane he [the prophet] thus avoids sectional discord. This is always backed up by specific injunctions to love one another, by calls to forget the narrow loyalties of the past, to abandon those things that divide them and to practise a new moral code of brotherly love. [68:237]

It is interesting to note that this explanation is similar to those theories of secularization that emphasize the undermining of religion's 'plausibility structure' by its fragmentation among different social groups, only it works in the opposite direction. In the case of segmented societies, the plausibility structure of discrete tribal and local units, in which 'local gods and spirits associated with particular clans, tribes or villages' [68:237] provide a degree of coherence, is challenged when it is confronted by the common external threat presented by the European incursion. The cargo cults with their demand for wider obligations can be seen as a corresponding search for plausibility at a more universalistic level.

Worsley completely rejects the concept of charisma as part of his theoretical tool-kit, and his reason for this provides a useful introduction to the final section of this chapter, which is concerned with the problem of rationality. This problem has been touched on at various points in the preceding argument (for instance, in the discussion of 'realistic' and 'unrealistic' goals of radical movements), but it merits special attention. Charisma, Worsley argues, is an irrational notion in Weber's sociology: but in a Marxist perspective the cargo cults can be seen as 'rational' reactions to the 'irrational' fluctuations of a capitalist market economy (to which Weber had of course attributed the characteristic of formal rationality). Thus Weber is first stood on his head, and then dismissed. Conceptual somersaults of this type are quite common in discussions of rationality, and the purpose of this section will be to try to identify criteria on which the distinction between rational and irrational actions can be made.

Worsley maintains that irrationality is built into the whole scheme of Weber's sociology of action. His argument runs as follows. By rationality Weber meant the adoption of the best means suited to 'the achievement of an end or the fulfilment of a set of values'. [68:267] This is a broad rendering of Weber's distinction between action that is *zweckrational*—oriented to a choice between a set of individual ends and the most efficient or 'expedient' means to achieve them [64:115]—and action that is *wertrational*—oriented to some absolute value and thus not calculating means on the grounds of their efficiency. Worsley goes on to claim that

> . . . Weber leaves out of his scheme, as something extra-scientific, the analysis of the objectives or goals of action. He

implies that we can say nothing meaningful about ends; we can merely take them as given, for science cannot help us when it comes to choosing between what are only matters of faith or arbitrary selection . . . now we observe that irrationalism is built into the *whole* scheme, for the entire province of the ends of action is treated as beyond the reach of science. . . . Weber, by limiting his definition of rationality to mere calculation of the relation of means to ends, excludes evaluation of the objective rationality of the ends. [68:267-8]

In this passage Worsley tells us much about his own definition of rationality: 'analysis' and 'evaluation' are used synonymously, and 'objective rationality' is a final thumb in the dyke that threatens to burst and swamp what Worsley 'takes as given'. [68:268, footnote] He really *cannot* mean that the goals of actions are in Weber's view beyond analysis. The passage he cites from *The Methodology of the Social Sciences* quite specifically argues that ends can be analysed in terms of the likelihood of their attainment, the unintended consequences that might ensue, and their 'cost' in terms of the 'cost' of other ends. Thus sociology can quite definitely analyse the goals of action, but what it cannot do—says Weber—is to preëmpt the choice of different goals: 'To apply the results of this analysis in the making of a decision, however, is not a task of the acting, willing person: he weighs and chooses from among the values involved according to his own conscience and his personal view of the world.' [63:53] Science can, however, indicate what values are implied in the choice of certain goals and rejection of others; and even here it does not merely analyse values by empathetically identifying what their content is: 'it can also "judge" them critically. This criticism can of course have only a dialectical character, i.e. it can be no more than a formal logical judgement of historically given value-judgements and ideas, a testing of the ideals according to the postulate of the internal *consistency* of the desired end.' [63:54]

Thus Weber allows the possibility of analysing the goals of actions, even to the extent of pointing out to an actor what his actions logically imply in terms of ultimate standards of value, but he rejects the jump from an 'is' to an 'ought'—the 'naturalistic fallacy', which derives value-statements from empirical

H

propositions—and sums up his position as follows: 'An empirical science cannot tell anyone what he *should* do—but rather what he *can* do—and under certain circumstances—what he wishes to do.' [63:54] Worsley quite explicitly *does* wish to evaluate the goals of actions and to state that those are 'rational' that conform to an 'objective reality'. These terms are taken as given, which leaves the precise criteria on which assessment is based somewhat unclear.

An article by Lukes has identified no fewer than ten meanings of the term 'rationality', and even he makes no claim to comprehensiveness. [47] This article, which provides a useful framework for discussion, sets out the problem facing the sociologist in terms of two attitudes that might be adopted towards a set of beliefs that appear on the face of it to be irrational. On the one hand he can adopt a critical attitude, taking it as a fact that the beliefs *are* irrational, and attempting an explanation of how they originated and how they came to survive. Or he can begin with the more charitable assumption that what appear to be irrational beliefs may, if understood in their context, prove to be rational. The first option suggests the staunch ethnocentricism of an Alice in Wonderland, and the second the credulity of Betjeman's mass observer who was unaware of the 'knowing winks' of his informants. We will concentrate on only *two* of the meanings of rationality listed by Lukes: others given are either of marginal importance, or (as, for example, in the case of Peter Winch) have already been discussed.

The first answer to the problem is to argue that the apparent irrationality of primitive religion and magic is removed if the beliefs are regarded as *symbolic*. An important recent proponent of this theory is J. H. M. Beattie. [7;8] Beattie considers magical and religious rites as being 'expressive and dramatic', and hence as being closer to a form of artistic expression than to scientific activity: 'Thus comprehending them is very much more like understanding a work of art, such as a play, than it is like understanding science.' [7:60] In understanding ritual and magic we must therefore examine 'levels of meaning' and regard these not primarily as offering explanatory theories of the universe but as 'dramatizing the universe'. [7:65] Beattie's solution is to claim that the problem of rationality is a non-problem since religious and magical actions can be placed in a separate category. However, this is only half an answer because there still remains the crucial question, which Beattie himself poses: 'in what sense, if any, can we say that people's institutionalized behaviour is symbolic if, as may well be the case, they themselves do not seem to know that it is?' [7:66]

One way of answering this is to point out that theories of primitive religion that regard it as an embryonic science *also* attribute orientations to magicians and myth-makers that they might not consciously hold. But in any case the anthropologist must decide what is the best interpretation, given the available evidence, rather than let his subjects carry out his analyses for him. Beattie argues that not only is the symbolic, expressive interpretation the most useful way of understanding ritual, but that most people *do* in fact regard it in this way when they take part in it. One of the pieces of evidence that Beattie puts forward in support of his view is that, having got a spirit medium to stage a trance (at considerable expense, Beattie adds) it was quite clear from the medium's behaviour that he was 'putting on an act' [7:71] This is one of the few concrete pieces of evidence that Beattie gives for his interpretation that ritual is a dramatic performance rather than an exercise in applied science—except where he attributes such orientations with phrases like 'The Nuer . . . knows, I *suspect*, that . . .' [7:70, my italics]—and it epitomizes the general problem of social context *versus* external criteria. Although Beattie is concerned to present an action frame of reference, such a framework can be used in criticism:

It is one thing to say that the rationale behind magical practices (as a general class) appears to be symbolism, but quite another to say that the agent is doing a special kind of activity called 'symbolling'. He is not; he is just doing what he believes to be instrumental. We misinterpret why men act if, from a consideration of what we believe the effects of the actions must be, we disregard the categories under which they act. [51:75]

The second solution to the problem of rationality stems initially from the work of Frazer, and maintains that primitive magical and religious beliefs are attempted explanations of phenomena.

This involves the claim that they satisfy certain given criteria of rationality by virtue of certain rational procedures of thought and observation being followed; on the other hand they are (more or less) mistaken and to be judged as (more or less) unsuccessful explanations against the canons of science (and modern common sense). [47:250]

Jarvie's solution to the problem of rationality is an attempt to establish a single criterion of rationality based on the instrumental, goal-directed orientation of such action. Thus the symbolic interpretation of magic is rejected because it 'simply involves reading a statement into an act.' [37:185]

The question of why primitive men, who in several ways use a highly rational technology to achieve their goals, should accompany this with magical practices is not to be answered by separating the activity into two discrete elements, one instrumental, the other expressive, because the two aspects are subsumed under the same category in the orientation of the actor:

> The primitive believes seeds would not grow if he did not chant, if they do not grow anyway he must have chanted wrongly. Good luck will come to him if he does things properly, bad luck is the result of either his own incompetence as a magician, or of malevolent magic performed against him by his enemies. The strength of the magical world-view is that it is a complete world-view, one that explains anything and everything in terms of magic, failed magic, or magical conspiracies. It combines very smoothly with even a sophisticated technology because it explains its success. [37:192]

Looked at in this way, the primitive farmer does not perform two actions—planting seeds (instrumental) and performing a ritual (expressive)—but he grows crops rather inefficiently and is not aware that ritual makes no difference to his success or failure. The problem is therefore not one of 'how on earth can they believe in magic?', but 'how do people with inefficient magical beliefs come to be critical of them?' This is a fairly strong neo-Frazerian interpretation.

Beattie and Jarvie take quite different approaches to the problem of rationality. Beattie, who is interested in all magical and religious ritual, sees it as falling in an entirely different category (similar in many ways to Pareto's category of 'non-logical action', and maintaining, with Pareto, that non-logical actions are often masked by 'the human tendency to "logicalize" non-logical activity and make it seem logical') [22:14], and thus he takes the discussion out of the category of rationality. Jarvie, who is above all concerned with magical ritual, sees it as rational to the extent that those who perform it do so in the pursuit of some goal: at the same time, since it is not based on the adoption of some standard or criterion of rationality, such as good evidence, reasonable doubt or critical appraisal of the techniques used, magic is distinct from science, where such tests can be made. For Jarvie, 'weak' rationality is action in pursuit of some goal (the only sense in which magical ritual can be called rational); 'strong' rationality is goal-directed action that is submitted to some criterion against which such action may be verified and assessed— and scientific actions entail, or may entail, the 'strong' sense of rationality.

Is there any satisfactory way in which we can draw a precise distinction between the 'ancient' and the 'modern' systems of rationality? An important place must be given to Robin Horton's discussion of African traditional thought and Western science, and although the idea of one kind of savage mentality confronting one kind of modern mind is only a convention, this does allow us to abstract certain features and make illuminating contrasts. Horton thinks that traditional African belief-systems are theoretical models akin to those of modern science, and that the supposed differences in the two modes of thought are a result of the different idioms used. Hence if we concentrate on the aims and methods rather than the content of the two sorts of theory, they present the following similarities: (1) a search for explanation by looking for the unity underlying apparent diversity, the order underlying apparent disorder, and the regularity underlying apparent anomaly; (2) placing things in a causal context wider than that provided by common sense; (3) playing a complementary role to common sense; (4) varying the theoretical level according to context; (5) explanation by means of abstraction, analysis and reintegration; (6) the use of analogy between puzzling observations to be explained and already familiar phenomena; (7) the restriction to only limited aspects of such phenomena; and (8) developing theoretical models that obscure the original analogies.

Horton's main aim is to break down the contrast between 'non-empirical' traditional religious thought and 'empirical' modern science. Traditional religious thought is argued to be just as interested in the natural causes of things as is science (so that the intellectual function of supernatural beings—like atoms, waves and similar concepts in science—is the extension of people's vision of natural causes). Also, traditional religious theory does more than postulate causal connexions that bear no relation to experience, since some of the connexions, by modern scientific standards, are almost certainly real ones. The argument is not that magical and religious thought are varieties of scientific thought, but that both types of thought aim and partly succeed in establishing causal connexions: of the two, scientific method is the more efficient and reliable way of arriving at successful statements about causality.

There is one distinction above all that Horton thinks is crucial in understanding these two different kinds of explanation: '. . . in traditional cultures there is no developed awareness of alternatives to the established body of theoretical tenets; whereas in scientifically oriented cultures, such an awareness is highly developed.' [33 no. 2:155] These alternatives he calls the 'closed' and the 'open'. The 'closed' culture of traditional societies is 'characterized by lack of awareness of alternatives, sacredness of beliefs, and anxiety about threats to them': the 'open' scientifically oriented cultures are 'characterized by awareness of alternatives, diminished sacredness of beliefs, and diminished anxiety about threats to them'. [33 no. 2:156]

Horton then lists a number of contrasts that are associated with the presence or absence of a vision of alternatives, and these can be listed as follows: (1) 'closed' rationality is characterized by magical attitudes, 'open' by non-magical attitudes; (2) in a system of 'closed' rationality ideas are seen as being bound to particular occasions, whereas in 'open' rational systems ideas are bound to other ideas, as they acquire autonomy and are regarded as something separate from reality; (3) unreflective thinking is a 'closed' situation, reflective thinking (thinking about thinking) an 'open' one; (4) diffuse motives characterize 'closed' rationality whereas segregated motives are found in 'open' rationality. There are also a number of differences connected with the presence or absence of anxiety about threats to the established body of theory, and these are: (5) a protective attitude towards established theory in a 'closed' situation, compared with a destructive attitude in an 'open' situation; (6) 'closed' divination versus 'open' diagnosis; (7) absence of an experimental method in a 'closed' system, and its presence in an 'open' system; (8) no confession of ignorance in a 'closed' situation, but confession of ignorance in an 'open' situation; (9) rejection of the notions of coincidence, chance and probability in favour of definite causal explanations and predictions in a 'closed' system compared with the acceptance of such notions in an 'open' system; (10) a protective attitude towards the category-system in 'closed' rationality, but a destructive attitude in 'open' rationality; (11) evaluative attitude towards time in a 'closed' system, compared with a neutral attitude towards time in an 'open' system.

Although the 'closed'/'open' distinction derives initially from Popper (and is given by Horton a somewhat narrower meaning) the basic insight contained in it is remarkably similar to Weber's distinction between substantive and formal rationality. The basis of Weber's argument in *The Protestant Ethic and the Spirit of Capitalism* was that economic activity and scientific innovation were gradually liberated from a substantively rational belief system in which the definition of normality in the social and natural order was articulated by and entrenched in the traditional religious institutions: this liberation happened as a result of the relegation of God and other supernatural agents from their immanent position in the natural order, and their replacement—particularly in Calvinism—by the notion of the natural order as a mechanism. Similarly, as God was pushed to a position of radical transcendence, the growth of non-religious, specialized idioms for explaining natural and social events and patterns became possible. The monolithic definition of 'what is normal', which had been underwritten and elaborated by medieval Catholicism and which had been applied to the whole spectrum of social activity—political, legal, economic, military—was restricted and tidied up considerably by placing formal restrictions on the role of religion in political and legal affairs, and by removing some of the traditional institutional blocks on activities in these different spheres. Finally, since the end of all knowledge

was no longer to conform to some immutable, divinely instituted cosmos, the search for knowledge acquired an autonomy
that made possible the calculation of different courses of action,
not on the basis of their contribution to or conformity with some
combined natural and normative order, but on the basis of their
relative efficiency (given a choice of empirical possibilities that is
assumed to contain no 'extraneous' evaluative criteria).

By means of the terms 'substantive' and 'formal', Weber distinguishes the belief systems of societies that correspond in many
of their features to those labelled here as 'closed' and 'open'. An
analogy might be a useful means of highlighting the distinction.
There are two main ways of storing and using information, the
library and the computer, and there are important differences
between these two methods. Information stored in a library has
to be 'prelocated' if it is to be useful: in other words, a library
works on the principle that every piece of material it handles can
be given a position in some overall scheme of classification, and
that position will serve to evaluate and set in context the item
concerned. There is not just *one* single classification system, but
every library must have *some* principle of classification, and this
will be devised in terms of the needs it serves. Furthermore,
classification systems *are* socially defined definitions of normality
to the extent that they evaluate as well as locate material in context: any sociology student who has browsed round a local
library that uses the Dewey system will have noticed that sociology is a near-neighbour of religion and a far cry from chemistry;
also, as the number of decimal points now used in classifying
sociology suggests, its growth was not anticipated. The basic
notion that this analogy with traditional belief-systems conveys
is that all knowledge is located according to some overall,
evaluative, socially defined scheme: all knowledge is *processed*
before it becomes part of the range of options available to members of a traditional society.

Before information is stored in a computer data-bank it is
often *cleaned*, and this is a very different process. 'Cleaning' raw
data before it is stored in a computer really involves *removing* the
evaluative, contextual meanings that are attached to the data as a
result of its being derived from research projects with different
goals and overall strategies. The only label needed on a piece of

data stored in a computer is where it originally came from, and as long as the data is fed into the bank in a form in which it can be 'understood' (which means that computer languages and operational procedures acquire an 'autonomous' status), it can be used in an immense variety of different ways. In contrast with the 'prelocation' principle of the library, which evaluates information before it is stored, computer data is not evaluated until a 'program' is fed in, and this typically happens *after* the 'clean' information has been fed in. While textbooks are flown across the Atlantic from the United States with their 'Library of Congress Catalog Card Number' on the reverse of the title page and then have to be reclassified before they can be placed in the library of the British Museum, the magnetic discs of computers are flown backwards and forwards continually and require no such culturally derived evaluation. Computers are 'open' in the sense that they specify no cultural context.

Lukes concludes that we must use two criteria of rationality, one universal and the other contextual. In the first place, Winch's position that the only available criteria of rationality are culture-dependent is either wrong or untestable: at any rate there is no way of imagining what it would entail for Winch to be right. All societies have distinctions between true and false, and all societies have language with operable logical rules (otherwise we would have no way of 'translating' their language to show that they did *not* have operable logical rules). Thus, in so far as we can 'translate' the concepts of primitive societies, and in so far as their magical and religious beliefs are logical and follow sound procedures, they are rational: if they are partially or wholly false, they are not rational. If beliefs are not directly verifiable or falsifiable by empirical means, then contextually provided criteria of *truth* will show whether the beliefs are 'consistent' or 'inconsistent', 'true' or 'false'—in other words, whether there are 'good reasons' for holding a particular belief. It can be argued (against Beattie) that some beliefs claim to be *true* and not just metaphorical; and it can also be argued (against Frazer) that some beliefs that are empirically falsifiable appear meaningful *in their context*. Taking this line of argument further, it has been suggested that to the extent that we can characterize two contextual styles—as 'closed' and 'open' systems of rationality—it is possible to synthesize the universal and contextual criteria of rationality with even greater precision. From the question 'Is religious activity rational?' there arises the question 'In what sense is it rational?' The dichotomy of 'closed' and 'open' rationality provides a useful device for specifying the universal and contextual criteria of specific belief systems.

REFERENCES

1 ABERLE, DAVID F. 'A note on relative deprivation theory as applied to millenarian and other cult movements', in THRUPP, SYLVIA L. (ed.), op. cit.

2 ABERLE, DAVID F. *The Peyote Religion Among the Navaho* (Aldine Publishing Co., Chicago 1966).

3 AHLER, JAMES G., and TAMNEY, JOSEPH B. 'Some functions of religious ritual in a catastrophe', *Sociological Analysis* vol. 25, no. 4, Winter 1964, pp. 212-30.

4 AMES, MICHAEL 'Ideological and social change in Ceylon', *Human Organization* vol. 22, no. 1, Spring 1963, pp. 45-53.

5 BALANDIER, GEORGES 'Messianismes et nationalismes en Afrique noire', *Cahiers Internationaux de Sociologie* vol. XIV, no. 1, 1953, pp. 41-65.

6 BARBER, BERNARD 'Acculturation and messianic movements', *American Sociological Review* vol. 6, no. 5, October 1941, pp. 663-9.

7 BEATTIE, J. H. M. 'Ritual and social change', *Man* vol. 1, no. 1, March 1966, pp. 60-74.

8 BEATTIE, J. H. M. 'On understanding ritual', in WILSON, BRYAN R. (ed.) *Rationality*, op. cit.

9 BELLAH, ROBERT N. *Tokugawa Religion* (Free Press, Glencoe 1957).

10 BELLAH, ROBERT N. 'Religious aspects of modernization in Turkey and Japan', *American Journal of Sociology* vol. LXIV, no. 1, July 1958, pp. 1-5.

11 BELLAH, ROBERT N. 'Epilogue: Religion and Progress in Modern Asia', in BELLAH, ROBERT N. (ed.), *Religion and Progress in Modern Asia* (Free Press, New York 1965).

12 BELLAH, ROBERT N. 'Meaning and modernization', *Religious Studies* vol. 4, nos. 1 & 2, 1969, pp. 37-43.

13 BURRIDGE, KENELM *New Heaven, New Earth* (Basil Blackwell, Oxford 1969).

14 COHEN, PERCY S. 'Theories of myth', *Man* vol. 4, no. 3, September 1969, pp. 337-53.

15 COHN, NORMAN 'Medieval millenarism: its bearing on the comparative study of millenarian movements', in THRUPP, SYLVIA L. (ed.) *Millennial Dreams in Action, Comparative Studies in Society and History*, supplement 2 (Mouton, The Hague 1962), pp. 31-43.

16 COHN, NORMAN *The Pursuit of the Millennium* (Paladin, London 1970).

17 ELIADE, MIRCEA ' "Cargo-cults" and cosmic regeneration', in THRUPP, SYLVIA L. (ed.) op. cit.

18 ELIADE, MIRCEA 'Survivals and camouflages of myths', *Diogenes* no. 41, Spring 1963, pp. 1–25.

19 EMMET, DOROTHY 'Prophets and their societies', *Journal of the Royal Anthropological Institute* vol. 86, part 1, January–June 1956, pp. 13–23.

20 EVANS-PRITCHARD, E. E. *Essays in Social Anthropology* (Faber and Faber, London 1962).

21 EVANS-PRITCHARD, E. E. *Theories of Primitive Religion* (The Clarendon Press, Oxford 1965).

22 FINER, S. E. (ed.) *Vilfredo Pareto, Sociological Writings* (Pall Mall, London 1966).

23 GEERTZ, CLIFFORD 'Modernization in a Muslim Society: the Indonesian Case', in BELLAH, ROBERT N. (ed.) *Religion and Progress in Modern Asia* (Free Press, New York 1965).

24 GELLNER, ERNEST 'Concepts and society', in EMMET, DOROTHY and MACINTYRE, ALASDAIR (eds.) *Sociological Theory and Philosophical Analysis* (Macmillan, London 1970).

25 GOLLIN, GILLIAN LINDT 'Theories of the good society: four views on religion and social change', *Journal for the Scientific Study of Religion* vol. 9, no. 1, 1970, pp. 1–16.

26 GUIART, JEAN 'Forerunners of Melanesian nationalism', *Oceania* vol. XXII, no. 2, December 1951, pp. 81–90.

27 GUIART, JEAN 'John Frum movement in Tanna', *Oceania* vol. XXII, no. 3, March 1952, pp. 165–77.

28 HILL, W. W. 'The Navaho Indians and the Ghost Dance of 1890', *American Anthropologist* vol. 46, no. 4, October–December 1944, pp. 523–7.

29 HOLLIS, MARTIN 'The limits of irrationality', *Archives Européennes de Sociologie* vol. VIII, no. 2, 1967, pp. 265–71.

30 HORTON, ROBIN 'Destiny and the unconscious in West Africa', *Africa* vol. XXXI, no. 2, April 1961, pp. 110–16.

31 HORTON, ROBIN 'The Kalibari world-view: an outline and interpretation', *Africa* vol. XXXII, no. 3, July 1962, pp. 197–219.

32 HORTON, ROBIN 'Ritual man in Africa', *Africa* vol. XXXIV, no. 2, April 1964, pp. 85–103.

33 HORTON, ROBIN 'African traditional thought and western science', *Africa* vol. XXXVII, no. 1, January 1967, pp. 50–71, vol. XXXVII, no. 2, April 1967, pp. 155–87.

34 INGLIS, JUDY 'Cargo Cults: the problem of explanation', *Oceania* vol. XXVII, no 4, June 1957, pp. 249–63.

35 JARVIE, I. C. 'Theories of Cargo Cults: a critical analysis', *Oceania* vol. XXXIV, no. 1, September 1963, pp. 1–31, and vol. XXXIV, no. 2, December 1963, pp. 108–36.

36 JARVIE, I. C. 'On the explanation of Cargo Cults', *Archives Européennes de Sociologie* vol. VII, no. 2, 1966, pp. 299–312.

37 JARVIE, I. C., and AGASSI, JOSEPH 'The problem of the rationality of magic' in WILSON, BRYAN R. (ed.) *Rationality*, op. cit.

38 DE KADT, EMANUEL 'Religion, the church, and social change in Brazil', in VELIZ, CLAUDIO (ed.) *The Politics of Conformity in Latin America* (Oxford University Press, London 1967).

39 KRADER, LAWRENCE 'A nativistic movement in Western Siberia', *American Anthropologist* vol. 58, no. 2, April 1956, pp. 282–92.

40 LANTENARI, VITTORIO *The Religions of the Oppressed* (Mentor Books, New York 1965).

41 LAWRENCE, PETER 'Lutheran Mission influence on Madang societies', *Oceania* vol. XXVII, no. 2, December 1956, pp. 73–89.

42 LÉVI-STRAUSS, CLAUDE *Structural Anthropology* (Basic Books, New York/London 1963).

43 LÉVI-STRAUSS, CLAUDE *The Savage Mind* (Weidenfeld and Nicolson, London 1966).

44 LÉVY-BRUHL, LUCIEN *Primitive Mentality*, translated by Lilian A. Clare (George Allen and Unwin, London 1923).

45 LINTON, RALPH 'Nativistic movements', *American Anthropologist* vol. 45, no. 2, April–June, 1943, pp. 230–40.

46 LONG, NORMAN *Social Change and the Individual* (Manchester University Press, Manchester 1968).

47 LUKES, STEVEN 'Some problems about rationality', *Archives Européennes de Sociologie* vol. VIII, no. 2, 1967, pp. 247–64.

48 MACINTYRE, ALASDAIR 'Is understanding religion compatible with believing?' in WILSON, BRYAN R. (ed.) *Rationality*, op. cit.

49 MALINOWSKI, BRONISLAW *Magic, Science and Religion and Other Essays* (The Free Press, Glencoe 1948).

50 PEEL, J. D. Y. 'Syncretism and religious change', *Comparative Studies in Society and History* vol. X, no. 2, 1968, pp. 121–41.

51 PEEL, J. D. Y. 'Understanding alien belief-systems', *British Journal of Sociology* vol. XX, no. 1, March 1969, pp. 69–84.

52 PHELAN, JOHN LEDDY *The Millennial Kingdom of the Franciscans in the New World* (University of California Publications in History, vol. 52) (University of California Press, Berkeley/Los Angeles 1956).

53 RADCLIFFE-BROWN, A. R. *Structure and Function in Primitive Society* (Cohen and West, London 1952).

54 SHAROT, STEPHEN 'A Jewish Christian adventist movement', *Jewish Journal of Sociology* vol. X, no. 1, 1968, pp. 35–45.

55 SHEPPERSON, GEORGE 'The comparative study of millenarian movements', in THRUPP, SYLVIA L. (ed.) *Millennial Dreams in Action, Comparative Studies in Society and History*, supplement 2 (Mouton, The Hague 1962), pp. 44–52.

56 SKLAIR, LESLIE *The Sociology of Progress* (Routledge and Kegan Paul, London 1970).

57 SMITH, MARIAN W. 'Towards a classification of cult movements', *Man* vol. LIX, Articles 1–22, January 1959, pp. 8–12.

58 SUNDKLER, BENGT G. M. *Bantu Prophets in South Africa*, 2nd edn. (Oxford University Press, London 1961).

59 TALMON, YONINA 'Pursuit of the millennium: the relation between religious and social change', *Archives Européennes de Sociologie* vol. III, no. 1, 1962, pp. 125–48.

60 TALMON, YONINA 'Millenarian movements', *Archives Européennes de Sociologie* vol. VII, no. 2, 1966, pp. 159–200.

61 THRUPP, SYLVIA L. (ed.) *Millennial Dreams in Action* (Mouton, The Hague 1962).

62 WALLACE, ANTHONY F. C. 'Revitalization movements', *American Anthropologist* vol. 58, no. 2, April 1956, pp. 264–81.

63 WEBER, MAX *The Methodology of the Social Sciences*, translated and edited by Edward A. Shils and Henry A. Finch (The Free Press, New York 1949).

64 WEBER, MAX *The Theory of Social and Economic Organization* (The Free Press, New York 1964).

65 WILSON, BRYAN R. 'Millennialism in comparative perspective', *Comparative Studies in Society and History* Vol. VI, no. 1 October 1963, pp. 93–114.

66 WILSON, BRYAN R. (ed.) *Rationality* (Basil Blackwell, Oxford 1970).

67 WINCH, PETER 'Understanding a primitive society' in WILSON, BRYAN R. (ed.) *Rationality*, op. cit.

68 WORSLEY, PETER *The Trumpet Shall Sound* (MacGibbon and Kee, London 1968).

69 ZYGMUNT, JOSEPH F. 'Prophetic failure and chiliastic identity: the case of Jehovah's Witnesses', *American Journal of Sociology* vol. 75, no. 6, May 1970, pp. 926–48.

I I

Secularization: the Variety of Meanings

IN CHAPTER 2 a number of early sociologists were shown to have theories of religion in which secularization was inevitable. These writers regarded the advance of science as a force inexorably erosive of traditional forms of religion, although their view of science as a replacement for religious explanations sometimes contained the strong notion that science could be constructed on quasi-religious lines. The view that secularization is inevitable must, however, be contrasted with the ideas advanced by other sociologists, which suggest that secularization may be improbable or even impossible. In any discussion of the secularization controversy it is important to specify that the conclusion of the argument depends to a considerable extent on its basic premiss: how we define secularization—and, perhaps even more fundamentally, how we define religion—largely determines whether or not such a process can be identified. To take two extreme positions as an illustration: if religion is defined solely in terms of institutional practice, then secularization must mean the decline of church membership and attendance and would seem to be a characteristic process, at least in Western European societies; but if, on the other hand, we define religion as some quantum of 'religiousness' within every individual, secularization would become impossible by definition and could only be used to refer to the changing content given to this universal feature of human psychology. Given the basic problem of definition in the study of secularization, it is important to consider the different uses that have been made of the concept.

Six different meanings of the term secularization have been explored by Shiner, [33] and they provide a valuable framework for any discussion of the topic. Shiner regards the Latin root *saeculum*, from which the term 'secular' derives, as having an ambiguous meaning itself. It could signify a great length of time (as in the phrase, *per saecula saeculorum*—'for ever and ever') or it could be used as a religiously negative term signifying 'this world' under the domination of Satan. However, as the church became more at home in 'this world' the term became more neutral, so that by the Middle Ages the term 'secular clergy' simply referred to those priests with ordinary parishes to serve as against those in religious orders. In the seventeenth century the term 'secularization' (*secularizatio*) was used to signify land transferred from ecclesiastical to civil control, and had a generally neutral meaning, though by the eighteenth century—when the transfer of church lands constituted a more extensive political programme—some of this neutrality was lost. In the nineteenth century the term 'secularism' was used to denote militantly atheistic associations, and perhaps because of this the idea of secularization was initially attacked by theologians, though later it was to become a positive plank in the arguments of 'secular' theologians.

The extent to which the sociological concept of secularization is value-neutral is a matter for debate. Martin's contention that the concept should be eliminated because it is 'less a scientific concept than a tool of counter-religious ideologies' [17:9] certainly has some force in the case of the early theorists of religion who incorporated a critique of religion and the assumption of inevitable secularization into their theories. Similarly, if it can be shown that the notion of secularization as a global process conceals the fact that diverse, even conflicting components are being lumped together into a blanket concept, then such a usage can be challenged on the basis of its lack of analytical precision. However, if it is possible to identify any definition of secularization which is precise enough to apply to empirical examples, there would seem to be a place for the term in this limited context.

The first definition treated by Shiner is that which specifies *the decline of religion*. By this is meant that previously accepted symbols, doctrines and institutions lose their prestige and influence; and the end point of such a process would be a religion-less society. One of the most influential of recent statements using this definition is that of Bryan Wilson, who defines secularization as a 'process whereby religious thinking, practice and institutions lose social significance'. [38:xiv] Wilson notes that religious change does not necessarily occur in similar ways in different societies, and points out that religious *practice* may atrophy, as it has done in the Scandinavian countries, or it may persist in a traditional form though with a different cultural significance, as it has done in the United States. Religious *institutions* may also show remarkable resilience—as they have done in the United States— though this may be at the expense of their bureaucratization. But religious *thinking*, he argues, is the area of most conspicuous change: men act less in terms of religious motivations and view the world in increasingly empirical terms. And even if, as some sociologists have argued, there remains a large measure of non-rational activity in modern industrial societies, this can be attributed more to 'irrational and arbitrary assumptions about life, society and the laws which govern the physical universe' [38:x] than to traditional religious dogmas. As we shall later discover, Wilson minimizes the importance of precisely the same area of 'invisible religion' on which Luckmann places such a strong emphasis in his argument. Denying that his use of the term secularization has any of the ideological implications criticized by Martin, Wilson simply takes it as a fact that religious thought, practice and organization have lost influence in Britain, the United States and other Western societies.

Nevertheless, Wilson clearly regards secularization as a broad development in modern societies. Statistics of religious participation provide 'some sort of index of secularization, taking that word at its common-sense value', [38:2] and on this measure it can be seen that organized religion in Britain has been losing its members fairly steadily since the last decades of the nineteenth century. An apparent exception to this process in the case of Roman Catholicism can be attributed to the influence of Irish immigration: 'Similar gains have also occurred in Muslims and Sikhs with the influx of new settlers from Pakistan and India.' [38:3] The relatively high level of baptisms, religiously performed marriages and burials represents the need to authenticate important rites of passage, and 'a man needs extraordinary presence of mind at death if he is to avoid religious officiation at his burial'. [38:7] The frequently encountered view that medieval

Catholicism represents the most comprehensive form of social legitimation ever attained by Christianity is used as a base-line from which the radical developments of Calvinism and other sectarian movements are traced.

One of the more implicit aspects of Wilson's argument opens up an important methodological issue, for he provides an epi-phenomenalist interpretation of the growth of post-Reformation sectarian movements. Such movements, he contends, interpreted Christian ideas 'in terms of the increasing rationality, order and organization which were necessary in their [members'] working lives'. [38:22] In complete contrast, the earlier sectarian move-ments (principally Adventist movements in the Middle Ages) 'were largely ecstatic emotional outbursts reinterpreting Christi-anity in primitive terms and with a literal demand for the fulfilment of Biblical promises'. [38:22] Contained in this argument is the implication that at some point in Christian history—presumably around the Reformation—sectarian protests ceased to be 'really' religious. This apparently precludes two important alternatives: (a) that it is equally important to interpret post-Reformation sects in terms other than those of their members' economic interests; and (b) that the economic basis of medieval millenarianism is of considerable significance.

The process within which Wilson incorporates the development of sects and denominations with a close affinity to particular social strata is that of 'the disenchantment of the world': different religious bodies increasingly act in a servicing role for distinct social groups, and this gradually involves them in a process of decline in response to social change, leaving only the shell of institutional persistence. An entirely similar process occurs as religious bodies lose their monopoly on the means of communi-cation. In this connexion, when the churches have recourse to the mass media in order to put their message across it tends to be done in such a way that any claims the churches might have to pre-eminence lose their validity. Wilson does not go as far as saying that 'the medium is the message', but this is his clear sugges-tion. Yet another instance of 'the disenchantment of the world' is to be found in the growth of ecumenicalism, which, far from being based on clear theological premises, represents more importantly the churches' response to the requirements of bureaucratic efficiency in the face of organizational decline. In brief, secularization involves the increasing denominationalism, pluralism and—for this is the key observation in Wilson's study—the increasing epiphenomenalism of traditional religion.

There are two main problems in this interpretation: firstly, if religion is in decline when was it at its peak? and secondly, is there a clear correlation between the three variables of 'thinking', 'belief' and 'practice'? The first problem can be described as that of the myth of a golden age of religion, and in different disguises it has already been encountered in the work of some of the early theorists of religion, which was discussed in chapter 2. For Hume the golden age was largely realized in classical Greece; for Gibbon it appeared in classical Rome, and for Comte it took the form of medieval Catholicism. The belief in a golden age of religion has been criticized as one of the 'utopian' aspects of the theories which treat secularization as religious decline because these tend to accept at face value 'Catholic laments about the period when men were truly religious. In this instance the backward-looking utopia of medievalism becomes the basis for writing about secularization.' [17:31] Usually the century adopted as the zenith of Western Christianity is the twelfth, with the twentieth century as the least religious of all. The usual technique is to take a 'handy historical tripod' [17:65] with one leg in the present, one in the nineteenth century and one in the twelfth. The twelfth century is depicted as the height of official Catholicism, any deviation from which can be regarded as secularization, and the nineteenth century contains the high 'peak' of mid-Victorian religion—another bench-mark against which the twentieth century decline of religious practice can be compared to give a clear indication of the secularization process.

I would add another leg to the tripod, which, though rarely used in secularization arguments, has some claim to represent an earlier 'peak' of religion. The fourth-century conversion of Constantine to Christianity and its subsequent adoption as the official religion of the Roman Empire followed a period in which those who had maintained their commitment to what was then a minority religion could just as validly be singled of as representatives of *real* religion as a twelfth-century Cistercian or a nineteenth-century Evangelical. Since the sanctions that could be used against a practicing Christian before A.D. 305 included, among other severe penalties, martyrdom and mutilation, it can be assumed that Christianity in this period was characterized by a particularly *virtuoso* level. It follows from this that the initial onset of secularization happened when Christianity became accepted as an established religion and the level of commitment demanded of members was consequently lowered. The institutionalization of Christianity and the formalization of its entrance procedures and internal structure are closely associated with the church's newly acquired role of legitimating the established social order. For some writers this development is virtually synonymous with the loss of Christianity's capacity to initiate change, and thus with its decline to the position of dependent variable:

> The church came to underpin the world of men and the values of the world corrupted it. Its very success was its downfall, for as it came to confuse the ordering of existence here and now under the rule of the church with the kingdom of God, it sacralized the world and lost its own perspective. It could no longer change the world, indeed it became the most potent force *resisting* change. [35:68]

However, even this early example of secularization is not without its paradoxical element. While the church at large may have found itself more at home in its secular environment from the beginning of the fourth century, it was at precisely this time that a movement with an other-worldly orientation originated. The monastic life as a distinct social and geographical phenomenon first originated in Egypt at the beginning of the fourth century and from there it spread rapidly to other parts of Christendom. We have already encountered the argument that 'It is no co-incidence that monasticism should have developed immediately after Constantine's conversion, at the very time when the persecutions ceased and Christianity became fashionable. The monks with their austerities were martyrs in an age when martyrdom of blood no longer existed; they formed the counter-balance to an established Christendom.' [36:45] Thus, concomitant with a process of institutionalization and this-worldly compromise in the church at large, it is possible to trace the origins of an other-worldly virtuoso protest movement. If the process of institutionalization is to be identified as one of secularization, then the origins of the monastic movement can only be termed a process of desecularization.

In effect, there is an 'ancient' and a 'modern' variant of the golden age theory of secularization. The 'ancient' version identifies the primitive church as the period of maximum religiosity and regards the emergence of Christianity as the established religion of the empire as evidence of secularization. Some theological versions extend this theory by seeing the Reformation as an attempt to reinstate the pristine purity of the first few centuries. The 'modern' version regards the twelfth-century predominance of Roman Catholicism in Western Christendom as the golden age of Christianity's monopoly of spiritual power, with the growing pluralism and denominationalism of the late medieval and Reformation period as the most significant onset of secularization.

The problem created by the packaging together of a number of criteria for assessing *real* religion and the use of such packages as bench-marks in history, is that any change or deviation from such 'peaks' constitutes secularization. As a result, Christianity seems to have been over-secularized: 'Unfortunately when change becomes automatically secularization then Europe has been secularized so often that it is difficult to see how any religion can be left.' [17:31] In some of these versions of the golden age of Christianity one can trace some of the same types of evaluation about what constitutes 'real' religiosity as those of the early evolutionists, whose contributions to the study of religion were assessed in chapter two. Evolutionist theories of what constituted the most 'real' form or religious belief and organization—evaluated in terms of its contribution to the maintenance of social cohesion—were often expressed in terms of some golden age of religiosity, whether it be the civic religion of classical antiquity or the all-embracing structure of medieval Catholicism. Theories of a golden age nearly always contain *some* mythical element: the theory of a golden age of religion is no exception.

A second use of the concept of secularization, which is identified by Shiner, is that of *the shift from 'other-worldly' to 'this-worldly' orientations* within religious groups themselves. In the sphere of ethics this is seen to involve the replacement of motivations towards a future life or to an ethical tradition by a pragmatic ethic in which present exigencies provide the major source of motivation. Much of Weber's concern with the removal of substantively rational considerations in the sphere of economic activity and their replacement by formally rational criteria fits into this perspective, and it has also been found useful in more recent empirical research. Pfautz, for example, has studied the testimonies of healings and other benefits which appeared in two of the official publications of Christian Science between the years 1890–1950 in order to determine whether the type of testimony given showed any overall change. [26] Weber's typology of social action was used as a basis for content analysis. *Affectual* motivation was interpreted as a general statement of benefit or a more explicit statement of specifically religious or magical benefit. *Value-rational* motivation was interpreted to include specific physical or mental healings, or changes in the testifier's way of life. *Traditional* motivation was used to identify cases in which the testimony explicitly stated that the writer's immediate parents were Christian Scientists; and *purposeful-rational* testimonies were those which referred to benefits of a material nature such as money or occupational promotion.

Using these indices, Pfautz attempted to draw a contrast between the use of affectual motivation, which emphasized 'the element of enthusiasm, ranging from general and developed religious satisfaction to such intense experiences as a redefinition of self and effects beyond the realm of reason' and purposeful-rational action, in which 'the citing of material benefits points up the fundamentally practical and worldly type of gain'. [26:249] However, since the act of testifying was officially defined by Christian Scientists as a logical proof of their doctrines, the procedure itself was basically value-rational in character. Allowing for more than one motivation in each testimony, Pfautz found that a fairly constant 90 per cent of testimonies over the period 1890–1950 contained this value-rational component. On the other hand, affectual motivations showed a rapid decline from 53 per cent of the 1890 testimonies to 21 per cent of the 1910 testimonies, thereafter remaining under 20 per cent: the first flush of 'enthusiasm' had apparently cooled by the 1920s. Traditional motivations showed a consistent rise, from none in 1890 (when Christian

Science was a new movement and there were no birthright members) to 21 per cent in 1950. There is solid evidence here for the operation of Niebuhr's 'generation effect' in the growth of denominations, though it is still only a secondary element in the testimonies. The purposeful-rational type of motivation showed a more marked increase, from a mere 4 per cent of the 1890 testimonies to 32 per cent of the 1950 testimonies. Although this evidence does not point to an unambiguous decline in 'other-worldly' motivations—since testifiers retained a religious world-view while discarding some of the more intense experiential aspects of it—it does suggest that 'this-worldly' evaluations of Christian Science increased considerably in importance.

Another sociologist who has given a provocative treatment to the way in which 'this-worldly' exigencies may be adopted as part of the programme of religious institutions is Peter Berger, who has even argued that the market model of *laissez-faire* economics (which Weber regarded as most typically formal-rational in its operation) is a useful approach to the analysis of the ecumenical movement. His analysis is clearly directed towards the increasing permeation of American denominations by the rational cal-culations of the wider social environment: 'it can be plausibly maintained that there are powerful social and economic factors pressuring American Protestant denominations towards an increasing rationalization of their activities. Simultaneously these factors enable the bureaucracies running these denominations to act in an increasingly rational manner.' [4:85]

Berger argues that interdenominational co-operation based on practical and largely pragmatic considerations was well established in American Protestantism before the start of the ecumenical movement as such, and that the theological rationale of ecumeni-calism represents a later development: 'In view of the chronology of these two processes in the United States, it is hard to avoid the impression that the theological rationale emanating from the ecumenical movement proper has served as an *ex post facto* ideological legitimation of a process of co-operation with appre-ciably more mundane roots.' [4:81] The situation of American Protestant denominations is seen by Berger in terms of the classic picture of competition between a large number of units in a free market. Using this economic analogy, it can be suggested that unrestricted competition has become increasingly impractical and expensive for those denominations that depend on a middle-class suburban market. As a result, cartels are formed which have the effect of reducing the number of competing units by amalgamation, and dividing up the market between the larger units that remain. Oligopoly rather than monopoly is the end result.

These large religious cartels co-operate in a highly rational fashion. They engage in market research, joint planning and a combined approach to specific tasks through the use of joint agencies. At the same time, many observers have noted the resurgence of denominationalism, which at first sight appears to be a countervailing movement to that of ecumenicalism. Berger nevertheless argues that this can be understood within his economic model. When product standardization occurs in a highly rationalized market situation, each individual producer typically engages in the technique of 'marginal differentiation'. In terms of most consumer products this usually means that marginal embellishments and slightly different packaging will be given to a product that is substantially the same as others in the market. Applied to the American Protestant denominations, a similar picture emerges of a fairly standardized 'central core' of theology with marginal differentiation of secondary features, such as the personalities of ministers and the design and furnishing of church buildings. Thus denominationalism can be seen as highly functional in a situation of competition together with product standardization. Theology then takes on a legitimating function with respect to the process of marginal differentiation, just as advertising is used in the marginal differentiation of other consumer products.

Using this sense of the word secularization, the process can be identified as the replacement of 'other-worldly' motivations by 'this-worldly' contingencies and criteria. In the specific example of the ecumenical movement, as Berger views it, the demands of rational organization in an environment characterized by economic motives and decisions have largely moulded the theological legitimations of the Protestant denominations involved in it. In order to present this as a general process of secularization, however, it would also be necessary to show that Christianity in an earlier period was devoid of 'this-worldly' concerns, and that these represent in some way a divergence from central religious traditions. In other words, we are once again involved in the search for a golden age of 'other-worldly' religiosity.

There is an important methodological point involved in this use of secularization. The substance of the argument put forward in chapter one was that the sociologist of religion must attempt to steer a path between the extremes of idealism and epiphenomenalism. To contend that the primary motivations of a religious group are 'other-worldly' is very close to the position that they are somehow untouched by the secular environment: to contend, in contrast, that they are primarily dictated by the 'this-worldly' concerns of the secular environment is to regard them as not *really* religious at all. Every religion originates in a social environment and attaches to some social location. It would therefore appear to be more satisfactory to regard both 'other-worldly' and 'this-worldly' concerns as complementary and equally authentic aspects of any one religious tradition rather than as two poles of the process of secularization.

A third use of the term secularization refers to *the 'disengagement' of society from religion*, or to the 'differentiation' of religious ideas and institutions from other parts of the social structure. Instead of religion's function being that of a primary source of legitimation for the whole of society, it becomes increasingly a matter of private choice, restricted to the sphere of religiously interested participants. As a consequence of this process religion loses its public role, and as a corollary society looks elsewhere for the source of its authority. On an institutional level the frequently posited trend is in many ways similar to that which is attributed to the family in a complex industrial society. Just as the multi-functional 'traditional' family (providing among other things governmental, religious, educational and economic services for its members) is seen as having been stripped of such non-essential functions and—according to some commentators—is thereby in a state of decay, so the traditional religious institutions which at one time were responsible for educational and welfare functions have been relieved of these activities by state agencies and—or so the secularization argument goes—find themselves more and more in a marginal position in industrial societies.

Much the same criticism can be levelled at the 'loss of function' argument in the case of religious institutions as that which has been levelled at the 'family crisis' argument. It might plausibly be argued that if these two institutional areas no longer have to maintain peripheral functions and are thus better able to handle their core functions, this represents an improvement in their capacity to service the social needs with which they are primarily concerned. The fact that educational and welfare functions have to a large extent been taken over by the state is not in itself an argument that religious institutions are in a state of decline. However, a concept which is closely related to the 'disengagement' thesis but which does not contain quite the same implications of decline is that of 'differentiation'. Parsons applies the concept of differentiation to both the family and the church in modern society and claims that there has been no necessary 'decline' in these two institutional areas:

> This differentiation does not, as is often contended, imply that either or both have lost much of their 'importance' in modern society. It means that the influence they do exert is not through organizational jurisdiction over certain aspects of life now structurally differentiated from them, but through the value-commitments and motivational commitments of individuals. In spheres outside their families and their churches, then, individuals have come to be by and large free of organizational control and in this sense to act *autonomously*, on their own responsibility. But this is by no means to say that their behaviour in these 'external' spheres is uninfluenced by their participation in the family and the church respectively'. [24:307]

It is important to note that the differentiation model does not preclude the possibility of religious decline through increasing marginality, but neither does it necessarily imply such decline. On this issue it simply leaves the options open. It can also be argued that Christianity contains within its own doctrinal framework the principle of differentiation between the community of believers and the social community as a whole. One of the arguments that has been made against the use of the church–sect typology in the study of religions other than Christianity is that they rarely exhibit the degree of differentiation from other social institutions on which this typology is based. Thus Robertson contends that it is inappropriate to apply a typology of religious *organizations* to non-Christian religions since only Islam has manifested the degree of organization necessary for such an analysis. And in the case of Islam, he continues, 'religion has historically been *organized but not differentiated*'. [28:122] In the following chapter we will consider Berger's analysis of the differentiation of religion from other institutional spheres, and the irony he sees in the notion that Christianity has been its own gravedigger, partly as a result of the doctrinal basis it provides for differentiation of the religious sphere.

Bellah incorporates the concept of differentiation in an evolutionary framework and postulates five ideal-typical stages in the development of religion. [3] He regards evolution as a process of increasing differentiation and organizational complexity, though he denies that this process is inevitable or irreversible, and he notes that complex and simple forms may coexist in the same society: his stages of development, therefore, are to be regarded as empirical generalizations rather than as points on a fixed historical continuum. *Primitive religion*, typified by Durkheim's 'elementary form' of Australian aboriginal religion, is characterized by the close relationship between the world of myth and the detailed world of everyday life. Religious action consists not of worship or sacrifice but of 'acting-out' in ritual, and there is no separate religious organization since religious roles tend to be fused with other social roles based on such criteria as age, sex and kin-group membership. Religion in primitive society reinforces the basis of social solidarity, and by its fluidity gives little leverage from which to change the world. The *archaic religion* of Africa and ancient India and China shows the development of a religious cult with gods, priests, worship, sacrifice and sometimes divine or priestly kingship. Mythical beings are more clearly characterized and are regarded as exerting an influence on the world, which leads to a more systematic and hierarchical view of the cosmos. Religious organization is still largely merged with other parts of the social structure, and the traditional structure of society is seen as being grounded in the divinely instituted cosmic order, leaving little tension between religious demand and social conformity.

Historic religion is a more recent phenomenon, and emerged in societies that were more or less literate. An important feature of this type of religion is the breaking through of 'cosmological monism' by emphasizing the transcendental status of the religious realm. As a corollary, the given empirical world takes on a subordinate status and for the first time world-rejection becomes an integral part of religious activity. It will be recalled that the definition of religion at the end of chapter 2 emphasized this aspect of bifurcation. That Bellah's evolutionary schema is not intended to represent a strict historical progression is well demonstrated by his examples of historic religion, which he dates from 1000 B.C. onwards in the case of religions in the Middle and Far East: historic religion stretches over a period of 2,000 years in the civilized world and incorporates the development of Islam in the seventh century A.D.

In historic religion the realm of the supernatural is 'above' the empirical world in terms both of value and control, and with the emergence of this demarcation between the two realms the goal of salvation becomes for the first time a central religious preoccupation. Demarcation also involves to some extent a process of 'demythologization', and a transcendent deity provides the basis for a universalistic belief system. Religious action is typically action in pursuit of salvation, and there is often an ideal of salvation which can be gained through withdrawal from the world. Accompanying these features of historic religion is the development of differentiated religious collectivities, and a delicate balance of forces between the religious and political leaderships is required if the religious legitimation of political authority is to be maintained. Thus the possibilities of tension, conflict and change emerged, based ultimately on the fact that political acts could be judged in terms of standards that the political élite could not in the last analysis control. In his study of religion and politics in centralized empires, Eisenstadt has pointed out that some form of *modus vivendi* did tend to emerge between political and religious leaders in societies with differentiated religious institutions, but he notes too that the same religious organizations could also serve as important foci of social change and political passivity. [8] Once the demarcation has been made between an empirical world and a transcendental realm the possibility exists for religious leverage and social change.

At this point Bellah ceases to base his ideal types on a number of historical cases and gives as his example of *early modern religion* the historical example of the Protestant Reformation. Typical of this stage of religious evolution is the collapse of the hierarchical structuring of the empirical and the transcendental, and the important belief that salvation is to be found not in withdrawal from the world but by pursuing worldly activities. Traces are found of developments in the direction of early modern religious forms in some of the historic religions, and contemporary movements in Roman Catholicism fit into a similar category, but only in Protestantism is this stage of religion found in a fully institutionalized form. One of the important symbolic components is seen to be the direct relationship between the believer and his transcendent reality, and religious action becomes identified with the whole of life. Not only is the cosmological hierarchy shattered, but the hierarchy within religious organizations themselves is rejected or substantially broken down. Both church and state are given a delimited area of authority, and neither is allowed to dominate the other or the whole of society. As far as the social implications of early modern religion are concerned, Bellah lines up with Weber and Merton in attributing a wide range of influence on economics, politics and science directly to the Protestant Reformation. For the first time, an inbuilt tendency to change in the direction of realizing religious values is institutionalized in the social structure.

There is some uncertainty as to whether *modern religion* represents a stage or a transitional phase, but its features are seen to include a flexible symbol system, not of the primitive monistic variety but one in which multiple structures of religious meaning have replaced the dualistic structure of historic religions. It has recently been pointed out that our own society has been obliged to invent the special term 'fundamentalist' for those who still take the traditional religious cosmologies seriously. [10:161] Bellah similarly finds evidence of a massive reinterpretation among religiously involved individuals of orthodox Christian doctrine, which leads him to conclude that religious symbolization is no longer the monopoly of groups that are explicitly labelled religious. Above all, the kinds of symbols used are regarded as a matter of personal choice rather than of institutionally defined orthodoxy. Religious organization thus adopts a more open and flexible pattern of membership, which is not equated with secularization:

> Rather than interpreting these trends as significant of indifference and secularization, I see in them the increasing acceptance of the notion that each individual must work out his own ultimate solutions and that the most the church can do is provide him a favorable environment for doing so, without imposing on him a prefabricated set of answers. And it will be increasingly realized that answers to religious questions can validly be sought in various spheres of 'secular' art and thought. [3:373]

Hence, to use the concept of differentiation as a device for analysing change in religious beliefs and organization need not necessarily imply a 'decline in religion' or the secularization of modern society. Differentiation is itself a neutral concept, as the article by Bellah amply demonstrates.

A fourth use of the term secularization refers to *the transposition of beliefs and activities* that were once thought of as having a divine point of reference to activities that have an entirely 'secular' content. In this process society is seen as taking over all the functions that were previously performed by religious collectivities and providing 'religious surrogates'. An example of this type of transposition might be the argument that Marxism provides a form of all-embracing cosmology and an eschatology similar to those of traditional Christianity. Robertson sees the use of such terms as 'surrogate religiosity' and 'functional equivalents' to religion in the context of the various definitions given to religion by different sociologists. [28:36–42] Those who use an *inclusive* definition will, he argues, tend to include 'isms' like Communism, nationalism, Fascism, together with humanism, secularism and psychoanalyticism—perhaps we might also include scientism—under the category of religions because they represent similar attempts to articulate an all-embracing system of meaning and an integrated way of life. Political 'isms' are thus seen as 'functional equivalents' because they are shown to have analogous functions for the societies in which they are found to those of religions in the more generally understood sense of the term.

'Surrogate religiosity' is the term given to the other 'isms' listed because these may often be espoused by individuals who have previously been strongly committed to some more traditional form of religious belief. The problem of incorporating equivalents and surrogates into the overall category of religion as defined *inclusively* is, of course, that it creates considerable confusion if one is interested in studying the factors involved when individuals transfer from a 'religious' 'ism' to a 'political-humanist' 'ism': for example, one might well be interested in studying whether individuals who belong to fringe political groups have also at some period belonged to marginal religious groups. There is sometimes too an *a priori* assumption in 'transposition' theories, which may be conveniently labelled 'the quantum theory of religiosity'. If it is assumed that within every human individual there exists a permanent core of religious motivation which has to find some continuous source of expression, then by definition some identifiable aspect of every individual's activity must have a religious basis, and the problem of 'equivalents' and 'surrogates' becomes a search for the most convenient place to pin it down. I think that Luckmann comes close to this idea when he contends that it is of the essence of man's human nature to engage in symbol-building of a religious kind.

On the other hand, the problem that immediately arises when an *exclusive* definition of religion is used—and the definition given at the end of chapter 2 (page 42) *is*, I would consider, an exclusive definition—seems to be that it rules out a number of contemporary systems of meaning and action which are of considerable interest to sociologists of religion and which one might wish to regard, at least marginally, as religious. It will not have escaped attention that in the previous paragraphs, when 'equivalents' and 'surrogates' were being distinguished, reference had to be made to 'the more generally understood sense of the term' religion, and to 'some more traditional form of religious belief'. Robertson similarly takes refuge in the phrases 'conventially and intuitively understood religion' and 'obviously-religious'. Nevertheless, if only to do justice to the self-definition of commitment which members of these related movements might wish to give—since it seems clear that they would for the most part firmly reject a religious label—we will exclude them from the category of religion, and thus question the basis of the 'transitional' sense of the term secularization since it seems to be founded on an over-generalized and spongy definition of religion.

The fifth meaning of secularization contains the idea that *the world is gradually deprived of its sacral character*, so that man increasingly discards magical images of his natural environment and comes more and more to regard it as capable of empirical scientific manipulation. At the end of this process it is possible to envisage a world emptied of supernatural meaning and one in which 'mystery' no longer played a part. This is very much the process that evolutionists such as Frazer identified and to which they devoted themselves with, at times, an almost missionary fervour, regarding the elimination of 'superstition' as the most pressing need of modern civilization. Much the same notion is contained in Weber's 'disenchantment of the world', though by this Weber specifically meant the removal of magical symbols rather than of all religion as such. Furthermore Weber, unlike Frazer, who saw more in common between primitive magic and modern science than between religion and science, regarded the Judaeo-Christian tradition and especially its Calvinistic form after the Protestant Reformation as exerting a major influence on this process. There was also a profound sense of irony in Weber's view that modern capitalism, having in significant respects been moulded by the Calvinist ethic, no longer needed its support. His remarks towards the end of *The Protestant Ethic and the Spirit of Capitalism* have already been compared with Frazer's tentative optimism about the progress of modern scientific thought (chapter 2, page 33). There, it was suggested, Weber left his options open on the question of whether a totally disenchanted society might lie at the end of the developments which had led to Western capitalism. However, there is no mistaking the sense of pessimism in his writing, and the paragraph quoted earlier ends on this note: 'For of the last stage of this cultural development, it might well be truly said: "Specialists without spirit, sensualists without heart; this nullity imagines that it has attained a level of civilization never before achieved".' [37:182]

The growth of economic and scientific rationality are linked, in Weber's perspective, with at least the *possibility* of a totally 'disenchanted' society. It is therefore interesting to find in the writing of a contemporary theologian the view that scientific activity itself presupposes a religious dimension. Langdon Gilkey suggests that if we look at the activity of scientific enquiry itself we find that it points beyond itself to an ultimate area of meaning for which religious symbols are alone adequate.

> [In the activity of scientific enquiry] . . ., I believe, as in any expression of human autonomy and creativity, elements of ultimacy or of the unconditioned appear as the background and presupposition of what is done. It is these elements, the experience of the ultimacy involved in the knowing process itself, which provide one of the major secular bases for religious discourse—even in the midst of the most secular of our enterprises, the enterprise of science. The activity of knowing, like any major cultural activity, points beyond itself to a ground of ultimacy which its own forms of discourse cannot usefully thematize, and for which religious symbolization is alone adequate. [11:40–1]

Gilkey goes on to argue that the peculiar language of myth and of religion is not only unavoidable but necessary in a scientific culture if its major issues are to be dealt with creatively. This, he argues, is because man's intellectual comprehension is different from his more existential self-understanding and because the links between these two aspects have to be articulated. There is more than an echo here of Spencer's view (outlined on page 29) that both religion and science are agreed in admitting that there is an Unknowable area that lies beyond the things of which we have knowledge, and that the function of religion is to prevent man from becoming too involved in his immediate concerns by awakening his consciousness of something beyond them. Perhaps there is corroboration in Gilkey's argument also for David Martin's observation that at conferences organized by secular theologians

> there is nearly always one person present more conservative than myself: and he is generally a physical scientist, a biochemist perhaps, or worst of all a physicist. I do not mean politically conservative, of course, but theologically conservative. So it would seem that while the theologians joyfully proclaim the death of God and the death of the Church in the name of 'modern man' the only two modern men present watch the whole exercise with sad and wondering eyes. [17:70]

Even on the more restricted level of definition—using 'disenchantment' to mean the elimination of magical beliefs and practices—the evidence does not point unequivocally in the direction of a society dominated by scientific, rational criteria. In his study of a working-class parish in Lyons, for example, Emile Pin found various forms of magic. [30:176] There is considerable evidence too of the importance of 'subterranean theologies' in contemporary England, which very often imply supernatural notions of cause and effect or the restoration of moral balance. [16:74–6] A more recent empirical study carried out in Islington found strong evidence of magical beliefs and other superstitions, and concluded that people felt most need for a 'God of the Gaps' in times of personal distress. [1] The evidence on particular superstitions suggested that 80 per cent of respondents knew which sign of the zodiac they were born under and between 9 per cent and 23 per cent 'really believed' in astrology: 6–8 per cent 'really believed' in superstitions generally.

Interest in astrology seems to be an area of considerable importance even in the most technologically advanced areas of Western society. An article by Christopher Driver ('Bibles and bazookas', *The Guardian*, 17 May 1969) gives an account of its popularity in California, typified by one student-initiated course at the Berkeley campus which used as its set book the 'Modern Textbook of Astrology'. The function of astrology in California, suggests Driver, is dual. On the one hand it provides an alternative source of self-definition among groups of individuals who are searching for such definition. A second and perhaps more significant function in the present context emerged from a conversation with a student specializing in anthropology and taking a part-time course in astrology. Was this to help in interpreting the world? asked Driver. No, was the reply, 'But perhaps to keep it sacred'.

A sixth and final definition of secularization given by Shiner is that which postulates *change from a 'sacred' to a 'secular' society*. The main proponent of this version has been Howard Becker, who traces a global movement in the whole of society rather than a more limited change in the area of religious beliefs and practices. Becker defines sacred society as one in which the members are unwilling and/or unable to respond to the culturally new

I

(defined in terms of the existing culture). 'There is present a high degree of resistance to change. Such a society incorporates and sustains an impermeable value-system, implying an absence of effective inter-societal communication, or in other terms, an isolated value-system.' [13:123] The secular society, in contrast, predisposes its members to welcome and respond to the culturally new, and thus there is a high degree of readiness for and capacity to change. In secular society there exists a permeable value-system, which is readily accessible and subject to other influences. According to this version, secularization involves the abandonment of a traditionally defined 'common universe of discourse' and the acceptance of change according to rationally based and utilitarian criteria. This represents a general theory of social change, which is beyond the scope of his inquiry, but in fact it is very close to— if not indeed synonymous with—the discussion in chapter 10 of the concepts of 'open' and 'closed' systems of rationality. The sacred society of Becker's typology is the counterpart of Horton's 'closed' system of rationality, in which there is a lack of awareness of alternatives, sacredness of beliefs, and anxiety about threats to these beliefs. Similarly, secular society and 'open' rationality share the capacity to accept alternative sets of beliefs without anxiety.

This has been adopted as a model for the analysis of secularization in Europe, especially when it is viewed in the light of the urbanization process in European societies. [13:124] Thus it appears that on the whole European rural communities have remained 'prescribed sacred' societies much longer than urban communities. This picture fits well with the observations of writers like Berger, who points out that in modern industrial societies traditional forms of religious allegiance and practice tend increasingly to be confined to the marginal areas of society, which have been least involved in the process of industrialization and urbanization: rural areas are seen as good examples of this marginality. It would also fit into Troeltsch's analysis of the emergence of the increasingly individualistic, subjectively based, fluid phenomenon of 'mysticism' in the late medieval towns and in post-Reformation towns and cities. Aquaviva, in similar terms, puts forward the view that although irreligion has been a persistent phenomenon in all ages, it is particularly associated from the eighteenth century onwards with the growth of urban settlements and urban influence: 'It seems to us evident, therefore, that throughout this period the radiating centres of dechristianization are nearly always the cities.' [2:211]

While urbanization and the decline of traditional religious institutions may be intimately related in the case of European Christianity, some of the assumptions of Becker's typology as a general theory of secularization and social change are open to question. The major implication of Troeltsch's observation, for example, is that although traditional religious institutions often lose their influence in an urban environment they are replaced by a more flexible and individualistic form of religion rather than by none at all. Only if we accept a definition of religion which emphasizes its traditional, socially prescribed characteristics does secularization make sense in Becker's use of the term. It would also appear to ignore the capacity for syncretism and value-conflict that several writers have identified in primitive societies, and to make no provision for the Weberian irony of a religious ethic which *itself* gave the impetus for a society characterized by its acceptance of change on utilitarian criteria. Even within the deeply embedded traditional framework of values which Becker attributes to 'sacred' societies there may exist a widespread acceptance of change. Japan is a good example of a society with a resilient traditional normative basis in which massive changes were made—though not without considerable strains in the social structure—after the Meiji restoration of 1870. [34:128] In short, tradition and sacredness, change and secularity *may* coincide historically but are analytically separable. The dichotomy between 'open' and 'closed' systems of rationality can be a valuable heuristic device for understanding the context of meaning into which specific beliefs and activities in particular types of society fit. When this dichotomy is combined with that of sacred versus secular, however, it becomes vastly more contentious, and perhaps impedes rather than advances our understanding. This, at least, is the view of one anthropologist: 'The contrast of secular with religious has nothing whatever to do with the contrast of modern with traditional or primitive. The idea that primitive man is by nature deeply religious is nonsense.' [5:x]

The problem of secularization thus reduces itself to one of

definition and to the rigorous use of value-neutral concepts. Two recent and highly influential contributions to the study of secularization and the place of religion in modern society have been those of Luckmann and Berger. Since they set their accounts solidly within the theoretical traditions of classical sociology and also make a strong claim for anchoring the sociology of religion in this central theoretical core, their work provides a useful reference back to the issues raised in chapters 1 and 2. A final chapter thus seems an appropriate place to examine the basic structure of their theories of religion.

REFERENCES

1 ABERCROMBIE, NICHOLAS; BAKER, JOHN; BRETT, SEBASTIAN; and FOSTER, JANE 'Superstition and religion: the God of the gaps', in MARTIN, DAVID, and HILL, MICHAEL (eds.), op. cit.

2 AQUAVIVA, S. S. 'The psychology of dechristianisation in the dynamics of the industrial society', *Social Compass* vol. 7/3, 1960, pp. 209–25.

3 BELLAH, ROBERT N. 'Religious evolution', *American Sociological Review* vol. 29, no. 3, June 1964, pp. 358–74.

4 BERGER, PETER L. 'A market model for the analysis of ecumenicity', *Social Research* vol. 30, no. 1, Spring 1963, pp. 77–93.

5 DOUGLAS, MARY *Natural Symbols* (The Cresset Press, London 1971).

6 DRIVER, CHRISTOPHER 'Bibles and bazookas', *The Guardian* 17 May 1969, p. 8.

7 EDWARDS, DAVID L. *Religion and Change* (Hodder and Stoughton, London 1969).

8 EISENSTADT, SAMUEL N. 'Religious organizations and political process in centralized empires', *Journal of Asian Studies* vol. 21, no. 3, May 1962, pp. 271–94.

9 FLINT, JOHN T. 'The secularization of Norwegian society', *Comparative Studies in Society and History* vol. VI, no. 3, April 1964, pp. 325–44.

10 GELLNER, ERNEST 'Our current sense of history', *Archives Européennes de Sociologie* vol. XII, 1971, pp. 159–79.

11 GILKEY, LANGDON *Religion and the Scientific Future* (SCM Press, London 1970).

12 GOODE, ERICH 'Some sociological implications of religious secularization', *Social Compass* vol. XVI/2, 1969, pp. 265–73.

13 GOODRIDGE, R. MARTIN 'Relative secularization and religious practice', *Sociological Analysis* vol. 29, no. 3, Fall 1968, pp. 122–35.

14 HILL, MICHAEL (ed.) *A Sociological Yearbook of Religion in Britain—4* (SCM Press, London 1971).

15 MACRAE, DONALD G. 'The Bolshevik ideology', in *Ideology and Society* (Heinemann, London 1961).

16 MARTIN, DAVID A. *A Sociology of English Religion* (Heinemann, London 1967).

17 MARTIN, DAVID A. *The Religious and the Secular* (Routledge and Kegan Paul, London 1969).

18 MARTIN, DAVID A. 'Notes for a general theory of secularization', *Archives Européennes de Sociologie* vol. X, 1969, pp. 192–201.

19 MARTIN, DAVID A., and HILL, MICHAEL (eds.) *A Sociological Yearbook of Religion in Britain—3* (SCM Press, London 1970).

20 MOHS, MAYO 'The new rebel cry: Jesus is coming!', *Time* 21 June 1971.

21 MOL, J. J. 'Secularization and cohesion', *Review of Religious Research* vol. 11, no. 3, Spring 1970, pp. 183–91.

22 PALMS, ROGER C. *The Jesus Kids* (SCM Press, London 1972).

23 PARSONS, HOWARD L. 'The prophetic mission of Karl Marx', *Journal of Religion* vol. XLIV, no. 1, 1964, pp. 52–72.

24 PARSONS, TALCOTT *Social Structure and Personality* (Collier–Macmillan, London 1970).

25 PFAUTZ, HAROLD W. 'The sociology of secularization: religious groups', *American Journal of Sociology* vol. LXI, no. 2, September 1955, pp. 121–8.

26 PFAUTZ, HAROLD W. 'Christian Science: a case study of the social psychological aspect of secularization', *Social Forces* vol. 34, no. 3, March 1956, pp. 246–51.

27 PRATT, VERNON *Religion and Secularization* (Macmillan, London 1970).

28 ROBERTSON, ROLAND *The Sociological Interpretation of Religion* (Basil Blackwell, Oxford 1970).

29 SALISBURY, W. SEWARD 'Religion and secularization', *Social Forces* vol. 36, no. 3, March 1958, pp. 197–205.

30 SCHNEIDER, LOUIS *Sociological Approach to Religion* (John Wiley and Sons, New York 1970).

31 SHAROT, STEPHEN 'Secularization, Judaism and Anglo-Jewry', in HILL, MICHAEL (ed.) op. cit., 1971.

32 SHINER, LARRY 'Toward a theory of secularization', *Journal of Religion* vol. XLV, no. 4, 1965, pp. 279–95.

33 SHINER, LARRY 'The concept of secularization in empirical research', *Journal for the Scientific Study of Religion* vol. VI, no. 2, 1967, pp. 207–20.

34 SKLAIR, LESLIE *The Sociology of Progress* (Routledge and Kegan Paul, London 1970).

35 WAAL, VICTOR DE *What is the Church?* (SCM Press, London 1969).

36 WARE, TIMOTHY *The Orthodox Church* (Penguin Books, Harmondsworth, Middlesex 1964).

37 WEBER, MAX *The Protestant Ethic and the Spirit of Capitalism* (Unwin University Books, London 1930).

38 WILSON, BRYAN R. *Religion in Secular Society* (Watts, London 1966).

39 WILSON, BRYAN R. 'When union means weakness', *Observer* 6 July 1969.

40 ZELDIN, MARY-BARBARA 'The religious nature of Russian Marxism', *Journal for the Scientific Study of Religion* vol. VIII, no. 1, 1969, pp. 100–11.

12

The Synthesis of 'Classical' Sociology in Contemporary Theories of Secularization

LUCKMANN BASES his analysis of religion in contemporary society on the observation of a problematic relationship between the individual and the social order: individual existence in society, he argues, has reached a critical point in the contemporary world. The unifying perspective of Luckmann's work is drawn from the theoretical insights of Durkheim and Weber, both of whom were very much concerned with the fate of the individual in a modern social environment and both of whom gave religion a key place in their explanations.

> For Durkheim, the symbolic reality of religion is the core of the *conscience collective*. As a social fact it transcends the individual and is the condition for social integration and the continuity of the social order. At the same time, only the internalization of that objective reality by the subject makes man into a social and, thereby, a moral and genuinely human being. For Durkheim man is essentially *homo duplex* and individuation has, necessarily, a social basis. The problem with which we are concerned here is seen by Durkheim in a universal anthropological perspective and is articulated by him, correspondingly, in a radical manner. For Weber, on the other hand, the problem of the social conditions of individuation appears in a more specific perspective—that is, in the historical context of particular religions and their relation to historical societies. [23:12]

The relative contribution of Durkheim's and Weber's ideas to the synthesis which Luckmann puts forward is amply illustrated in this quotation, for a Durkheimian emphasis is traceable throughout the argument. As an example of this, both Durkheim and

Weber are regarded as being in agreement that the question of the individual in modern society is related fundamentally to the secularization of the contemporary world, and that the problem of individual existence in society is a 'religious' problem. This is a perspective which can be traced much more clearly in Durkheim's thought than it can in the work of Weber, who tended to regard religion as yet another problematic aspect of any type of society rather than as the central point of reference and key to our understanding of social order. It is well to remember Bellah's *caveat* that 'Max Weber made no claim to have the key to the reality which lies behind the façade of religious symbolization'. [2:91]

Having established the important place which religion occupied in 'classical' sociology, Luckmann's next step is to note the lack of any well-articulated links with this theoretical foundation in much recent sociology of religion. There is an active field of research in parish sociology, in demographic and statistical analyses of churches and of institutional participation, and in studies of church organization; indeed, there has been a remarkable growth in the past two decades of specialized institutes and journals. What appears to be lacking—and here we may refer back to the criticism of 'religious sociology' in chapter one—is the 'informing' of this research by the broader theoretical concerns that characterized the work of sociologists like Durkheim and Weber. As a result, much research has been narrowly empirical and has been dominated by interest in the apparent decline of traditional religious institutions, often oriented towards an institutionally defined set of problems and strategies for their solution. The contributions of Weber and Durkheim to the sociological study of religion have thus tended to be shelved and parcelled off—Weber's as an exercise in historical sociology rather than as part of his general theory of society, and Durkheim's as referring solely to primitive society.

For a number of years, the sociology of religion appears to have been 'out in the cold', and its 'rediscovery' in the postwar years was initially as an applied science, almost a form of market research, which ecclesiastical entrepreneurs might make use of. The situation that Luckmann depicts—and it would need to be qualified by pointing to important exceptions to this general trend—is best described as one of rampant schism. Denominational 'sociologies' of religion grew up in Catholicism, Protestantism and, Luckmann suggests, Judaism, which as well as being parochial tended more importantly to exclude matters of 'faith' from their research to the extent that they took certain theological positions as given rather than attempting to relate these to different social patterns. Above all, 'religion' and 'religious institution' became synonymous, and the church became the main focus of research.

The effect of this perspective is very marked in the analysis of secularization. Divorced from a well-founded theory, the process of secularization comes to be seen as something involving the shrinking influence of the churches, which consequently take on the role of islands of religion in a sea of secularism. This type of explanation, says Luckmann, is closely related to the dominant view of the increasing specialization of institutions in modern complex societies. But it could only be maintained if it were also argued that the institutional form of religion found in churches was able to satisfy religious needs completely. Can church attendance in fact be equated with a comprehensive index of religiosity? Luckmann thinks not, and goes on to reverse the approach of religious sociology by suggesting that church-oriented religion is on the *periphery* of modern society. Church attendance is a more markedly rural phenomenon; it involves women more than men only to the extent that they are non-working women; and the occupational groups most involved in church religion tend to be 'traditional'. This is at least the case in Europe, but in the United States there is the paradoxical situation of a 'modern' society with a high degree of institutional religious practice, where religion appears to play anything *but* a peripheral role. However, this may be understood as a case in which religion has adopted a 'secular' ethos and functions rather than retaining a traditional belief-system and structure. Thus it can be argued that traditional church religion has been pushed to the periphery of modern life in both Europe and the United States. Given this basic premiss, the two questions for Luckmann are: how did this happen? and, have there been any replacements for traditional religion?

The idea that urbanization and industrialization are sufficient

in themselves to account for the process of secularization is rejected, along with the naïve argument that the rise of science is
the root cause. We must go beyond these partial explanations and
look at the wider social-structural changes underlying secularization: thus we must see religion not just as an institutional phenomenon but as a source of norms which give significance to the
integration and legitimation of everyday life in society. From this
viewpoint, secularization can be regarded as the shrinking relevance of the values of *church* religion for such integration and
legitimation in a modern society, and the survival of church
religion can be attributed to the support of 'remnants' within
modern society of a past social order. The most interesting line
of enquiry—often obscured by the survival of traditional religious
institutions—is whether a new *kind* of religion has developed in
modern societies.

In order to treat institutional religion as one type within a
more general category of religion, it is first necessary to give a
general definition of religion. This can be done by locating the
sociology of religion in the sociology of knowledge, where use
has been made of the concept of 'symbolic universes' of meaning,
which are articulated by different social groups in order to en-
capsulate and interpret their experience. 'Symbolic universes are
socially objectivated systems of meaning that refer, on the one
hand, to the world of everyday life and point, on the other hand,
to a world that is experienced as transcending everyday life.
[23:43] These symbolic universes may be regarded as umbrellas
of meaning by means of which men make sense of their experience
and under which they encounter each other—clearly, a religious
cosmos would come within this category and we would need to
ask under what conditions its social basis became institutionalized. Pushing this analogy, we are interested in the process by
which umbrellas of meaning are embodied in an ecclesiastical
roof.

Luckmann's use of the term 'objectivations' to identify the
products of subjective experience that come to be shared by
members of a social collectivity (and in becoming socially significant take on more than the sum of a number of subjective experiences) is perhaps best paraphrased by the Durkheimian
concept of 'collective representations'. Men are seen as interpret-

K

ing and translating their experience into meaningful reality through the mechanism of socially given objectivations, and the significance of religion as a symbolic universe is that it has reference to a *transcendent* segment of reality whereas other meaning systems do not transcend the everyday life of man. The process of locating subjective experience in an interpretive scheme and thus giving it 'meaning' is used by Luckmann in such a way that the interpretative scheme he speaks of is very similar to the notion of 'culture' in other sociological contexts. A scheme of interpretation, he argues, results from 'sedimented past experiences', [23:45] and man transcends his biological nature by constructing a socially maintained universe of meaning. This, for Luckmann, is a fundamentally *religious* process, although the way in which religion is objectivated socially and institutionalized allows for a range of more specific types of religion.

However, most men do not construct a universe of meaning entirely from scratch since they are born into a social environment in which these universes already exist. By the process of socialization a historical universe of meaning is internalized, and this has immense importance for the legitimation of the established social order. Because the social order is regarded as intrinsically valid and obligatory, it can be seen as a manifestation of a transcendent and universal order that provides a world view:

> The world view, as a transcendent moral universe, has an obligatory character that could not be approximated in the immediate context of social relations. . . . We may say, in sum, that the historical priority of a world view provides the empirical basis for the 'successful' transcendence of biological nature by human organisms, detaching the latter from their immediate life context and integrating them, as persons, into the context of a tradition of meaning. We may conclude, therefore, that the world view, as an 'objective' and historical social reality, performs an essentially religious function and define it as an *elementary social form of religion*. This social form is universal in human society.' [23:52–3]

In short, the explanation put forward by Luckmann is very closely related, if not identical, to that of Durkheim, in that religion is seen as the key factor in endowing society with moral

authority. Because religion is given this broad function of providing a sacred cosmos, it can also be argued that a specialized
institutional carrier of this cosmos (for example, in the form of a
church-type organization with a set of specialized religious roles)
is not *necessarily* implied whenever religion is found, and may only
be expected in societies with a fairly complex and differentiated
structure. Indeed, it may be maintained that the more specialized
that religious expertise becomes, the more threatened is the
integrating function of the sacred cosmos for the society in
question. And it is only when religion is the major concern of
specialized social institutions that an antithesis between 'religion'
and 'society' develops, with important consequences: for once
the sacred universe and the 'world' each attain a substantial
degree of autonomy and become largely self-regulating within
their own spheres, the possibility of change and conflict arises.
Here Luckmann notes that the Judaeo-Christian tradition
represents an extreme case of the institutional specialization of
religion.

At the individual level, Durkheim's explanation again appears
in a reinterpreted form. Using the observation that the sacred is
something which is 'set apart' by men's attitude to it, Luckmann
suggests that the sacred cosmos is distinguished from the rest of
the world-view and given a particularly central place in the world-
view. When institutional specialization occurs it is assumed that
the religious institution will adequately meet the needs of individual religiosity, and the sacred cosmos is mediated in a
formalized and expert manner by religious specialists. At the same
time, the monopoly exercised by these 'official' models of the
sacred cosmos is supposed to appear subjectively plausible to
individual adherents, and it is at this point that a major problem
arises.

The 'official' model of the sacred cosmos, it is argued, can be
undermined from the point of view of its subjective plausibility
by three factors. Firstly, the 'official' model, being the property
of experts and specialists, is a complex set of formulations, which
has somehow to be transformed by the individual into the subjective relevance of his own experience. This may well be integrated into a meaningful whole in which subjective identification and 'official' models are compatible, but there is always a

danger of the two aspects getting out of joint, thus undermining the subjective plausibility of the 'official' model. Perhaps an example of this would be the elaborate theological rejection of mechanical means of contraception by the Roman Catholic hierarchy, which has increasingly been confronted by the demand on the part of sections of the laity for a more meaningful interpretation of doctrine that would match their subjective experience. Secondly, the 'official' model sets out highly specific norms of belief and activity, and this might well serve to weaken the integrating function of the sacred cosmos. The segregation of religious roles from the broader network of roles in a society means that the religious component declines in significance through its more demarcated area of competence. An example of this might be found in the analysis of religion as a 'leisure-time pursuit'. [28] Thirdly, since the formulation of the 'official' sacred cosmos is the task of experts who may be segregated from the everyday life of members of society, there may be a gap between 'official' concerns and the concerns of typical members of society. Once again, the *Humanae Vitae* debate is an example of the gap that may exist between theological experts and ordinary laity.

The idea that complete congruence between the 'official' model of religion and subjective images of ultimate significance could exist relies on the notion of perfect socialization of the individual into the institutional religious system. It is a theological ideal but an empirical impossibility: all the same, Luckmann accepts the golden-age theory of Christianity when he notes that medieval Catholicism came nearest to attaining this goal. 'Official' and subjective congruence is least probable in a complex industrial society where the operation of religious institutions on a bureaucratic basis means that the 'sacred' plausibility of the institution is endangered by its 'secular' activities. In addition, the embodiment of the sacred cosmos in an institution means that questions of ultimate concern may tend to be 'frozen' and immutable, and thus become irrelevant for subsequent generations. The mere fact that institutional religion becomes a specialist concern in a complex society means that it becomes more circumscribed and compartmentalized rather than operating on a diffuse level, and global claims become much less plausible. Furthermore, in complex societies religious institutions, which all make *some* claim to authenticity, tend to compete with each other, and this has the effect of undermining the validity of their universalistic claims. This observation marks a significant point of common ground between a number of sociologists who are agreed that competing religious institutions render the universalistic claims of religion *per se* problematic. Luckmann himself sees the process as a loss of the church's monopoly on the definition of an obligatory sacred cosmos.

Drawing on an economic—and firmly intellectualist—image, Luckmann sees the individual in a modern society selecting different themes or products from a range of 'ultimate' meanings and building them into a rather precarious private system of 'ultimate' significance. Recent evidence suggests that this may be most characteristic of consumers of the 'ultimate' models provided by cults, who tend rather to 'shop around' within a cultic milieu. The religious form of mysticism, Troeltsch originally contended, is an extreme and disparate form of religious individualism and privatization; and for Luckmann, the type of religion associated with this 'private sphere' is very close to Troeltsch's idea of 'parallel spontaneities': Troeltsch saw 'mysticism' as resting primarily on emotions and sentiments that were sufficiently unstable to make articulation difficult. Furthermore, the extreme subjectivity meant that no form of social obligation could be defined. [8] Thus the modern theme of religion is that of individual 'autonomy' and subjective self-realization, both of these fitting comfortably into the prevailing individualism and pragmatism of Western society.

While supporting the retreat into the private sphere and endowing subjective experience with a sacred quality, this 'invisible religion' also supports a process of secularization in modern industrial societies, but it does *not* seek to legitimate these societies, as traditional forms of religion have done. Luckmann's definition of secularization signifies the retreat by traditional religion from public, social significance. However, following Durkheim's analysis, religion is seen as lying at the very centre of man's experience of his natural and social environment, and thus secularization cannot mean the total removal of religious symbols and activities from the world. Man will always be involved in the activity of constructing a sacred cosmos in order to render his experience ultimately meaningful, and if this is how we identify religion, then religion becomes *the* human activity above all. Secularization in the sense of a removal of the sacred cosmos becomes by definition impossible. At its most fundamental level, religion will always be present as the primary agent of social cohesion in any society. But it is also clear that certain *forms* of religion are of declining influence and can thus be regarded as implicated in the process of secularization. The traditional institutional form of religion seems most exposed to this process, and Durkheim gave a parallel explanation when he noted the effect that Roman Catholicism had exerted in particular historical conditions to bind together social groups, adding (in a formula that Luckmann paraphrases as a decline in 'plausibility') 'but the necessary conditions are no longer given'. [13:374] Both Durkheim and Luckmann trace the root of this development to the growing individualism and freedom of conscience demanded by men in an industrial society, which does not fit readily into the dogmatic and disciplinary ethos of traditional religion, thus undermining the social basis of such religion. Secularization applies to this specific historical movement rather than to the primary function of religion, which is retained with a different content.

Peter Berger begins his analysis of secularization at the same point as Luckmann by noting the dialectical relationship between man and his society: [5:3] society is a product of human activity and consciousness and yet man is also a product of his society (a perspective that is usefully summarized in the phrases 'man in society' and 'society in man'). [3:chaps 4 and 5] Man and society are thus in a state of continual interplay. Man creates both physical and mental products as a result of his activities, and these products gradually take on a reality over and above their individual contributors, which then reacts back on the subjective consciousness of men. These three processes Berger calls externalization, objectivation and internalization, and his model is once more broadly based on a Durkheimian view (especially in the way that 'objectivations'—or collective representations—impinge on the individual members of a society), though the concept of alienation is implied in the notion that men 'heap up' the products of their own activities in the form of an externalized and imposing objective reality. The collective product of man's own activity is what we call culture, and this includes both the tools that man uses to shape his natural environment and the language and symbols by means of which he shapes his social relations. Since our perception of society itself is part of this culture, we must always regard society both as a product of its component human members and as an objectivated reality that confronts those members. Society, as Durkheim argued, is not just made up of individuals, but is also a source of *coercion* over individuals, and this occurs in part when social norms are internalized by the members of society. Successful socialization implies that there is symmetry between the objective world of society and the subjective world of the individual.

Individuals in a society organize their experience into a meaningful pattern, and hence, says Berger, they construct a meaningful world or *nomos*, which is shared by the group and which has an internal logic propelling it towards greater generality and comprehensiveness. This 'social enterprise of world-construction' [5:23] is the way in which men protect themselves against meaninglessness, and the social order takes on a sheltering quality. It can be seen in those situations—death, for example—where the problem of meaning arises with great clarity and renders precarious the maintenance of the *nomos*. The drive towards generality, however, means that there is a tendency for the *nomos* to be identified with some ultimate truths inherent in the universe and thus to merge with the *cosmos*: this is a source of strong stability for the *nomos* because it provides it with an external source of legitimacy. This merging of *nomos* and *cosmos* that Berger indicates gives more precision to the concept that Luckmann depicts more generally as the establishing of 'symbolic universes' of meaning.

Religion—which Berger also sees as the establishment of a sacred cosmos—is of crucial importance in the process of maintaining a meaningful model of the world, for 'religion is the audacious attempt to conceive of the entire universe as being humanly significant'. [5:28] Since religion appeals to a stable criterion of ultimate reality, which is beyond the changing reality of human society, it is a key source of legitimation. The most primitive form of religious legitimation is the one that sees the social order as a mirror image of the sacred cosmos, so that participation in the social order necessarily involves participation in the divine cosmos. There are colourful images of this type of legitimation in some of Shakespeare's plays, where any disturbance of the natural and social order (the murder of Caesar, for example) results in a corresponding and often amplified disturbance in the cosmic order. There is also a great deal of similarity between the close interpenetration in primitive religion of *nomos* and *cosmos* and Weber's description of traditional Indian and Chinese culture as being part of a 'magic garden'. Judaism represents a decisive break in this macrocosm/microcosm scheme: with the belief in a transcendent God the first step is made in the direction of a secularized view of the social order.

But whatever the link between *nomos* and *cosmos*, religious legitimation always serves to maintain some socially constructed reality, both on the individual level—for example, by making marginal situations like death meaningful and thus reintegrating individuals who are confronted by these situations into the social order—and on the social level, an example of which might be some crisis in a broader social context, such as war or economic crisis, in which religious legitimations will often become prominent. [9] It is very strongly denied at this point in the argument that the theory implies a sociologically determinist view of religion. It does not mean that any particular religious system is merely the effect or 'reflection' of social processes: 'Rather, the point is that the *same* human activity that produces society also produces religion, with the relation between the two products always being a dialectical one. [5:48] In this passage Berger provides one solution to Durkheim's paradox, discussed in chapter 2 (page 40). Thus religion may at different times be a dependent variable or an independent variable, the important link being between the socially constructed *nomos* and *cosmos*. Some degree of congruence will be maintained between these levels of meaning; indeed, for *nomos* and *cosmos* to be meaningful there must be such a strain towards congruence between them—there must exist what Berger terms a 'plausibility structure'.

In this sense both religion and society can be seen as autonomous variables in a dialectical relationship, so that if the plausibility structure is challenged, the result might either be the redefinition of the religious belief system (in which case religion would be the dependent variable) or it might be an attempt to adapt the social environment so that it became congruent with the belief system (in which case society would be the dependent variable). As an example of the former, one might cite the gradual retreat of traditional religion from authoritative pronouncements on substantive scientific matters after the nineteenth-century controversy over biological evolution. An example of the latter might be the importance in sectarian and communitarian 'island formations' of maintaining a social environment that corresponds with central tenets of the religious belief system, and thus protects the plausibility of the belief system.

Berger then goes on to apply his general theory of religion to the historical process of secularization, which he defines as 'the process by which sectors of society and culture are removed from the domination of religious institutions and symbols'. [5:107] In this definition both the structural and the cultural components of the process are included, and although secularization may be viewed as a 'global phenomenon' of modern societies, attention is directed to the lack of uniformity in its distribution. There can be no single causal explanation of the process of secularization, but the perspective that Berger himself adopts is to consider the extent to which the Western religious tradition may have *contained* the seeds of secularization throughout its history. This, he suggests, is not a new interpretation, and the idea that Protestantism played an important role in the growth of the modern world is very much bound up with it. If we look at the impact of early Protestantism we can detect a significant 'enclosure' movement in relation to the sacred which has been termed 'the disenchantment of the world'. God becomes a totally transcendent divinity and the operation of the sacred in the world is both restricted and systematized. This is in contrast to the traditional belief system of Roman Catholicism, in which the sacred is mediated to man through a number of channels—including the sacraments, saints and angels. The implications of Protestantism for the growth of a secular mentality are most important: 'A sky empty of angels becomes open to the intervention of the astronomer and, eventually, of the astronaut.' [5:113]

However, Berger does not interpret the onset of secularization as an event that is attributable to Protestantism alone, since the 'disenchantment of the world', which is furthest advanced in Protestantism, had its roots in the religion of the Old Testament. In contrast to the religious beliefs of surrounding cultures—in which the continuity between an empirical and a supra-empirical world meant that the natural world was thoroughly permeated by sacred forces—Israelite religion contained the distinctive feature of a transcendent divinity standing *outside* the world. Furthermore, the intervention of the divinity in human affairs was thought to take place in historically specific contexts, and the sphere of ethics was 'rationalized' to the extent that magical elements were discarded from it and a system of moral law established. Against this background, the dominant form of Western Christianity can be seen to have strong elements of *de*seculariza-tion, and this suggests an interpretation that is closely related to Hume's 'oscillation theory' of religion. The strict monotheism of Judaism was mitigated in Christianity by the doctrine of the Incarnation, by which Christ acts as mediator; in addition, the multiplicity of angels and saints modifies the conception of divine transcendence. This, says Berger, amounts to a 're-enchantment of the world'. At the same time, the formation of a specifically religious institution in the shape of the Christian church had the effect of segregating from religious influence the rest of society's institutional framework, which then became defined as 'the world'—a realm in which the sacred had no jurisdiction. Having made this initial break, the potential for secularization in import-ant spheres of social activity became well established, and the result of this historical process has been the gradual removal of larger and larger segments of society from traditional religious influence. This is the process of differentiation, which was discussed in chapter eleven.

With the segregation of religion to its discrete institutional sphere, there has occurred a concomitant challenge to the credi-bility of religion. The structure of plausibility that links religion with its social location has been broken down: partly this has been due to changes in the infrastructure, but partly also elements of the religious tradition in the West have acted as independent forces which have altered the structure of plausibility, and the impact of Calvinism on the growth of capitalism may be cited as just such an episode. The interaction of religion and society produces paradoxical results: thus, while religious elements may be seen as important formative influences on the modern secularized world, this world largely precludes the impact of religion as an independent influence. 'We would contend that here lies the great historical irony in the relation between religion and secularization, an irony that can be graphically put by saying that, historically speaking, Christianity has been its own gravedigger.' [5:127] Secularization, which was originally located in the capitalist economic structure, has gradually invaded other areas of society. Religion's 'complicity' in the growth of this key area of secularization was, of course, very much the focus of Weber's analysis of the rise of capitalism, and his pessimism over this ironic paradox has already been emphasized.

Accompanying the growth of autonomous secular areas is an increasing pluralism in the area of religious beliefs and institutions. Instead of one religious tradition maintaining a monopoly there is a situation of competition between different religious groups, and in the case of the ecumenical movement Berger makes use of the models of classical economics to point to the appearance of a free competitive *market* in religion whenever the situation of pluralism arises. In this market situation the laity of any religious group come to be seen as consumers and are thus given an important role: the 'rediscovery of the laity' has even happened in traditional religious institutions like Roman Catholicism, though it is considerably more marked in the Protestant denominations. Pluralization makes it more and more difficult for religion to maintain its plausibility because society as a whole can no longer be enlisted to give it social confirmation. This happens because individuals who do *not* accept religious beliefs are no longer a socially segregated group representing a minor threat to the traditional religious system, but are distributed in many different areas of society. As a result, it becomes difficult to maintain the boundaries of a socially confirming group of believers except through the mechanisms that Berger calls 'ghetto' or 'island' formations: in their sectarian form these were analysed in chapter 4. Outside such sectarian or quasi-sectarian groups the maintenance of religious belief-systems becomes a subjective, privatized enterprise. There exist a whole range of competing religious legitimations of aspects of the world rather than a single overarching set of religious symbols to legitimate 'the world'. The interpretation that Berger gives to the process of secularizations ends with a picture of contemporary religion that is identical to the 'invisible religion' of Luckmann: religion has become pluralistic and privatized, a matter of choice and a source of sacred symbols from which men may construct their own 'invisible' religions.

To end this book with a detailed account of the work of two contemporary sociologists might appear to present their theories as a definitive solution to the study of religion in industrial societies. In fact, my intention was quite different. Luckmann and Berger, far from indicating where the sociology of religion should stop, have performed the much more valuable function of suggesting a direction in which it might go. Above all, they base their work on an explicit awareness of where the sociology of religion has come *from*. In this chapter I have tried to indicate some of the continuities between 'classical' sociology and the work of Berger and Luckmann, which is centred on the axiom that there can be *no* sociology of religion without such a central theoretical foundation. The limited aim of this textbook originated from a similar search for continuities and firm roots in sociological theory, but I have found that much of the task consisted in hacking away the tangle of misinterpretations and second-hand versions that obscures this theoretical basis.

My emphasis throughout has been on the analysis of theoretical roots in the Weberian tradition. The reason for this was not only the evident productiveness of Weberian theory in substantive research but also the fact that in this theoretical tradition in particular the problems encountered and insights gained overlap a whole range of sociological sub-specialisms: the relevance of the concept of charisma for the study of both religious and political movements is an excellent example. Sociology at large is often regarded as an imperialistic discipline, which swallows up its academic neighbours (though the process now seems to have been reversed in some universities). Within sociology, however, the sociology of religion is undoubtedly the most imperialistic specialism. Religion is not only a central concern of sociological theory: it is *the* central concern.

REFERENCES

1 ARCHER, MARGARET SCOTFORD, and VAUGHAN, MICHALINA 'Education, secularization, desecularization and resecularization', in MARTIN, DAVID, and HILL, MICHAEL (eds.) *A Sociological Yearbook of Religion in Britain—3* (SCM Press, London 1970).

2 BELLAH, ROBERT N. 'Christianity and symbolic realism', *Journal for the Scientific Study of Religion* vol. 9, no. 2, 1970, pp. 89–96.

3 BERGER, PETER L. *Invitation to Sociology* (Penguin Books, Harmondsworth, Middlesex 1966).

4 BERGER, PETER L. 'A sociological view of the secularization of theology', *Journal for the Scientific Study of Religion* vol. VI, no. 1, 1967, pp. 3–16.

5 BERGER, PETER L. *The Social Reality of Religion* (Faber and Faber, London 1969).

6 BERGER, PETER L. *A Rumour of Angels* (Allen Lane The Penguin Press, London 1970).

7 BOLLE, KEES W. 'Secularization as a problem for the history of religions', *Comparative Studies in Society and History* vol. 12, no. 3, 1970, pp. 242–59.

8 CAMPBELL, COLIN 'The cult, the cultic milieu and secularization', in HILL, MICHAEL (ed.) *A Sociological Yearbook of Religion in Britain—5* (SCM Press, London 1972).

9 CLEMENTS, KEVIN 'The religious variable: dependent, independent or interdependent?', in HILL, MICHAEL (ed.) op. cit. 1971.

10 COGLEY, JOHN *Religion in a Secular Age* (Pall Mall, London 1968).

11 COX, HARVEY 'The epoch of the secular city', *Social Compass* vol. XV/1, 1968, pp. 5–12.

12 CUTLER, DONALD R. (ed.) *The World Year Book of Religion. The Religious Situation. Volume I* (Evans Brothers, London 1969).

13 DURKHEIM, ÉMILE *Suicide* (Routledge and Kegan Paul, London 1970).

14 FENN, RICHARD K. 'The secularization of values. An analytical framework for the study of secularization', *Journal for the Scientific Study of Religion* vol. VIII, no. 1, 1969, pp. 112–24.

15 FENN, RICHARD K. 'The process of secularization: a post-Parsonian view', *Journal for the Scientific Study of Religion* vol. 9, no. 2, 1970, pp. 117–36.

16 GLASNER, PETER E. 'Secularization: its limitations and usefulness in sociology', *The Expository Times* vol. LXXXIII, no. 1, October 1971, pp. 18–23.

17 GREELEY, ANDREW M. 'After secularity: the neo-Gemeinschaft society: a post-Christian postscript', *Sociological Analysis* vol. 27, no. 3, Fall 1966 pp. 119–27.

18 HERBERG, WILL *Protestant—Catholic—Jew* (Doubleday Anchor, New York 1960).

19 HERBERG, WILL 'Religion in a secularized society: some aspects of America's three-religion pluralism', in SCHNEIDER, LOUIS (ed.) *Religion, Culture and Society*, op. cit., pp. 591–600.

20 HILL, MICHAEL (ed.) *A Sociological Yearbook of Religion in Britain—4* (SCM Press, London 1971).

21 KALLEN, HORACE M. 'Secularism as the common religion of a free society', *Journal for the Scientific Study of Religion* vol. IV, no. 2, 1965, pp. 145–51.

22 KRAUSZ, ERNEST 'Religion and secularization: a matter of definitions', *Social Compass* XVIII/2, 1971, pp. 203–12.

23 LUCKMANN, THOMAS *The Invisible Religion* (Macmillan, New York 1967).

24 MACINTYRE, ALASDAIR *Secularization and Moral Change* (Oxford University Press, London 1967).

25 NELSON, BENJAMIN 'Is the sociology of religion possible? A reply to Robert Bellah', *Journal for the Scientific Study of Religion* vol. 9, no. 2, 1970, pp. 107–11.

26 PARSONS, TALCOTT 'Religion in a modern pluralistic society', *Review of Religious Research* vol. 7, no. 3, Spring 1966, pp. 125–46.

27 PARSONS, TALCOTT 'Christianity and modern industrial society', in SCHNEIDER, LOUIS (ed.) *Religion, Culture and Society*, op. cit., pp. 273–298.

28 PICKERING, W. S. F. 'Religion—a leisure-time pursuit?', in MARTIN, DAVID (ed.) *A Sociological Yearbook of Religion in Britain* (SCM Press, London 1968).

29 ROBBINS, THOMAS 'Eastern mysticism and the resocialization of drug users: the Meher Baba cult', *Journal for the Scientific Study of Religion* vol. VIII, no. 2, Fall 1969, pp. 308–17.

30 SCHNEIDER, LOUIS (ed.) *Religion, Culture, and Society* (John Wiley and Sons, New York 1964).

31 SCHWEIKER, WILLIAM F. 'Religion as a superordinate meaning system and socio-psychological integration', *Journal for the Scientific Study of Religion* vol. VIII, no. 2, 1969, pp. 300–7.

32 STARK, RODNEY, and GLOCK, CHARLES Y. 'The "new denominationalism"', *Review of Religious Research* vol. 7, no. 1, Fall 1965, pp. 8–17.

33 SYKES, RICHARD E. 'An appraisal of the theory of functional–structural differentiation of religious collectivities', *Journal for the Scientific Study of Religion* vol. VIII, no. 2, 1969, pp. 289–99.

34 YINGER, JOHN MILTON 'Pluralism, religion, and secularism', *Journal for the Scientific Study of Religion* vol. VI, no. 1, 1967, pp. 17–30.

Select Bibliography of General Works on Sociology and the Sociology of Religion

ARON, RAYMOND *Main Currents in Sociological Thought*, 2 vols. (Weidenfeld and Nicolson, London 1968).

BABBIE, EARL R. 'The religious factor—looking forward', *Review of Religious Research* vol. 7, no. 1, Fall 1965, pp. 42–51. *Comment* by Gerhard Lenski, pp. 51–3.

BARNES, HARRY ELMER *An Introduction to the History of Sociology* (University of Chicago Press, Chicago/London 1948).

BECKER, CARL L. *The Heavenly City of the Eighteenth Century Philosophers* (Yale University Press, New Haven 1932).

BECKER, HOWARD *Through Values to Social Interpretation* (Duke University Press, Durham, N.C. (1950).

BENDIX, REINHARD *Max Weber: an Intellectual Portrait* (Methuen, London 1966).

BENSON, PURNELL HANDY *Religion and Contemporary Culture* (Harper and Brothers, New York 1960).

BERGER, PETER L. *Invitation to Sociology* (Penguin Books, Harmondsworth, Middlesex 1966).

BERGER, PETER L. *The Sacred Canopy* (Doubleday, New York 1967). (English edition see below.)

BERGER, PETER L. *The Social Reality of Religion* (Faber and Faber, London 1969).

BIERSTEDT, ROBERT *Émile Durkheim* (Weidenfeld and Nicolson, London 1966).

BIRNBAUM, NORMAN, and LENZER, GERTRUD (eds.), *Sociology and Religion* (Prentice-Hall, Englewood Cliffs 1969).

BROTHERS, JOAN (ed.) *Readings in the Sociology of Religion* (Pergamon, Oxford 1967).

BROTHERS, JOAN *Religious Institutions* (Longman, London 1971).

DAVIS, KINGSLEY *Human Society* (Macmillan, New York 1965).

DEMERATH III, NICHOLAS J., and HAMMOND, PHILLIP E. *Religion in Social Context: Tradition and Transition* (Random House, New York 1969).

DURKHEIM, EMILE *The Elementary Forms of the Religious Life* (George Allen and Unwin, London 1954).

ELDRIDGE, J. E. T. (ed.) *Max Weber: The Interpretation of Social Reality* (Michael Joseph, London 1970).

ETZIONI, AMITAI *A Comparative Analysis of Complex Organizations* (Free Press, New York 1961).

FINER, S. E. (ed.) *Vilfredo Pareto, Sociological Writings* (Pall Mall, London 1966).

FLETCHER, RONALD *The Making of Sociology. A Study of Sociological Theory: Volume 1. Beginnings and Foundations; Volume 2. Developments* (Michael Joseph, London 1970).

FREUND, JULIEN *The Sociology of Max Weber* (Allen Lane The Penguin Press, London 1968).

GEERTZ, CLIFFORD 'Religion. Anthropological study', *International Encyclopaedia of the Social Sciences*, pp. 398–406.

GERTH, H. H., and MILLS, C. WRIGHT (eds.) *From Max Weber: Essays in Sociology* (Routledge and Kegan Paul, London 1948).

GINSBERG, MORRIS *On the Diversity of Morals* (Mercury Books, London 1962).

GLOCK, CHARLES Y., and STARK, RODNEY *Religion and Society in Tension* (Rand McNally, Chicago 1965).

GLOCK, CHARLES Y., and STARK, RODNEY *Christian Beliefs and Anti-Semitism* (Harper and Row, New York/London 1966).

GOULD, JULIUS, and KOLB, WILLIAM L. *A Dictionary of the Social Sciences* (Tavistock, London 1964).

✓ HERBERG, WILL *Protestant—Catholic—Jew* (Doubleday Anchor, New York 1960).

HILL, MICHAEL (ed.) *A Sociological Yearbook of Religion in Britain—4* (SCM Press, London 1971).

HILL, MICHAEL (ed.) *A Sociological Yearbook of Religion in Britain—5* (SCM Press, London 1972).

HOULT, THOMAS FORD *The Sociology of Religion* (Holt, Rinehart and Winston, New York 1958).

HUGHES, H. STUART *Consciousness and Society* (Vintage Books, New York 1958).

JOHNSON, HARRY M. *Sociology: a Systematic Introduction* (Routledge and Kegan Paul, London 1961).

KNUDTEN, RICHARD D. (ed.) *The Sociology of Religion* (Appleton–Century–Crofts, New York 1967).

LENSKI, GERHARD *The Religious Factor* (Doubleday Anchor, New York 1963).

LESSA, WILLIAM A., and VOGT, EVON Z. *Reader in Comparative Religion: an Anthropological Approach* (Row Peterson and Company, Illinois/New York 1958).

LUCKMANN, THOMAS *The Invisible Religion* (Macmillan, New York 1967).

MARTIN, DAVID A. *Pacifism* (Routledge and Kegan Paul, London 1965). ✓

MARTIN, DAVID A. *A Sociology of English Religion* (Heinemann, London 1967).

MARTIN, DAVID A. (ed.) *A Sociological Yearbook of Religion in Britain* (SCM Press, London 1968).

MARTIN, DAVID A. (ed.) *A Sociological Yearbook of Religion in Britain—2* (SCM Press, London 1969).

MARTIN, DAVID A. (ed.) *Fifty Key Words in Sociology* (Lutterworth, London 1970).

MARTIN, DAVID A., and HILL, MICHAEL (eds.) *A Sociological Yearbook of Religion in Britain—3* (SCM Press, London 1970).

MARWICK, MAX (ed.) *Witchcraft and Sorcery* (Penguin Books, Harmondsworth, Middlesex 1970).

MEHL, ROGER *The Sociology of Protestantism* (SCM Press, London 1970).

MERTON, ROBERT K. *Social Theory and Social Structure* (The Free Press, New York 1957).

MITZMAN, ARTHUR *The Iron Cage: an Historical Interpretation of Max Weber* (Alfred A. Knopf, New York 1970).

NISBET, ROBERT A. *Émile Durkheim* (Spectrum Books, Prentice-Hall, Englewood Cliffs 1965).

NISBET, ROBERT A. *The Sociological Tradition* (Heinemann, London 1967).

NOTTINGHAM, ELIZABETH K. *Religion and Society* (Random House, New York 1954).

O'DEA, THOMAS F. *The Sociology of Religion* (Prentice-Hall, Englewood Cliffs 1966).

O'DEA, THOMAS F. *Sociology and the Study of Religion* (Basic Books, New York/London 1970).

THE OXFORD DICTIONARY OF THE CHRISTIAN CHURCH, edited by F. L. Cross (Oxford University Press, London 1963).

PARSONS, TALCOTT *The Structure of Social Action* (The Free Press, New York 1937).

PARSONS, TALCOTT; SHILS, EDWARD; NAEGELE, KASPAR D.; and PITTS, JESSE R. (eds.) *Theories of Society* (The Free Press, New York 1965).

RAISON, TIMOTHY (ed.) *The Founding Fathers of Social Science* (Penguin Books, Harmondsworth, Middlesex 1969).

REX, JOHN *Key Problems of Sociological Theory* (Routledge and Kegan Paul, London 1961).

✓ ROBERTSON, ROLAND (ed.) *Sociology of Religion* (Penguin Books, Harmondsworth, Middlesex 1969).

ROBERTSON, ROLAND *The Sociological Interpretation of Religion* (Basil Blackwell, Oxford 1970).

SCHARF, BETTY R. *The Sociological Study of Religion* (Hutchinson, London 1970).

SCHNEIDER, LOUIS (ed.) *Religion, Culture, and Society* (John Wiley and Sons, New York 1964).

SCHNEIDER, LOUIS *Sociological Approach to Religion* (John Wiley and Sons, New York 1970).

SIMMEL, GEORG *Sociology of Religion*, translated by Curt Rosenthal (Philosophical Library, New York 1959).

STARK, WERNER *The Sociology of Religion. A Study of Christendom* (Routledge and Kegan Paul, London 1966–72):

 Volume I. Established Religion (1966);
 Volume II. Sectarian Religion (1967);
 Volume III. The Universal Church (1967);
 Volume IV. Types of Religious Man (1969);
 Volume V. Types of Religious Culture (1972).

TROELTSCH, ERNST *The Social Teaching of the Christian Churches*, 2 vols, translated by Olive Wyon (George Allen and Unwin, London 1931).

VERNON, GLENN M. *Sociology of Religion* (McGraw-Hill, New York 1962).

WACH, JOACHIM *Sociology of Religion* (Chicago University Press, Chicago 1944; Phoenix edition 1962).

WEBER, MAX *Ancient Judaism*, translated and edited by Hans H. Gerth and Don Martindale (The Free Press, New York 1952).

WEBER, MAX *The Religion of India. The Sociology of Hinduism and Buddhism*, translated and edited by Hans H. Gerth and Don Martindale (The Free Press, Glencoe 1958).

WEBER, MAX *The Theory of Social and Economic Organization*, translated by A. M. Henderson and Talcott Parsons (Free Press, New York 1964).

WEBER, MAX *The Religion of China. Confucianism and Taoism* (Macmillan, New York 1964).

WEBER, MAX *The Sociology of Religion*, translated by Ephraim Fischoff, introduced by Talcott Parsons (Methuen, London 1965).

WEBER, MAX *Economy and Society*, 3 vols., ed. by Guenther Roth and Claus Wittich (Bedminster Press, New York 1968).

WILSON, B. R. *Sects and Society* (William Heinemann, London 1961).

WOLFF, KURT H. *The Sociology of Georg Simmel* (Free Press, New York 1950).

YINGER, JOHN MILTON *Religion, Society and the Individual* (Macmillan, New York 1957).

YINGER, JOHN MILTON *The Scientific Study of Religion* (Collier-Macmillan, London 1970).

Name Index

(Italics indicate names on list of references)

273

Subject Index